children's inquiry

Using Language to Make Sense of the World

Judith Wells Lindfors

Teachers College
Columbia University
New York, NY 10027

Published by Teachers College Press, 1234 Amsterdam Avenue, New York, NY 10027

Library of Congress Cataloging-in-Publication Data

Lindfors, Judith Wells.
    Children's inquiry : using language to make sense of the world / Judith Wells Lindfors.
        p.   .cm. — (Language and literacy series)
    Includes bibliographical references and index.
    ISBN 0-8077-3836-0 (pbk.). — ISBN 0-8077-3837-9 (cloth)
    1. Questioning.   2. Speech acts (Linguistics).   3. Children—Language.   4. Inquiry (Theory of knowledge).   5. Communication in education.   I. Title.   II. Series: Language and literacy series (New York, N.Y.)
 P95.52.L56   1999
    306.44—dc21   98-55089

ISBN 0-8077-3836-0 (paper)
ISBN 0-8077-3837-9 (cloth)

NCTE stock number 06366

Printed on acid-free paper
Manufactured in the United States of America

06   05   04   03   02   01   00   99   8   7   6   5   4   3   2   1

Contents

PART II: Expression

PART III: Participants

Preface

The word *inquire* means different things to different people. Dictionary definitions (which attempt to capture people's usage) cluster into two main groups: those that do not specifically entail language, and those that do. In the first group, *to inquire* is "to seek knowledge" or "to make investigation"; and *inquiry* is "seeking for truth, information, knowledge." In the second group, the language group, *to inquire* is "to seek to learn by asking," or "to seek information by questioning" or "a person (or persons) addresses another (or others) to obtain information"; and *inquiry* is "the action of asking."

This book is about children's inquiry in the second sense, the language sense. It is an exploration of inquiry *acts*. As you will see in the coming chapters, I define an act of inquiry as *a language act in which one attempts to elicit another's help in going beyond his or her own present understanding.* My interest is in how children develop and use the language of inquiry in their learning lives. Clearly my definition is less a definition of inquiry than it is a demarcation of the territory to be probed in this book. People explore their world in many ways: they observe, they read, they ponder, they write, they listen. They also turn to others and intentionally engage them in their own attempts to understand. It is this turning-to-others that I focus on here and I do so with reference to children: inquiry as language acts by which children bring others into their sense-making.

You might wonder why I don't just call this a book about children's questions. After all, this is what educators have called this in the past. The problem is, they have called lots of other things "questions" too—language acts that had nothing to do with children trying to bring others into their attempts to understand the world. "Just who do you think you are?" is a question, and so is "Could ya pass me the salt?" but neither one has anything to do with anybody trying to understand something. So *question* includes too much. But it also excludes too much, for children engage others in their probing in lots of expressive ways besides asking questions. For example, they contest, they negotiate, they agree, they compare, they evaluate, they generalize, they disagree, they predict, they reflect . . . on and on it goes. Throughout this book, a major contention is that children's inquiry acts are different from those we have called questions. And so, if we are to hear children's inquiry acts, we must listen in a new way, for we are likely to hear only that which we know to listen for.

The picture of inquiry that I am painting in this book is one possibility among many. Another author would have created a different picture of children's inquiry—its nature, its development, and its possibilities and potential power in classrooms. My purpose in writing this book is not to amass all existing research on children' s inquiry and present it in a well-ordered, comprehensive way. My purpose is, rather, to propose a view of children's inquiry that I believe is promising in the insights it might afford. I am attempting to construct an integrated conceptualization of inquiry that focuses on inquiry's purposes, expressive ways, collaborations (in partnerships among participants), individual styles, and contexts. I believe that the view I am proposing may help us hear children's inquiry acts in classrooms: may help us recognize children's inquiry, appreciate it, and above all, foster it.

This book is exploratory, rather than informing, in its intent. True, there is much information in these pages, but I include it in order to construct new territory, not in order to comprehensively survey existing territory. Its material is more ideas than information *per se*.

If pressed to categorize this book by genre, I would call it an extended exploratory essay. Those of you who are familiar with my *Children's Language and Learning* (1987) will recognize at once that an exploratory essay is a quite different kind of book from the earlier one, which was an expository text. I find it fitting that my dictionary defines *essay* as "an attempt," for this book is my attempt to understand children's inquiry. It is only my most recent attempt: children's inquiry has been a major fascination for me throughout my professional life, and an area I have been exploring with my graduate students in a seminar for 20-some years.

Different kinds of text engage readers in different ways. My expectation is that reading an informing text (such as *Children's Language and Learning*) will involve a different kind of connection for a reader from reading an exploratory text such as this one. My own connection with the reader as I have worked on this book has been different too. I always feel a reader's presence as I write, but never have I had a writing experience in which the reader's presence felt so close, collegial, and dialogic as during the writing of this book. I have felt companionship as I wrote;

I hope you will feel it as you read. I hope you will talk back to me—challenge, inquire, wonder, reflect on the ideas you find in the coming pages.

This book is itself an act of inquiry for me: it is my inquiry about children's inquiry. I have turned to many others for help as I have tried to push my understanding of children's inquiry deeper. You will doubtless hear many of the voices of those who have helped me:

> children I have listened to over the years,
> children I have read about in the research of others,
> students with whom I have been dialoguing for 25 years,
> colleagues, both near and distant, with whom I dialogue face to face and in writing.

With such a range of voices influencing my own understanding, it will perhaps not surprise you to find a variety of types of writing in the coming chapters. You will find transcripts (from homes and from classrooms) and my discussion of them; class exercises; information (e.g., research findings) offered in support of some assertion or suggestion; stories of various kinds—anecdotes, episodes from my classes; and reflections and wonderings of my own. Sometimes my voice is one of reason; other times, of passion. Sometimes my voice speaks tentatively; other times with deep conviction.

I believe that inquiry is universal, a part of what it is to be human. Over the past decade a similar suggestion has been proposed for narrative. The presence of narrative across cultures suggests that to be human is to create and respond to story. Barbara Hardy (1977) calls narrative "a primary act of mind" (p. 12), a fundamental way we understand and construct our experience in the world. However, within this universal presence of narrative, there is wonderful *cultural* variation in the sorts of stories told and in the manner and contexts of their telling. And within these cultural norms, the *individual* creates and tells and responds to story. And so the suggestion is that narrative is at once a universal and a cultural and an individual phenomenon.

I believe that inquiry is like this also—another "primary act of mind" perhaps. I take very seriously the suggestion that curiosity is innate, and that the child is, from birth, oriented toward trying to understand his or her world with the help of others. And those others—being human and thus inquirers themselves—demonstrate and engage the child in the community's ways of inquiry: its purposes, its expression, its ways of collaboration, its individual styles, its contexts. There is much the inquiring child must learn, for inquiry acts are acts of imposition. How does the child impose on more expert (often adult) others politely, without offending? I believe that inquiry acts and events are deeply and complexly rooted in the primary relationships of self and other within a culture.

Believing this, as a mainstream individual myself, I have not attempted in this book to probe inquiry's ways in cultures different from my own. To do so would be the ultimate example of a fool rushing in where angels fear to tread. The dangers are real: unintentionally overlooking, misinterpreting, diminishing, or oversimplifying are but a few. Although the classroom transcripts I rely on in this book include some cultural diversity in the participating children, the home (parent-child) transcripts are all from mainstream families. This is the kind of inquiry interaction I know best. In these parent-child transcripts, I can hear the sounds of inquiry—can hear how adult and child are collaboratively constructing inquiry discourse. But I must leave it to others to explore inquiry in cultural contexts less familiar to me, for I could not hope to do justice in describing the richness and complexity to be discovered there.

My hope is that the framework I am proposing and trying to elucidate here, will serve as a helpful starting place for a consideration of inquiry within non-mainstream groups. Yet I worry that the predominantly mainstream orientation in the home transcripts might serve to further privilege an already privileged discourse. It is not my intention to trot out (yet again) mainstream interaction for scrutiny, in the process shoring up its privileged position. I implore you as you read the home transcripts and my discussion of them, to remember that these reflect one culture's ways of adult-child interaction, and that there is no suggestion here that these ways are either *normative* or *best* or necessarily the most helpful for children's learning in school or elsewhere. Such a misinterpretation of my intention would be most regrettable, given the current demographics that show increasing cultural diversity among children in our classrooms, but a continuing dominant mainstream orientation in our schools. In my state, for example, evaluation of teachers and children and schools is based almost exclusively on *standard*-ized test scores. What is it that is "standard" here? Whose ways are "standard"?

As I suggest in the coming pages, the classroom may offer the richest possible opportunities for all of us—teachers and children alike—to increase our awareness of both the cultural diversity and the individual distinctiveness in inquiry. If we afford children's inquiry a central place in our classrooms, we may come to see how the universal urge to understand the world with the help of others plays itself out in culturally and individually distinctive ways.

Acknowledgments

I have many people to thank:

- Bob Bolick, formerly of Harvester Wheatsheaf, who first expressed interest in the possibility of this book and actively encouraged me to write it;
- my fourth-floor colleagues: Colleen Fairbanks, Elaine Fowler, Julie Jensen, and Joan Shiring, who believed in this project from the beginning;
- my colleague Judi Harris, who—during our four-hour "breakfasts"—was always eager to discuss my ideas and writing progress;
- friends outside of academe—Daphne Apostolidis and Vivian Paley—who have been interested and supportive all along;
- an anonymous reviewer, who took my ideas seriously enough to push me to think harder about them;
- Hans van der Meij, who read and responded to an early version of Chapter 1.

Jane Townsend—friend, dialoguer, wonderer *par excellence*—read and responded to the final draft of this manuscript in its entirety. It is a better book because of her input. I am deeply grateful.

Reactions of the students in my Fall 1997 Children's Questioning course as they read this book in manuscript form have been helpful, inviting me into deeper and more diverse reflections about children's inquiry (and our own). I have learned much from our class discussions and from the weekly, individual Reaction Papers the students wrote, responding to the ideas of this book chapter by chapter. How I have appreciated our wondering community.

I thank The University of Texas Research Institute for the Faculty Research Assignment grant they provided for me to complete this book, and I thank Yetta Goodman, Sarah Hudelson, Chris Pappas, and Vivian Paley for the letters they wrote in support of my grant application.

To the parents and children whose voices fill these pages, my heart-felt thanks.

My two sisters, Shirley Thomas and Edith Cacciatore, have ever been supportive of their "little sister's" endeavors, but never more so than during my writing of this book.

My mother, Ruth Wells, the most wondering person I have ever known, may be the individual most responsible for my having written this book at all. To grow up in the company of one who lives with her own sense of wonder ever alive, is to be shaped as an inquirer in profound and lifelong ways. To call this person "mother," is to be blessed indeed.

It is my own children, Brenda, Susan, and Erik, who have been my most important teachers as I have tried to understand children's inquiry and its development. No reading, no study, no research has taught me *more* or *more powerfully* about the nature of children's inquiry than their daily lived demonstration.

And finally, thank you, Ben, for the "sabbatical" you provided, but even more for your absolute confidence that this book was worth the effort and that it would become a reality.

CHAPTER 1

Inquiry

Listen to four-year-old Jill and her mother as they read a bedtime story together.[1]

> MOTHER: (reading) "But the red squirrel pushed and shoved [the rabbit] until they were both settled snug and peaceful, high up in the tree under the stars."
> JILL: Where do rabbits really sleep?
> MOTHER: In their holes.
> JILL: Under the ground?
> MOTHER: Uh huh. "The next day—"
> JILL: Do they have nest-es?
> MOTHER: They build nests in trees.
> JILL: Squirrels do too?
> MOTHER: Uh huh.
> JILL: Do they lay eggs?
> MOTHER: Uhn uhn [no].
> JILL: But, who lays eggs?
> MOTHER: Birds.
> JILL: Ducks do too.
> MOTHER: Well, ducks are birds. Fish lay eggs.
> JILL: Uhn uhn [no]!
> MOTHER: Yes, they do. Right in the water.
> JILL: What else?
> MOTHER: Uh—what else lay eggs? Turtles lay eggs.
> JILL: Nuh uh!
> MOTHER: They do. Go ask Daddy. They do!

It has been said that we don't really know much about being human. "We can answer detailed questions about neuronal activity or neonatal reflexes, but we have very little to say about what it means to be human in the modern world" (Wertsch, 1991, p. 1). Surely there is much we do not know, but just as surely, there are some things we do know about "what

1

it means to be human"—some very important things, in fact. We know, for example, that to be human is to develop language and to do so in somewhat predictable ways that reflect our membership in the human species and in a particular culture. This is exactly what Jill is in the process of doing. Like virtually every child, she is figuring out—from an array of particular instances of language in use around and with her—how language works, its structures, relations, processes, but most of all its power, how language can work for her, to carry out her purposes in the world. It's a universal human thing to do, this figuring out of the complex system that is language, from myriads of specific instances of language in use. But so is it a culturally human thing to do: Jill is acquiring language within a particular community, inevitably using that group's language in that group's ways. There is, in a sense, no such thing as acquiring language, but only acquiring some community's ways of language. Jill's language will inevitably express the orientation, values, events, discourses, relationships of the community that nurtures her into its interactive ways.

I believe that whatever the community within which a child develops language, he[2] will use it throughout life to carry out three fundamental, compelling human urges: to connect with others, to understand his world, and to reveal himself within it (see Lindfors, 1990). The three come through loud and clear in Jill's conversation with her mother. Some scholars have called these three urges social, cognitive (or intellectual), and expressive (or personal) (Rogoff, 1990). The labels hardly matter, but the categories surely do, for they identify major and continuing kinds of work that language does for us. To be human in the world is both to hold these compelling purposes, and to develop and use language to carry them out.

This book is about inquiry. It is a focus that would seem to place it squarely within the second of those three human urges—the cognitive or intellectual one: to understand our world. And so it does, but this is only part of the story. Because we inquire *of others* in order to further our understanding, inquiry is as much a social act as it is an intellectual one. We can hear both in Jill's talk: we hear her trying to figure something out, but we also hear her maintaining connection with her mother. In our acts of inquiry, we reach out to another.

But even this is not all. In my inquiry act, *I* seek to go beyond; *I* seek to connect with another. My *self* is there, in the act. It is an act that arises in my own noticing, wondering, perplexing, seeking, going beyond. The sense that I am making is mine alone, unique and individual; the focus, intention, expression—all my*self* in the act. Again think of Jill, of how strong her personal presence is as she tries to further her understanding with her mother's help.

A central theme of this book is that inquiry acts are the perfect language microcosm, simultaneously and inevitably acts of connection, of understanding, of personal expression.

LANGUAGE ACTS

To act is to do something; to perform a language act is to do something by means of language. Jill and her mother are not emitting verbal sounds; they are "doing things with words," carrying out purposes that are important to them (Austin, 1962; Searle, 1970). *Languaging* is perhaps the term we need, for the notion that is central to this book is not language-as-knowledge (words, sentence structures, phonemes, genres *known*), but language-as-doing (words uttered, sentences spoken and interpreted, genres constructed, communication purposes carried out).

I am defining language acts as the seamless union of four aspects: communication *purpose* (or intention), *expression* (of purpose, of content, of stance), *participants*, *context*. We will consider these four in a general way in this chapter, and in subsequent chapters, will focus on each in relation to inquiry acts specifically.[3] For now, think of a single language act as being a turn in a conversation. It's a notion we'll modify a bit as we go along (e.g., extending it to written language), but for now the domain of "a language act" is a conversational turn.[4]

Aspects of Language Acts

Purpose. Purpose is the beginning. Every language act arises in an individual's communication purpose and is an attempt to carry it out. Our purposes are many and diverse. We comfort, persuade, entertain, inform, request, encourage, insult, promise, invite . . . and yes, we inquire. Our purposes may be conscious or not; they may be expressed as long stretches of talk (or writing) or as short stretches—perhaps only a single word or exclamation; they may be carried out directly or indirectly, honestly or deviously; they may be expressed effectively or ineffectively and may be successful or unsuccessful in the end. But whatever their diversity, there is—must be—purpose.

Notice that an individual listens purposefully no less than he speaks purposefully. As we expect in a conversation between two people, Jill and her mother alternate between speaking and listening turns. In both roles, they engage in purposeful language acts. As listener, Jill or her mother interpret the other's talk in terms of what she perceives the speaker's purpose to be and probably in terms of her own purposes as well. To interpret is to engage in a language act.

The focus of this book is inquiry, a particular subset of language acts. It is communication purpose that defines an act of inquiry: it is a language act in which one attempts to engage another in helping him to go beyond his present understanding. But when we think further about this general definition, it is clear that it encompasses many more specific purposes. What comes to mind immediately is the inquirer who, like Jill, is seeking information. But don't our inquiry acts sometimes seek confirmation of an idea, or explanation of some phenomenon? And what about wondering, that stance of openness to a world of possibilities? Aren't wondering acts attempts to engage others in our own going beyond? Do these acts come into classrooms? What do they sound like when they do? These issues are the focus of Part I.

Expression. We may think first of someone uttering verbal sounds. But clearly this is not enough. In order for those verbal sounds to constitute a language act, the individual must be saying something about something. Jill and her mother know this. They do not simply make noises back and forth. They express their ideas and feelings to one another.

Examples abound of utterances that sound like language acts but are not—drunken babbling or a parrot's mimicry, for example. My "reading" a written Swahili text aloud would be another example. I do not know Swahili, but I do know its sound-symbol correspondences and stress patterns, both of which happen to be quite regular. When I utter the sounds encoded in Swahili written text, I am producing sounds, but I am not engaging in language acts. There must be message as well as sound. Noise is not enough. Yet sound (or some overt expressive means) is necessary. To be engaged in thinking about some important idea is not to be engaged in a language act, an act of communication. The language act brings meaning and expression together: we *say* (expression) *something about something* (meaning).

It is possible to conceptualize the "expression" (the saying or writing or signing with the hands) and "meaning" separately, as two aspects of one entity. However, in the reality that is language acts, there is no separation.

> Language can . . . be compared with a sheet of paper: thought [meaning] is the front and the sound the back; one cannot cut the front without cutting the back at the same time; likewise in language, one can neither divide sound from thought nor thought from sound. (Tannen, 1989, p. 16)

Jill asks, "Where do rabbits really sleep?" Is this meaning? Yes. Is it expression? Yes.

The word *meaning* is not so easy as it might first appear, for it has many aspects. We often think first of the semantic aspect. The basic notion here is that the speaker of any language possesses a kind of mental lexicon or dictionary—a body of particular meanings that get expressed as words or as parts of words (such as past tense or plural) in his language. A major problem with this view, however, is that it suggests such neutrality: find the right meaning/word, select it, say it, and you have "expressed meaning." But word meanings aren't neutral. They live in our minds as the accumulation of the communication contexts in which we have encountered them, retaining echoes of those contexts and communication partners and events. These live in our speech as well as in our minds. Our words cannot be neutral, for it is living, breathing, feeling people who speak and interpret them. Words in dictionaries are neutral enough, but once words get up off the page and are uttered out of people's mouths, they are imbued with feelings, values, opinions, caring. They respond to the particulars of the moment—time, place, topic, partners, and so on. Dictionary meanings tend to be general fillers for slots: the suggestion is that *fancy, wasp, dance* express certain specified meanings and one places them in conversation in appropriate slots. All very simple and crisp and clean. But words in conversation are never general, always particular.

> The word does not exist in a neutral and impersonal language . . . (it is not, after all, out of a dictionary that the speaker gets his words!), but rather it exists in other people's mouths . . . serving other people's intentions: it is from there that one must take the word and make it one's own. (Bakhtin, 1981, pp. 293–294)

There is nothing neutral or impersonal about Jill's "Nuh uh." It's a word she might never find in a dictionary at all. But she has found it in other conversations. She brings it into this one as her word, carrying out her intention, and that "Nuh uh" necessarily retains the tone—the feel—of earlier encounters.

As we consider this expressive aspect of language acts in relation to inquiry acts specifically, we will not confine ourselves to interrogative forms, those so-called wh-questions (e.g., where, what, when, why) and yes/no questions and polar questions (i.e., interrogatives in which a choice is specified, X or Y). The meanings and sounds that inquiry makes out of people's mouths in real acts of communication go well beyond these favored forms. I am trying to find out what your phone number is whether I use an interrogative ("What's your number?") or a command ("Tell me your phone number") or a statement ("I need your phone number"). Clearly, syntactic form is not the issue. The focus is meaning and purpose, whatever their expressive form.

Why, then, do we invariably think of inquiry acts as questions (i.e., interrogative forms)? We know that, just as I can use a variety of forms to find out your phone number, so I can use question forms in ways that have nothing to do with inquiry at all. When I look at you angrily and say, "Ya wanna fight?" I am challenging you, not seeking your help in understanding something. When I ask, "Can I borrow your pencil?" I am not seeking information; I am seeking the use of your pencil. Why then, does this strong sense of inquiry = question persist? Do we sometimes fail to hear children's inquiry acts in classrooms when those acts are not expressed in question form? What are inquiry's other ways of expression—of seeking information, confirmation, explanation; of wondering; of making sense with the help of others? We will explore these matters in Part II.

Participants. These are the persons in the act, the interactants. They speak, listen, and respond to one another in coordinated ways, thus creating a text together.

In thinking about participants in language acts, we need to consider both the text-construc*tors* (the individuals) and their text-construc*ting* (their collaborative activity). The first is *style* —individual voices within the text; the second is *dialogue* —the partners' cooperative text-making. We hear two quite distinctive voices as Jill and her mother share their bedtime story. We also hear their turn-by-turn connection as they create this particular text, different from any they have ever constructed before. Although we can in principle separate style and dialogue, as people actually communicate with one another, there is no such separation. Two sides of a piece of paper again.

Through their language acts, participants in a conversation create text. They also create a relationship. Or, to put it another way, the relationship they build in their interaction is part of the text they create together. They may, like Jill and her mother, be in close proximity, or they may be far apart, as in an author-reader relationship. The relationships may be intimate or distant, friendly or hostile, symmetrical or asymmetrical, but whatever the specific character, there will be a relationship among the participants. These relationships are not peripheral to "the language act"; rather, they are an inevitable part of it, necessarily expressed in the participants' text. Language acts create and express interpersonal relationships every bit as much as they create and express content, information, message.[5]

In Part III we will consider interactants' style (the individual) and dialogue (the collaboration) as these relate to acts of inquiry. But this brief general introduction hints at some questions about participants within inquiry events: How do individual inquiry acts (single conversational turns) contribute to the making of larger dialogic texts—whole conversations that are exploratory in their intent? Do students and teachers create such events in classrooms? What do these events sound like? How are they "built"? What are the sounds of individual voice in inquiry acts and events? Is there such a thing as individual inquiry style—participants' own characteristic ways of inquiring that allow us (especially as teachers) to say, "Yes, that's Jill all right!"

Context. Time and place come to mind first. We say with a shrug, "Well, of course. People engage in language acts at some particular place and some particular time." But context turns out to be quite complex, both because it includes more than time and place, and also because it is dynamic and ever shifting.

First, what does context include in addition to time and place? It includes all the meanings, values, understandings, personal histories, and expectations that each participant brings to the event. It is in terms of one's rich social, intellectual, emotional past that one expresses and interprets what's going on in an interactive event (e.g., a conversation, a lesson, a meeting). It is not simply the physical environment that situates an interaction. Every interaction is also situated in the intellectual, social, and emotional understandings and feelings of the participants who create the interaction.

Further, context is not static. Underlying every language event is the question, "What's happening here?" The expressive and interpretive behavior of participants is guided by their sense of what kind of event they are carrying out and what purposes they are trying to accomplish. "We're having an argument" is a different context from "We're maintaining closeness" or "We're playing one-upmanship," or "We're sharing a bedtime story." These are all different "answers" to the question "What's happening here?" But these change in subtle ways as the partners continue to interact. The question "What's happening here?" is not one that the participants "answer" once and for all in a conversation. "Each moment is a place you've never been," says Strand (quoted in Kehl, 1983, p. 30). And so as the participants interact, the "happening" alters, shifts, reshapes itself, becoming a place the partners have never been before.

Inevitably there is an interdependence between text and context:

each conversational turn is guided by the speaker's sense of what kind of an event he is participating in, but each conversational turn also contributes to the participants' "definition" of what's happening. Jill and her mother talk in ways that are appropriate to "We're doing bedtime story." Yet this particular one extends their notion of what "doing bedtime story" can be. Context shapes text and text shapes context.

I looked up *context* in my dictionary one day and found that it comes from *contexere*, "to weave together"—*com-*, "together"; *texere*, "to weave." In a sense, the context question, "What's happening here?" is a question about what is woven together in interaction events. Woven together are time and place, and us, the participants—our meanings, our expression, our purposes, our selves. Context turns out to be less a physical reality than it is an interpretive one, and a dynamic, ever-shifting one at that.

What are inquiry's contexts? How do speakers' acts of inquiry shape their notions of what's happening? And how do these notions, in turn, shape the talk, the inquiry acts themselves? What do teachers and students weave together in inquiry acts and events in their classroom communities? It is such context questions that will be the focus of Part IV.

A Bedtime-Story Conversation

Now let's return to Jill and her mother and their bedtime story with attention to the purpose, expression, participants, and context of their language acts. Mother is reading Jill a book called *The Lively Little Rabbit* as they sit on Jill's bed together. The excerpt I've selected is heavy in inquiry acts, that is, conversational turns in which Jill engages her mother in her attempt to extend her understanding. Here is the text again, with turns numbered for easy reference in the subsequent discussion.

Text No. 1: Nest-es

1. MOTHER: (reading) "But the red squirrel pushed and shoved him [the rabbit] until they were both settled snug and peaceful, high up in the tree under the stars."
2. JILL: Where do rabbits really sleep?
3. MOTHER: In their holes.
4. JILL: Under the ground?
5. MOTHER: Uh huh. "The next day—"
6. JILL: Do they have nest-es?
7. MOTHER: They build nests in trees.
8. JILL: Squirrels do too?

9. MOTHER: Uh huh.
10. JILL: Do they lay eggs?
11. MOTHER: Uhn uhn [no].
12. JILL: But, who lays eggs?
13. MOTHER: Birds.
14. JILL: Ducks do too.
15. MOTHER: Well, ducks are birds. Fish lay eggs.
16. JILL: Uhn uhn [No]!
17. MOTHER: Yes, they do. Right in the water.
18. JILL: What else?
19. MOTHER: Uh—what else lay eggs? Turtles lay eggs.
20 JILL: Nuh uh!
21 MOTHER: They do. Go ask Daddy. They do!

Purpose. Clearly a major purpose for Jill throughout this episode is inquiry: to engage her mother's participation in her own attempt to understand her world. Jill's overarching purpose is to find out more about the "home life" of various animals she is familiar with. Each turn is slightly different in its specific purpose and advances the conversation in a slightly different way. Jill's purpose in #2 seems to be to resolve a sensed contradiction between the imaginative situation pictured in the book and the real-world situation she knows. In #4 she elaborates, pushing further. She seems to be seeking new information in #6, #10, and #12, whereas in #8 and #14 she extends the information her mother has given her to a new instance. In #16 and #20 she rejects the information her mother has given. Seeking new information, clarifying, confirming, rejecting, connecting, applying—all these are inquiry acts, for in each one Jill is attempting to engage her mother's help as she tries to figure out the nesting ways of various animals. Clearly, information-seeking is not the only way children engage others in their sense-making efforts.

Jill is not the only one who is working purposefully in this episode. Mother, too, has an overarching purpose (to help Jill understand) and she carries it out, turn by turn, in each one responding to Jill's inquiry act.

It is easy to see that this conversation serves other purposes besides inquiry: it reinforces the partners' closeness and reaffirms their relationship, it connects them in their carrying out a nightly, shared ritual, and so on. That is the way of communication—to serve multiple purposes simultaneously. But it is also easy to see that inquiry is a dominant purpose in this episode and that it guides the individual language acts that comprise it. Each act has its own purpose that contributes to the overarching one.

Expression. What about the expression of meaning in this episode, the saying-something-about-something? It is possible to consider the expressive forms Jill and her mother use. Our usual expectation is that inquiry acts will be in question (interrogative) form. Often they are, as in many of Jill's turns in this conversation. But often they are not, as in Jill's #14, #16, and #20.

As is so often the case with children's inquiry, Jill's expression of what she knows is certainly as impressive as her expression of what it is that she is trying to figure out. Her inquiry acts are possible because of what she knows already. In fact, an important part of that knowledge is knowing what it is that she doesn't know and needs to. She could not ask, "Where do rabbits really sleep?" without already understanding that rabbits do sleep, that their ways of sleeping may not be as pictured in the book, that everyday life and life as portrayed in books are often different, and so on. She knows that she can use her mother to resolve her sensed discrepancy and provide the particular information she needs, she knows what the missing pieces are that she needs, and she knows just how to use language to get these pieces from her mother. This is quite a bit of knowing, though it doesn't even scratch the surface for the one "simple" question, "Where do rabbits really sleep?"

An even more impressive feature of Jill's meaning is that it is meaning-*making* that she expresses—activated meaning, meaning in progress. Jill is not engaged in a hunting-and-gathering mission here, filling some mental storehouse with bits of information against some far-off winter. She is not accumulating; she is actively constructing. And so her expression involves confirming, opposing, seeking, relating, connecting, elaborating—all by way of building. Meaning as process, not as thing. Expression in meaning-*making*. Language *acts.*

This pair's expression does not confine itself to meaning as it relates to the physical world—to rabbits and squirrels and fish, to sleeping and building nests and laying eggs. Jill and her mother also express relationships—to each other and to the construction of knowledge. Their experience of many similar inquiry conversations in the past has built shared expectations—about their respective roles as inquirer and inquirer's helper in inquiry events such as this one, about how certainty and tentativeness are expressed, about how initiating and responding moves are carried out. Notice that although Jill is the partner with lower status in this asymmetrical relationship, in this kind of situation it is accepted as appropriate that she assume a dominant role, directing the discourse and vehemently rejecting her mother's information. This is *this* pair's understanding of this type of event. Other partners might operate with different shared notions of the personal relationships and roles in such a conversation and how they should be expressed. The meaning and expression in this episode have as much to do with interpersonal relations as they have to do with "content."

There is feeling, too. Meaning isn't—can't be—neutral. In their expression, Jill and her mother convey how they feel about what they mean and say. Definitions of words in dictionaries (actual or mental) don't tell how we feel about those words when we use them in actual communication events. Dictionaries can't capture the vehemence of "uhn uhn" in #16 and its perfunctoriness in #11, or the different levels of intensity in the meaning/expression of "they do" in #17 and #21. But in this conversation, the words-as-spoken necessarily convey these: now perfunctory, now vehement; now tentative, now authoritative, and so on. These are the inevitable thrusts that words have in conversations—the stances, attitudes, feelings, and kinds of involvement they convey. These are inevitably expressed, interpreted, and responded to in talk. They are part of the meaning that is expressed in all language acts, including acts of inquiry.

Participants. When partners interact, they necessarily come together, yet remain separate and distinct. Both of these aspects are very evident in the "Nest-es" example. The two voices (or "speaking personalities") are quite distinct: the voice of a determined, feisty four-year-old; the voice of a supportive, willing mother who is ready to hold her own against a feisty four-year old when necessary. But notice how these two "speaking personalities" (Bakhtin, 1981, p. 434) connect with one another in this interaction. There is coordination in their moves. They know how to take each other. Their turns play off each other appropriately, especially in the oppositional turns (16–20). The tension is right: the partners know how hard to push and pull, thrust and back off, without jeopardizing the interaction. Each partner knows who she is dealing with and each language act reflects this other-awareness.

The interconnectedness of the text these two partners construct is very evident in the turn-to-turn linkings. There is a tight initiate-respond pattern with responses closely contingent on initiations: seek-information $\longrightarrow$ provide information; assert $\longrightarrow$ challenge; challenge $\longrightarrow$ counter (#15 to #17); inform $\longrightarrow$ extend (#13 to #14). Turns are closely tied to one another.

The interconnectedness is also evident in the more general patterns of movement through the conversation. Topics get introduced and then expanded, elaborated, extended: where rabbits really sleep moves beyond simple "holes" to where these are and what they are like; and egg laying gets extended to a variety of animals and even gets contested—an important way of pushing a topic further. Thus each language act is not only a response to the one immediately preceding it; it also resonates across larger stretches of text. There is cooperation—a coming-together of these distinct individuals—and this cooperation occurs within and also creates context.

Context. For me, this example demonstrates rather dramatically why it is that time and place, in and of themselves, do not define context. This conversation happens at a particular time (7:30 p.m.) and in a particular place (Jill's bedroom), but the *context*—the contribution of these to the question "What's happening here?"—is not time and place per se, but rather the *significance* that these have for this pair. The notion of time that is relevant is not 7:30 p.m., but rather just-before-bed storytime; and the relevant notion of place is not bedroom, but the-place-where-we-do-bedtime-stories. Specific time and place situate the event psychologically and emotionally as well as physically.

Jill and her mother would have no difficulty answering the context question, "What's happening here?" They would say, "We are having a bedtime story." What does this answer weave together in this event? The threads surely include a host of shared expectations that derive from this pair's history of bedtime story events: expectations for their respective roles in relation to one another and to story text; expectations for how to introduce, and pursue, topics; expectations for how to connect story text with "life text"; expectations for how to construct their own text jointly—how to connect their conversational turns, and so on. The threads include the knowledge both partners bring to the event—knowledge of the physical world (of fish and birds, of squirrels and rabbits), of each other, of language. The threads include feelings, too—valuings of information, of ways of expression, of each other, of the construction of knowledge in inquiry dialogue.

As Jill and her mother create their *text* turn by turn, they also create and recreate *context*. Each conversational turn brings them to a new place in the communication event. The new question becomes, "Now what is happening?" Many of Jill's turns answer, "Now what I'm doing is eliciting your help in figuring out X"; many of her mother's turns answer, "Now what I'm doing is providing the help you seek." We readily see the reciprocal relationship of text and context in this conversation. The understanding that this is "doing bedtime story" shapes the kind of turn-by-turn talk that occurs; and the talk itself is yet another instance of "doing bedtime story," further defining (out of the partners' mouths) what "doing bedtime story" can be. Thus text and context continually create each other.

*   *   *

As this "simple" bedtime story text demonstrates so clearly, purpose, expression, participants, and context do not live in separate boxes. They are not combinable distinct elements so much as perspectives or vantage points from which to consider the wholes that are acts of language. All four are present in language acts.

The conversation between Jill and her mother also demonstrates that although each language act within it has its own kind of completeness, it also has a certain incompleteness. That is, we can sense that each language act is but a part of a larger whole that it contributes to:

- Each language act has its own specific purpose (e.g., to seek or provide help in clarifying, confirming, extending); but it also echoes the overarching purpose of the larger text (to advance Jill's understanding of the domestic ways of animals).
- Each language act is a particular expression of particular meaning—has its own "completeness" as a conversational turn; but it is also a link, at once responding to the expression that has preceded it and inviting the response that will follow.
- Each language act is expression by an individual, but it bespeaks the presence and participation of another.
- And each language act reflects and contributes to the context-of-the-moment, but also to the overarching context question, "What's happening here?"

I have used this particular conversation to demonstrate the defining features of language act—purpose, expression, participants, context—and to show their interconnection. The conversation is an inquiry episode, that is, a stretch of conversation on a given topic, with inquiry as its overarching purpose. One partner (Jill) engages another (Mother) in her own attempt to go beyond her present understanding. Each inquiry act within this episode serves, in its own way, that overarching purpose. In this text we can see language carrying out the three human urges mentioned earlier: to connect with others, to understand the world, to reveal oneself within it. To use language at all—to speak or write or sign—in conscious awareness of another's presence is to engage in an act of connection. But inquiry acts often go beyond this. They exert a pull on the partner for a verbal response. These acts tilt toward the partner in a special way. Often they hang in the air rather like unresolved chords do in music. The pull exerted by Jill's inquiry acts that are in interrogative form is obvious. Less obvious is the pull of her rejections (#16 and #20) and of her comment, "Ducks do [lay eggs] too." (#14) In a different conversation, guided by a different overarching purpose and a different context, these utterances might not be inquiry acts at all. But within *this* conversation they are, and they exert inquiry's pull on the mother. Within *this* conversation "Ducks do too" has an exploratory cast, a searching quality, an inquiring "accent" that echoes the overarching purpose that frames it. "Ducks do too" has the thrust of "How 'bout ducks?" And Jill's "uhn-uhns," in *this* conversation, are a way of saying, "But this doesn't fit in the structure I'm building." Often "no" moves are attempts to end discussion, but in this instance they are not. Jill is not saying "No! That's final." She is inviting Mother to come back at her, which Mother does by providing support for her claim. Given that inquiry acts are deliberate attempts to engage another's help in one's going-beyond agenda, it is perhaps not surprising that the pull for another's active participation is especially strong. It is a social pull, a pull into connection with another.

The intellectual urge that is getting played out in this inquiry text is perhaps too obvious to require comment. Going beyond present understanding is, after all, what Jill's acts are for, the reason she engages in them at all.

To connect, to understand, and to reveal oneself. The sounds of self—Jill's and Mother's voices—resound strongly in this text. But not only this pair, not only this text. Inquirers are activators, movers and shakers, and they shape discourse in powerful ways. They introduce agendas and use others to help carry them out. We expect the individual's understandings, interests, inclinations, topics, agenda, and expressive ways to take center stage. The inquirer tends to call the plays. Not surprising, then, if the plays themselves and also the voice that calls them should reveal the caller, the self in talk.

Acts of inquiry stand as the ultimate acts of going beyond: going beyond present understanding (intellectual); going beyond self to engage (the help of) another (social); but ever going beyond *as self* (personal).

A RATIONALE

The four aspects that define language acts for us are not new. I have not invented them. My intention in this book is to bring these various threads together in a focus on language acts of inquiry.

Why do this? Why focus just on acts of inquiry when there's a whole world of language acts of many kinds all around us? Why select inquiry acts out of this vast whole?

The first reason I have already mentioned: This subset of language acts is particularly fascinating because inquiry acts so seamlessly join, in perfect balance, the intellectual and social and personal, that combination that makes us human. The microcosm again. Inquiry acts are a clear expression of those deep and continuing urges that define us as humans: to connect, to understand, to reveal self. The three are perfectly wedded in acts of inquiry.

A second source of fascination is the imposing nature of these acts and the constant need for the inquirer to manage this imposition. Imposition is built into inquiry acts: The inquirer uses the partner(s) to help him carry out his agenda, his purposes. A major theme throughout the work of the sociolinguist Deborah Tannen is the double bind. Speakers are constantly attempting to balance two competing, contradictory pulls: affiliation and autonomy, what Tannen (1984) calls involvement and considerateness respectively. On the one hand, we want to come close to our partners, to say, in essence, we are alike. This is the pull of affiliation. But on the other hand, we want to preserve both our own and our partner's independence and autonomy, to behave respectfully toward the partner. And so we also say, in essence, we are not alike and I respect our difference and separateness. We want to be together with another, but without imposing or being imposed on. Tannen recalls one researcher's characterization of human beings one with another as rather like two porcupines "trying to get through a cold winter. They huddle together for warmth but find that their sharp quills prick each other, so they pull away and get cold. They have to keep adjusting their closeness and distance" (Tannen, 1984, p. 18).

Inquiry acts present a wonderful challenge in regard to the double bind. They are imposing acts. They are controlling acts. They not only "require" the conversational partner to verbally help the inquirer with his sense-making, but they also set up the "slot" for the partner's response to fill in order to mesh with the inquiry. (Jill's inquiry acts provide good examples.) Very controlling moves indeed. And so these acts are particularly sensitive, having everything to do with interpersonal relationships. Who has the right to impose on whom? How is this to be done without alienating the partner (whose cooperation is essential to the successful execution of the inquirer's agenda)? These acts need to be managed with care because our relationships with others can be jeopardized, especially when the inquirer is a child (lower status, less powerful) and the partner being imposed on is an adult (higher status, more powerful). Yet our urge to make sense of the world is strong and continuing, and so we keep eliciting others' help despite the risks involved in imposing. We do this through our acts of inquiry, each act requiring a wonderfully delicate balance, a perfect tension, between our urge to understand (which leads us to impose) and our urge to maintain relationships (which leads us not to impose).

Obviously there are other kinds of language acts that impose on the partner. Requests pressure the partner to do something (or to refrain from doing something). Also, in many conversational routines the initiator's turn determines (to a considerable extent) the form and content of the partner's next turn. For example, a greeting "requires" a greeting in return; a call "requires" an acknowledgment; an assertion often pulls for a counterassertion, and so on. Familiar scripts offer more specific examples: "Knock, knock" requires "Who's there?" and "Know what?" requires "No, what?" But these controlling acts, being either requests for action or else routinized exchanges, offer less-rich verbal material for study than inquiry acts do. With requests, it is often enough if one carries out a physical act in response; talk is not the issue. And in performing verbal routines, one simply decides whether he will or will not play the game; one does not use language to *manage* the game. But in inquiry acts, management of this delicate communication game is all. Talk *is* the issue. How to be close in ways that suggest we are intimate enough that I have the right to impose, while at the same time maintaining that distance we call "respect"? How do I engage in an imposing act without it being perceived as an imposition? To study inquiry acts is necessarily to study the double bind, that central tension in all interaction: autonomy and affiliation.

Third, inquiry acts are basic to an area of abiding interest and concern in our society: how children learn. It is an interest both theoretical and practical, an area fascinating in its own right, but also one with profound implications for decisions we make about the learning environments we provide for children in our society. Children's inquiry acts provide a window to their thinking, allowing us to glimpse what they are making sense of and how they are doing it, how they understand and how they use others to help them. It is an imperfect, murky window to be sure, but it's the best we've got.

Fourth, the time is right. Others have thought about inquiry acts before now. Just as I am not the first to reflect on language purposes, expression, participants, and contexts, so I am not the first to consider acts of inquiry. Researchers and scholars from a variety of disciplines have been interested in (some aspect of) inquiry acts. In one issue of *Questioning Exchange: A Multidisciplinary Review,* J. T. Dillon (1987) hints at this range in his introductory remarks to the book review section, which, in that particular issue, included reviews of books "from a dozen fields" including "education, psychology, logic, philosophy of science, linguistics, discourse analysis, computer science, socio-linguistics, hermeneutics, survey research" (p. 151). Surely the label "inquiry act" would convey something different to scholars in each of these fields, but Dillon's list indicates that the range of different disciplines that have contributed to scholarly discussion about inquiry is very wide indeed. (For two substantial literature reviews, see Van der Meij, 1986, and Townsend, 1991).

Beyond this range of scholars interested in inquiry per se is yet another group interested in children's development of inquiry: for example, psychologists interested in children's "curiosity" behavior and its expression over time, educational psychologists interested in children's expression of inquiry in classroom settings, developmental psycholinguists interested in children's development and use of particular interrogative structures that play important roles in inquiry, developmental sociolinguists interested in the interactive contexts in which children participate in inquiry events. And so the question arises: Why now? If so many others have already studied a variety of aspects of inquiry acts and the development of inquiry in children, then why engage in yet another examination?

There are several answers, the first being that it is precisely *because* of this large and diverse body of work that a reconsideration of inquiry is both possible and called for: possible, because there is much material to work with, and called for, because that material exists rather as free-floating bits looking for a comprehensive, coherent structure. Interesting bits and pieces, even in abundance, are not enough. My hope is that the language-act framework I am suggesting will provide a useful structure for considering inquiry.

Besides the bits-and-pieces limitation of the existing research on inquiry and its development in children, there is a fundamental form/function confusion that mars much of this work, and it is a confusion we now have sufficient understanding to deal with: the confusion of *interrogative* (question form) with *inquiry* (communication purpose). We will deal with this matter in depth in Chapter 4, but it is important to point out here that this confusion has resulted in a large body of work that "thinks" it is about inquiry (especially about increasing children's engagement in it), but is actually about getting children to say more interrogatives in certain situations, for example, in classrooms. You can, of course, play with variables in ways that will increase the number of question forms children produce or alter the kinds of questions children ask (e.g., constraint-seeking questions in 20-question games) without in either case (amount or type) doing anything at all about *inquiry*—children's own real attempts to engage others in helping them understand. This body of research that confused interrogative form with inquiry act missed much of what it was trying to understand and foster. Inquiry, as we've seen already in Jill's "Nest-es" transcript, expresses itself in other forms than interrogative. To recognize inquiry only when it expresses itself as "when," "where," "why," and so on is to miss much that is inquiry.

This is not to say that the study of interrogative form makes no contribution to our understanding of inquiry acts; but it is to say that we must not equate "inquiry" and "interrogative"—not think that a study of the one provides insights about the other. As we'll see in Chapter 4, this turns out to be a more complex and interesting issue than may appear from this brief comment. At this time in our history, we're in a good position to understand and appreciate more fully the contribution that a consideration of interrogative form does make to a study of inquiry acts, and also to recognize more clearly the ways in which it does not contribute but may, in fact, confound. And so the consideration of inquiry in this book is a reconsideration in which it may be possible to examine inquiry acts holistically, as language acts, and do so without falling into the form-function confusion that has beset much work in this area.

There are several important voices that have not been taken into account in earlier discussions of children's *questioning*, but that have much to contribute to a consideration of children's *inquiry*. Vygotsky and (especially) Bakhtin are two important voices you will hear in the coming pages. I find it an interesting paradox that so much of American research and scholarship that announces its focus as "questioning" turns out to have very little to say about inquiry as I define it here; whereas much of Vygotsky's and Bakhtin's work, although explicitly purporting to be about something other than inquiry (e.g., inner and outer speech, multivoicedness, genre) offers powerful insights and new perspectives on acts of inquiry.

The final reason for this consideration of inquiry underlies all the others. That reason is the importance of inquiry in classrooms. I believe that an exploration of inquiry—its nature and, especially, its power—has profound educational implications.

It matters that the social, intellectual, and personal join in the child's acts of inquiry. We have heard for so long that our business is to educate "the whole child" that the words have become a vacuous cliché. "Yeah, yeah," we say to ourselves. To reconsider inquiry acts in classroom settings may be to put life and meaning back into the words "whole child." There is nothing so *whole* in the human being—child or adult—as engaging others (social) in one's own act of going beyond present understanding (intellectual) and doing so as self, for reasons that are one's own (personal).

- The classroom supports the *social* nature of inquiry. There the child has many others to engage in his exploring, his meaning-making,

his going beyond. He has others to join him in collaboratively constructing inquiry texts.

- The classroom supports the *intellectual* nature of inquiry. Indeed,
  we take the intellectual to be the primary business of classrooms.
  It's what we are about, consciously and deliberately, in school. It's
  how the institution defines itself: as a learning place.
- The classroom supports the *individual* nature of inquiry. It is a community comprised of and appreciative of distinctive individuals—
  voices—within it. Here there are many voices. Here there are many
  ways of carrying out this social and intellectual act that we call
  inquiry. The presence of a range of distinct, individual voices in the
  classroom may help the child to hear and appreciate his own—his
  voice, his "speaking personality" that makes its distinctive mark
  on this community.

I know of no place that holds such power and promise for children's inquiry development as does the classroom. And to develop ways of inquiry is to develop one's humanness—social, intellectual, personal. It
matters that these three come together and receive support in classroom
communities.

It matters that inquiry acts are acts of imposition. How to manage
imposition in our interactions with others is central to language, and it is
central in a way that reaches deep, deep into human relationships, for it
has to do with balancing concern for self and other. This is the very heart
of human relationships: me and you. Us.

Classroom communities may be the best of all possible places for
children to learn how to manage imposition, which means learning how
to maintain that delicate balancing of self and other. In many mainstream
homes, parents try very hard to respond to their children's inquiries without suggesting that these acts are imposing. Oh, it is true that even the
most well-intentioned parent sometimes loses patience with the child's
endless "Why?" But many parents try to remain patient no matter how
persistent the child is, thus suggesting that inquiry acts do not impose.
This suits such parents' notion that good parenting involves accepting
and supporting children's curiosity. But for children who come from such
homes, it may be that the classroom is a particularly good place for learning that inquiry acts are acts of imposition, the various ways in which
they impose on another, and, especially, ways to manage this imposition
"politely," that is, taking into account both self and other, and expressing
yourself in a way that conveys this two-way respect.

The classroom has much to offer the child as he learns to deal with this most basic aspect of all interaction (not just inquiry):

- I think of the teacher as an inquirer herself, one who initiates genuine inquiries, but does so in ways that voice respect for the children from whom she seeks help with her own understanding.
- I think of the many inquiry acts and events the child will participate in as both inquirer and responder. The child plays out his own inquiries and gets responses, but also hears the myriad of others' inquiries and the various responses they receive. It is the presence of many voices here, each one distinctive, that offers the possibility of the child becoming aware of how self-other relations get managed respectfully (or not) in inquiry discourse.

It *matters* that the child have opportunities in the classroom to learn to impose respectfully in his inquiry.

It matters that inquiry acts are absolutely fundamental in children's learning. The one place in American society that exists explicitly for the purpose of fostering children's learning is the school. Surely the school supports other aspects of a child's development also; and surely other institutions (e.g., home, church) support the child's learning. Nonetheless, it is school that, in our society, takes the child's learning as its reason for being.

I believe that there is no single human activity more fundamental and powerful in one's learning than inquiry. We hear much about the Zone of Proximal Development these days, that particularly promising cognitive area where a child can go further with another's help. This is where inquiry lives. Vygotsky (1978, 1986) points out that it is neither what the child can do independently already, nor what is way beyond the child's current ability, that is most promising for the child's learning at any given moment. Rather, the place of promise is that area just beyond the child's reach. Acts of inquiry occur at this very place. The child controls this "zone" through his or her acts of inquiry. These acts bring the helping other—often the teacher—to that perfect place, the going-beyond-with-help place. I believe that more often than not, children "know" that place better than we adults do. The child "knows" where he is, though he may not know that he knows it. But his inquiry act tells us where he is and wants to go, and brings us to that place to help him.

And so it *matters* that children's inquiry acts and the conversations they engender be central to the life of a classroom. These are the heart of a child's learning, and they are our best hope of recognizing how we can help. Helping-in-learning is what I understand teaching to be.

It matters that we invite new voices into the discussion. These new voices can help us hear, recognize, appreciate, and foster the language of inquiry. It matters that we hear the sounds that inquiry makes: what it is and also what it isn't. It matters that we be able to distinguish between real inquiry discourse and a host of pretender events in the classroom, events such as whole-group discussions that have much to do with teachers' control and students' performance, but little to do with the *inquiry* of either. It matters that inquiry acts, not question forms, propel and shape classroom discourse. New voices in the dialogue help us identify the purposes, expression, participants, contexts of inquiry acts, help us hear and distinguish the sound of inquiry and the sound of pretense, the sound of exploration and the sound of performance.

Perhaps these voices go beyond helping us hear what inquiry is and isn't, to helping us envision what it can be in our classrooms. This may matter most of all.

PART I

Purpose

In this book, it is communication purpose that defines an act of inquiry: *the speaker's attempt to elicit another's help in going beyond her own present understanding.* In Chapter 2, we focus on *purpose* or, more accurately perhaps, on purposes, for there are many kinds of inquiry acts. For example, some are information seeking in their intent, whereas others seek to explore, to reflect, to wonder. Whatever the specific purpose, however, the inquiry act will in some way constitute the speaker's attempt to bring another into her own act of understanding. Because inquiry is an act of purposeful communication and *not* a linguistic structure, we select conversational turn (rather than sentence) as the unit of interest.

In Chapter 2, we will consider early aspects of children's inquiry development and then, in Chapter 3, we will focus on the classroom, trying to differentiate between acts and events that do carry out inquiry purposes, and those "pretender" acts and events that only appear to do so.

CHAPTER 2

Inquiry Purpose

What other starting point could there be than *purpose*? It is, after all, one's communication purpose that gives rise to any language act: It is because we want to accomplish something in interaction with another that we speak or write at all.[1]

But when we examine inquiry in a deliberate way, as we do now, attempting to understand its development in children, there are additional reasons to begin with communication purpose. The first thing we need to do is decide how to identify the unit we are after. It is purpose that motivates this decision. I have heard some researchers liken the task of studying a particular phenomenon to that of making rabbit stew: The first step in both is to catch the rabbit. Catching real rabbits is a lot easier than catching the "rabbits" we are interested in, for real rabbits are recognizable, distinct entities: Here is one rabbit and over here is another. But language acts (including acts of inquiry) are not obvious units. The question is, how shall we define the unit of interest in such a way that we can listen to a conversation and say, "Here is one inquiry act and here is another." Communication purpose will be the basis of this decision, and the starting point for our consideration of inquiry.

After establishing the unit, we will focus on two kinds of inquiry acts that carry out rather different purposes: information-seeking and wondering. We'll do this in two parts, first, by contrasting two conversations that exemplify the difference, and then, in the next section, by characterizing each of these types of inquiry.

Finally, we'll turn our attention to the early development of inquiry. What are the beginnings of this communication purpose in children? How does inquiry develop over time? To address the first of these questions, we'll examine the development of (verbal) inquiry's precursors during the child's first year, and to address the second, we'll consider two basic notions that will, in subsequent chapters, guide our exploration of children's continuing inquiry development.

Purpose is our starting point, then, as we begin to explore inquiry. As you will see, it is the basis for

- identifying acts of inquiry in conversation;
- defining inquiry acts of information-seeking and of wondering;
- understanding the beginnings of inquiry in children.

THE UNIT

What is *"an* act of inquiry?" The basic unit in any exploration must meet two conditions: It must have internal unity, must make sense as an entity, recognizable and distinct from other entities; and that unity must be of a kind that is relevant to the particular focus of interest. Our interest is communication, and the unit that is most relevant for us is *conversational turn.*

Often we encounter studies in which *sentence* is selected as the basic unit. Surely the sentence would meet our first condition: It is an identifiable distinct entity. But a sentence is a unit of formal grammar, not a unit of communication. So, although the sentence has unity, it is the wrong kind of unity for an exploration of inquiry acts. We need a unit of communication, not a unit of grammar.

Conversational turn provides the relevant basic communication unit for this exploration. Bakhtin (1986) calls this *utterance.* Unlike a sentence, an utterance is not an abstract language *form;* rather, it is a language *act.* We can consider its purposes, expression, participants, context. But the grammatical unit *sentence* has none of these. It exists in a social vacuum as a theoretical possibility, not as an actual social occurrence.

One might object to this argument, saying that conversational turns are made up of sentences. But this is not so. When a conversational turn and a sentence coincide, that is simply accidental. Often a conversational turn is smaller than a sentence. Jill's "unh uh" would be an example. And often a conversational turn is more than a sentence (several sentences carrying out one purpose). Also, conversational turns may include elements that are not grammatical units at all—"uh," repeats, mispronunciations—all of which have nothing to do with sentences (syntactic units) but a great deal to do with utterances (e.g., indicating the mental state of the speaker). The unity of a conversational turn is the communication work it is doing, not the language structures it uses to do that work. Jill's "unh uh," whatever its status as a grammatical entity, is doing the important communication work of disagreeing with her mother. And so conversational turn (or utterance) has the kind of inherent unity we need, unity that resides in its existence in actual (oral or written) conversation. Inquiry acts, like all language acts, are not grammatical structures. They are purposeful communication acts: they serve the speaker's purpose of getting another's help in her attempt to (further) understand.

I rely entirely on Bakhtin (1986) here, both in describing the unit that is a language act (utterance or conversational turn) and in arguing its relevance. The unit is his, not mine. I am simply appropriating it. (See Todorov, 1984, for a slightly different description.)

Bakhtin was adamant in distinguishing between language structures on the one hand—words (lexicon), sentences (syntax), sounds (phonology) — and communication on the other. He drew a sharp distinction between words in dictionaries and words "out of people's mouths." Only the latter are communication. The units people actually speak or write in interaction with one another are utterances, conversational turns. They will necessarily include linguistic elements, but these are simply the raw materials used in communication. I think of the linguistic elements (words, sentences, sounds) as being rather like the paints an artist uses. What the artist is trying to do is create an artwork. She uses paint to accomplish this, but paint is not the point. If we were to catch the artist working at her easel and ask, "What are you doing?" she would not answer, "I am using paint." She would say, "I am painting a picture." So, too, if we asked a speaker engaged in a conversation, "What are you doing?" her answer would not be "I am saying words" or "I am saying sentences" or "I am making sounds." Rather, she might tell us "I am trying to convince X that . . ." or "I am telling X about the time I . . ." or "I am encouraging X to . . ." or, in the case of an inquiry act, "I am trying to get X to help me figure out . . ."

Bakhtin (1986) characterizes utterances according to three features: boundaries, finalization (or completion), and expressive aspects. Boundaries *define* utterances (i.e., identify them with certainty), whereas completion and expressiveness *describe* utterances (i.e., tell what utterances are like).

> The *boundary* criterion for utterance is simply stated:
> The boundaries of each concrete utterance as a unit of speech communication are determined by a *change of speaking subjects*, that is, a change of speakers. Any utterance—from a short (single-word) rejoinder in everyday dialogue to the large novel or scientific treatise—has, so to speak, an absolute beginning and an absolute end: its beginning is preceded by the utterances of others, and its end is followed by the responsive utterances of others . . . (Bakhtin, 1986, p. 71)

Thus utterance is a unit that is relatively easy to identify, especially if it is a written utterance (an essay, a telephone message, a letter, a bumper sticker, a poem). The researcher who tape-recorded and subsequently transcribed the Jill "Nest-es" episode had an easy time deciding the bounds of each utterance, the points at which speakers changed. It is not always quite so easy. In many conversations there are overlaps in turns (two or more people speaking at once), imperfections of all sorts (hesitations, backtrackings, bumblings), aborted utterances (conversational turns that seem to stop in the middle), interruptions, and so on. Nevertheless, conversation bounded by the speech of others is about as clear and convenient a unit as we could find.

However, clarity and convenience are not the reasons to choose it. We choose utterance because of a dialogic principle: The speaker has carried out her purpose for that moment in the conversation and has turned the conversation over to someone else. Bakhtin (1986) sometimes speaks of utterances as links in a dialogic chain. This metaphor works well in characterizing the interlinking boundedness of utterances; that is, conversational turns are individual, distinct units, yet each one is connected to preceding and subsequent turns.

The partners, too, are linked, and this linkage is reflected in their dialogue. Each one's utterance reflects the other's presence. In each turn the speaker *turns* to the partner, and this "quality of turning to someone, is a constitutive feature of the utterance; without it the utterance does not and cannot exist" (Bakhtin, 1986, p. 99). We can see this turning to someone in Jill's utterances in the "Nest-es" transcript. Whether questions, observations ("Ducks do [lay eggs] too"), or protests ("Uhn uhn!"), each turn is positioned in relation to the partner. If we read just Jill's utterances aloud (or just her mother's) it would sound like one part of a telephone conversation. We would sense a partner's presence. Each of Jill's utterances is bounded by her mother's, each one carries out her purpose, and each one inclines toward and connects with her mother's contributions. Thus, though each utterance is the contribution of a single speaker, it is dialogic, not monologic, for it whispers the presence of another.

Turn-taking is a fundamental principle in interaction. Conversational turn is a unit that squares with our sense of how conversations work. We expect that speaking turns will move back and forth among participants. Like most "rules" (expectations) that guide human behavior, turn-taking in conversation may be more evident in the breech than the observance. We often follow a turn-taking, one-speaker-at-a-time pattern, but often we do not. We know how to violate this turn-taking expectation, for example, with "back channel talk" (the "um-hms," "ohs," and "ahs" that we say in accompaniment to a speaker's turn), with acceptable interruptions (e.g., finishing a partner's sentence or chiming in on the partner's predictable speech), and so on. We know to what extent we can violate this turn-taking principle. We know how to repair the conversation when turn-taking violations threaten it. All these attest strongly to our expectation of turn-taking as a guiding principle. And it is one which guides speech events involving any number of participants (e.g., in church services, lessons, meetings, bull sessions): however many participants there are, we still expect the event to be managed according to some kind of turn-taking organizational scheme. Thus Bakhtin's utterance is the relevant unit for communication events involving any number of participants.

To consider conversation as a set of alternating turns is to consider it from the outside: it is to watch turns move back and forth between speakers. But when Bakhtin (1986) considers the second aspect of utterances—their completion (or finalization)—he is looking at the "inner side of the change of speech subjects" (Bakhtin, 1986, p. 76), the unity of the conversational turn from within itself. When one speaker's utterance is complete, there is a change of speaker. But what makes an utterance complete?

The determining factor for completion is getting the job done, carrying out one's purpose at that point in the interaction.

> In each utterance—from the single-word, everyday rejoinder to large, complex works of science or literature—[it is] the speaker's *speech plan* or *speech will,* which determines the entire utterance, its length and boundaries . . . what the speaker *wishes* to say. (Bakhtin, 1986, p. 77)

As with the feature of boundaries, so with the feature of completion: a dialogical principle is central. "The first and foremost criterion for the finalization [completion] of the utterance is *the possibility of responding to it . . .* of assuming a responsive attitude toward it" (Bakhtin, 1986, p. 76). *Completion* here is not complete in the sense of final and forever, once and for all. It is completeness in the sense of enough for now. Enough is enough when there is the possibility of a partner's response and the speaker turns toward the partner(s) in anticipation of that response.

Consider the "Nest-es" transcript again. The "inner side" completeness of each utterance is evident. In each of Jill's turns she provides enough to allow, indeed, to invite, her mother's response. Jill's intention for many of her utterances could be phrased as "to get mother's help in finding out X." In other utterances her purpose is to add her observation or to protest. In every case it is her purpose—what she "wishes to say [do]" in the conversation—that makes her utterance complete.

Bakhtin's (1986) third aspect of utterance, which he calls *expressiveness,* brings warm-blooded, feeling human beings into the act. He insists that no utterance is neutral. Sentences, those syntactic structures that live in grammar books, are neutral, and words out of dictionaries are neutral too. But utterances, "words out of people's mouths," are never neutral. They necessarily express "the speaker's subjective emotional evaluation of the referentially semantic content of his utterance" (Bakhtin, 1986, p. 84). They also express "how the speaker (or writer) senses . . . his addressees . . . those to whom the utterance is addressed" (p. 95). The speaker has a relationship to the content and to the partner(s) in the event, and her utterances express how she feels about both. Sentences, on the other hand, are neutral because they do not come from people's mouths. There is no human, no voice, and therefore no "evaluative accent" as Bakhtin calls it. But when words are spoken in real dialogues, they must be spoken *in some way*, for example, angrily or cheerfully or condescendingly or ironically or perfunctorily. "Intonation is the sound that value makes" (Clark & Holquist, 1984, p. 10). There is no speaking without this "intonation" that indicates how the utterance is to be taken.

We hear this expressive aspect loud and clear in the "Nest-es" text. We cannot hear Jill's and her mother's actual voices, but the words printed on the page suggest the evaluative accents. We hear Jill's voice—now quizzical, now determined, now protesting; and we hear Mother's voice—now the voice of the provider, now the clarifier, now the authority. These evaluative accents are not in the words as dictionary entries, but only in the words as Jill and her mother *voice* them in their utterances.

Notice that this expressive aspect of utterance, like the first two (boundedness and completion), bespeaks dialogicality, a turning to someone. It is not by itself that Jill's "Where do rabbits really sleep?" has a challenging accent; rather, it expresses challenge in relation to what her mother has just read. It is not standing alone that Jill's "Uhn uhn!" and "Nuh uh!" express protest; rather, these utterances express protest in opposition to her mother's immediately preceding assertions. And her mother's provider and clarifier voices provide and clarify in response to Jill's quizzical, seeking voice, and that voice changes to an authority voice in response to Jill's protests. "Evaluative intonation" (expressiveness), like boundedness and completion, resonates with the speaker's awareness of the other in a dialogic event. Expressiveness has that essential "quality of turning to someone" (Bakhtin, 1986, p. 99). It is dialogic.

The final point to make about utterances is that each one combines the repeatable and the unrepeatable. Bakhtin (1981, 1986) saw many aspects of life as playing out a constant tension between centripetal and centrifugal forces, that is, between those forces that pull inward toward a steady and stabilizing center, and those that pull outward, seeking to destabilize. The linguistic aspects of language—the semantic and syntactic and phonological/graphemic elements we inevitably use in talking or writing—these are the *repeatable*. But the use we make of these means in communicating with others is *unrepeatable*, absolutely unique. Think again of the artist. Her paints, brushes, canvas are all repeatable. But the paintings she creates out of these are unrepeatable, each one unique. So too with us as we communicate with others. Jill and her mother use words that they have used before and will use again. They also use sentence structures that they have used before and will use again—interrogatives, exclamations, declaratives. And there is nothing new in the consonant and vowel sounds they produce. All these linguistic elements are givens in the language system they are using (English). Yet using these means, Jill and her mother create utterances that are altogether new. They have learned their words from the mouths of others in other social events, but they use them in ways that are their own, actualizing their own communication purposes.

ACTS OF INQUIRY

Let's move now from considering language acts in general, to considering inquiry acts specifically: those language acts whose purpose is to engage another in one's attempt to understand. I am using two texts to demonstrate key aspects of inquiry utterances. Both are inquiry texts, that is, each one not only includes numerous inquiry utterances, but also has inquiry as its overarching purpose, the purpose that frames and guides the entire conversation. Inquiry *utterances* do not occur only in inquiry *texts*. They also occur in texts that have some other framing purpose (e.g., to tell a story or to play out an imagined situation in sociodramatic play). But the two focal texts of this chapter are, like Jill's "Nest-es" transcript, inquiry texts: In each one, the purpose of the text as a whole is to try to understand something, reflect on something, figure something out with the help of one or more other people.

The two texts are very different. The first is another bedtime-story conversation between Jill and her mother. The second is a literature discussion among 15 eleventh-grade students and their teacher. It is a more complex and "messy" event than Jill's bedtime conversation. The texts differ in many ways, including age and number of participants and type of interaction event. However, as you will see, they differ especially in the type of inquiry acts that dominate each one. I present the two texts together (below) because the contrast between them highlights those different types of prevalent inquiry utterances which give each text its own distinctive rhythm and tone. Another way to say this is that the two texts play out different ways of being dialogic in inquiry, different ways of "turning to someone" for help in going beyond present understanding. Again purpose is the determining factor: in their utterances, the participants in these two events turn to others differently because their inquiry purposes are different. The dominant inquiry purpose in the first text is *information-seeking*, and in the second text it is *wondering*.

Text No. 2: Hospital

Four-year-old Jill and her mother[2] are conversing during a bedtime story reading of one of Jill's favorite books, *Curious George Goes to the Hospital* (Rey & Rey, 1966). They are in Jill's bedroom. They have come to the place in the story where Curious George, a mischievous monkey, has just been taken to the operating room for the removal of a puzzle piece that he swallowed.

1. JILL: Mommy, when I went to the hospital, did I cry when they first put that thing on me? (She is pointing to a picture of Curious George on the operating table being given ether.)
2. MOTHER: Uh-huh.
3. JILL: How do you know? Did you hear me?
4. MOTHER: I knew you were crying when you went in the room.
5. JILL: Why?
6. MOTHER: 'Cause you were afraid. You were like little Betsy, weren't you? Right? That's right. (Betsy is a child in the story who is a very frightened patient.)
7. JILL: I just went one time before, right?
8. MOTHER: Uh-huh.
9. JILL: But sometimes when you're just sick and you don't got to get your tonsils out, you don't use that thing, do you?
10. MOTHER: Unh-unh [no].
11. JILL: What do you do when you go to the hospital when you're just sick?
12. MOTHER: Well, it depends on what's wrong with you. Sometimes you just rest there until you get better and sometimes you need an operation.
13. JILL: What's an operation?
14. MOTHER: That's when they cut you open and take something out of you—
15. JILL: Yuk!
16. MOTHER: —or fix it or put something inside of you and sew you back up and then you're good as new! (#14 and #16 constitute

one turn for the mother. Jill's "Yuk" interrupts and overlaps her mother's turn.)

17. JILL: If I go, I hope I go to rest.
18. MOTHER: Yeah.
19. JILL: That's my favorite part in the hospital.
20. MOTHER: Yeah.
21. JILL: Have you been to the hospital before?
22. MOTHER: Huh?
23. JILL: Have you been to—how many times have you been to the hospital?
24. MOTHER: I've been to the hospital three times.
25. JILL: Uh-oh! Three?
26. MOTHER: Uh-huh.
27. JILL: OK. What was the first one?
28. MOTHER: The first time was when I was a little girl. I was eleven years old. And I went to the doctor—to the hospital—because I had rheumatic fever.
29. JILL: What's rheumatic fever?
30. MOTHER: Well, it's where—
31. JILL: You just had to rest?
32. MOTHER: Just had to rest.
33. JILL: That's good.
34. MOTHER: I had to lay in bed a long time and they took lots of blood tests and stuff but that's all. Took lots of medicine and rested and then I had hepatitis.
35. JILL: What's hepatitis?
36. MOTHER: Well, that's where your liver gets sick inside of you and I had to just rest again.
37. JILL: And then?
38. MOTHER: And the other time I went was when I had a little baby girl.
39. JILL: Oh. (laughs)
40. MOTHER: Named Jill.

Text No. 3: Gertrude

An 11th-grade English class of 15 students and their teacher are discussing *Hamlet*.[3] Silca's opening question shifts the discussion to a consideration of Gertrude, the queen (Hamlet's mother), who married the king's brother shortly after the king's death. In this transcript, a dash (—) indicates an interruption and ellipses (. . .) indicate an utterance that ends by trailing off. The students chose their own names for the research study from which this excerpt comes. Silca, Miranda, and the teacher are female; Fidel and Tree are male.

1. SILCA: Um, did the queen have a choice on who she was, when she remarried? Like, did he ask her, "Will you marry me?" and she said, "Yes," or was, was it kind of just planned?
2. TEACHER: See, we don't really know that. Um, do you mean like the government, would they plan it, is that what you mean?
3. SILCA: No, I mean like, did she have a say in her second marriage? 'Cause I mean Hamlet's like blaming his mom.
4. TEACHER: Um-hm [Yes].
5. SILCA: It's kind of, he's kind of like copping out or something. He's like, instead of saying it to—
6. FIDEL: Well, maybe it was the only way she could stay queen.
7. SILCA: —instead of saying it to, to his new father.
8. TEACHER: Right. He goes after his mother.
9. SILCA: Yeah.
10. TEACHER: Yeah, I, I think, well, judging from just some clues, I think she must have had a say. I mean the fact that Hamlet would be so angry about her remarrying at all suggests that she had a choice. Um, I mean, and I can't imagine why she, you know, why she wouldn't have a choice unless it were something that were dictated by the government. But since—
11. SILCA: 'Cause I thought they were, I don't know, I didn't think that they were asked, that it was all arranged. Like maybe, um . . .
12. TEACHER: Yeah. I don't, I don't think there are very many textual clues to suggest that. Although really we just get Hamlet's perspective on it, that's true. Fidel?
13. FIDEL: Maybe she was marrying him 'cause that was the only way that she could stay queen.
14. TEACHER: It seems like a good possibility.
15. TREE: That's not what *he* thinks, though.
16. TEACHER: Hamlet? What do you think he thinks?
17. TREE: He thinks that, that she was probably part of it. I, that's what I think.
18. TEACHER: Do you think that's why he's so angry with her and why he's so, um, in a way cruel to her?
19. TREE: I mean, if, if your mother married, married your uncle two months after your father died, and you know that your father killed, your uncle killed your father—
20. TEACHER: Right.

21. TREE: —you know that there was probably something going on even when your father was still alive.

22. TEACHER: Good. It does seem that they're in cahoots. Um, and that does seem to be a lot of Hamlet's motivation, you know, to, when he says that he's gonna set a mirror up so that Gertrude can see her inmost self, he seems to suggest that he wants, you know, that he's gonna reflect this to her, and whether he's reflecting what Gertrude herself is like or whether what, is what Hamlet perceives Gertrude, um, as being like.

23. MIRANDA: It seems that in that whole part where he, where he was talking to her about, um, setting a mirror up and all that, he seems to be, I don't know what it really, um, really self-righteous or—

24. TEACHER: Uh-hm [Yes].

25. MIRANDA: —or, I don't know.

26. TEACHER: Yeah. He even says that, doesn't he?

27. MIRANDA: I don't know.

(Turns #5 and #7; #19 and #21; and #23 and #25 are single turns overlapped by #6, #20, and #24 respectively. In the following discussion these single turns are indicated as #5/7, #19/21, and #23/25.)

In Text No. 2 Jill is trying to enlist her mother's help in learning more about hospital experience. Each of Jill's utterances is an act of inquiry contributing to this overarching purpose. Her mother's purpose is to provide the help Jill seeks. Carrying out this agenda is not all these two are doing: they are also sharing a bedtime story, being close, and reaffirming their relationship. But their joint endeavor of helping Jill build understanding of hospital experience is a major purpose of this text and reverberates in all the utterances within it. It produces overtones, an overriding tone that resonates in the utterances of the whole.

In many of Jill's utterances she seeks specific information from her mother: She seeks facts (Did I cry?), seeks explanations and reasons (Why?), seeks support (How do you know?), seeks confirmation (. . . right? When . . . you don't use that thing, do you?). But she does other things too by way of building her understanding: She reacts to the information she is getting (Yuk!), she evaluates it (That's good), she connects it to her own life (If I go . . . That's my favorite part . . .)—all-important ways of using language toward further understanding. Notice that we might not consider some of these conversational turns to be inquiry acts if we had chosen a different unit from Bakhtin's utterance (e.g., if we had chosen interrogative). But all of Jill's utterances are turns that keep turn-

ing toward her mother for support in her meaning-making. Thus they
are inquiry utterances, resonating with the framing purpose of this inquiry text.

Mother's turns provide information, but do so in ways that turn the
conversation back toward Jill again. Her turns bring momentary closure
to each seek-information/provide-information pair, but they do so in a
way that suggests active waiting, a way that seems to say, "What next?"
or "Now what do you want to know?"

Notice the burst-pause rhythm of this text, with Jill primarily responsible for the bursts and her mother for the pauses. The boundedness
(outer side) and completion (inner side) features of the utterances here
are determined by the purposes of the participants. Those features give
rise to the burst-pause rhythm. The dominant pattern in the alternation
of turns (boundedness) is one of seek/provide. The completion within
most of Jill's turns is her specification of what she seeks from her mother
(her questions), thus providing the "possibility of [her mother] responding." Her "Yuk!" and "Uh-oh!" are emotive, knee-jerk responses, with
a quite different kind of completion from that in utterances #17 and #19
in which Jill works on the information her mother has provided by relating it directly to herself ("If I go, I hope I go to rest." "That's my favorite
part; . . .") Notice how her mother's "Yeah" responses in #18 and #20 support Jill's reflective pause before her next initiating "burst," "Have you
been to the hospital?" Each of Jill's inquiry acts carries out her "speech
plan or speech will"—her purpose at that point in the conversation, as
she works to build her understanding in concert with her mother.

Inevitably there is expressiveness in the partners' conversational
turns—their feeling, caring voices in the inquiry utterances of this inquiry
text. You can hear Jill's "accent" or "intonation" expressive of concern
(#1), of disgust (#15), of premonition (#25), of perseverance, and so on.
There is real caring expressed here about hospital experience, about her
mother, about the work they are doing together in carrying out the inquiry purpose(s) of this conversation. Her mother's voice expresses its
nonneutrality too. She provides the information Jill seeks, but does so in
a voice that reassures.

The 11th graders' text has a very different rhythm. Its flow is different
largely because its dominant purpose is different and, as with Jill's hospital text, the rhythm has much to do with the boundedness, completion,
and expressiveness of the purpose-guided utterances within it.

Jill's purpose was to gather information in order to further her understanding of hospital experience. But information gathering is not the purpose of the 11th graders' literature discussion. The students and teacher
in this event are exploring possibilities. Though this involves trying to get

clarification of whether or not Gertrude had a choice of husband, for the most part these students and their teacher already have the necessary information. Now they seek to play with it, to reflect on it from various perspectives. The rhythm of this text expresses the play-with-possibilities purpose that frames it. Whereas Jill's purpose was closure—to get each bit she needed, bit after bit, resulting in the text's burst-pause rhythm— the exploratory purpose of the Gertrude discussion is to keep the discussion open. This results in a text in which utterances do not bring finality in burst-pause pairs. Rather, it is one in which each utterance holds the discussion open, hanging suspended in the air. The purpose as the conversation proceeds from turn to turn is to maintain "opensure." Each turn "turns to" the participants as an invitation to add a further possibility to the pool or to reflect on a possibility already suggested.

The "inner side" of the inquiry utterances here—their "quality of completion"—also reflects purpose. The participants are playing with possibilities relating to Gertrude's role, something Shakespeare indicates little about in *Hamlet*. The ambiguity invites speculation. An utterance is complete when (the speaker believes) it has carried out her purpose at that point in the interaction. Some inquiry utterances in this text seek clarification; their completeness is the specification of the point that needs to be clarified (#1, #2, #3, #16, #18). Other utterances attempt to provide clarification: Their completion is the provision of what (the speaker thinks) the other seeks (#10, #17, #19). The purpose of some utterances is to suggest possibilities: Their completeness is the articulation of the possibility being suggested (and perhaps a reason for considering it) (#5/7, #6/13, #15, #17). Other utterances serve to offer a further reflection on a possibility already put forward (#10, #11, #12, #19/21, #22). Still other utterances serve to encourage the consideration of possibilities (#4, #8, #14, #20, #24, #26). These utterances are the teacher's. Notice how minimal they are. The teacher wants the students to be the ones to carry this exploratory discussion, so she gives just enough to affirm them, without taking over the discussion. Her support is not only for the specific contributions made, but also for the endeavor itself. In this discussion, each utterance is complete when it has carried out the speaker's purpose at that point in the conversation. Together the utterances are threads that weave an inquiry text of an exploratory kind.

The participants' exploratory stance is expressed throughout. Here is Bakhtin's nonneutrality (expressiveness) once again. A tone of tentativeness sings its way through this text. The participants' talk expresses reflection and possibility, not finality. The talk is rough draft, not final draft in form (Barnes, 1986). Some utterances trail off (#11), others are full of hesitations and repetitions and self-corrections—possibilities being born as the words are spoken. It is the talk of reflection. No neatness here, no decisiveness, no finality—which is precisely the point of this discussion. The participants' heavy use of tentativeness markers contributes to the exploratory "accent" of this interaction: "I mean like . . . ," "kind of," "we don't really know," "he's kind of like . . . ," "or something," "well maybe . . . ," "I think, well . . . ," "I can't imagine . . . ," "unless it were . . . ," "I don't know," "like maybe," "it seems like," "probably," "in a way," "if," "he seems to suggest," "whether . . . or whether . . ." (See Feldman & Wertsch, 1976 for a discussion of tentativeness markers.)[4] We tend to wince at the "sloppiness" or "laziness" of these teenagers' "kind of" and "I mean like." These are imperfections, surely, yet perhaps they are the necessary imperfections of rough draft talk. How different are these accents from those of Jill and her mother! The boundedness, completion, and—especially—expressiveness are different largely because the inquiry purposes are different in the two texts. Utterances shape themselves according to the purposes they attempt to carry out. Sometimes the dominant inquiry purpose is to seek information; sometimes it is to wonder.

TWO TYPES OF INQUIRY ACTS

I have defined inquiry utterances as those conversational turns in which a speaker tries to engage another in her attempt to build further understanding. Clearly this is a very broad definition and includes inquiry acts of many kinds. It is not my goal to play surveyor of this vast terrain, plotting out all the corners of its territory. That would be the ultimate impossible task of fairy tales. My goal is instead to select two maximally different types of inquiry acts to explore, by way of getting a sense (not a map) of the terrain. The two types of inquiry acts are information-seeking and wondering.

Information-Seeking

Most of Jill's utterances in the "hospital" text are information-seeking utterances. I am using *information* in a rather global sense here to include facts, clarifications, justifications, explanations, confirmations. Jill elicits bit after bit from her mother, working toward the goal of building her understanding of hospital experience. *Working* is a key word. Information-seeking utterances sound very much like work—deliberate, effortful, focused, moving toward a specific end. It is work that *has* a goal; it isn't itself the goal. Information-seeking is product oriented, if you like. It is oriented toward what one is wanting to know. There is a no-

nonsense quality that gets played out in the boundedness, completion, and expressiveness of these inquiry acts. In each information-seeking utterance the speaker says, "Here is what I need from you," and she knows when the partner has satisfied that need. Each of Jill's new information-seeking utterances suggests that her mother has satisfied the last one and so now Jill can move on to a new one. Notice how well the partnership works in this transcript. Jill and her mother share a history that includes many such episodes. Theirs is a practiced partnership in a practiced event: bedtime-story conversation.

The sequence #29 to #33 is interesting. In #29 Jill asks, "What's rheumatic fever?" but then, as soon as her mother begins to answer, she interrupts with, "You just had to rest?" This is a recasting of her question in terms of her operation-versus-rest categories. Jill seems to be recasting her question from #29 toward the specific type of information she seeks: not some general definition or description of rheumatic fever, but one that fits the operation-versus-rest framework she has built for understanding hospital experience. This is work, all right—work directed toward finding out what Jill wants to know in the way she wants to know it.

It is important to stress that Jill's information-seeking utterances (like those in the earlier "Nest-es" transcript) are not part of a hunting-and-gathering mission. A building metaphor more aptly captures the work being done than a gathering metaphor does. The building in Jill's text is clear. She is constructing a larger structure about hospital experience. She is not accumulating free-floating bits, but rather is integrating and relating them. One striking aspect of Jill's building work is the way she uses the information she gets in the first part of the conversation, to construct the operation-or-rest structure she uses in organizing subsequent information.

Not all of Jill's utterances in the "Hospital" text seek information. Utterances #15, #17, #19, #33, and #39 carry out other purposes. It is perhaps unfortunate that all of Jill's information-seeking utterances are questions and all her other utterances are not; this may reinforce a mistaken notion that information-seeking utterances must be in interrogative form. But to think this would be to confuse sentence and utterance, falling into the very trap Bakhtin cautions us to avoid. An interrogative is a type of sentence, a grammatical structure; an information-seeking utterance is a conversational turn that carries out a particular type of inquiry purpose in discourse. It happens that speakers often use interrogatives to do their information-seeking work (for reasons we'll consider in Chapter 4). But it is the work being done, not the form being used to do it, that identifies the utterance as information-seeking. Jill could have used other forms. For example, in #1 ("... did I cry when they first put that thing on me?")

she could have said, "I bet I cried when they put that thing on me"; in #9 ("But sometimes when you're just sick . . . you don't use that thing, do you?") she could have deleted the tag ("do you") at the end; in #31 ("You just had to rest?") she could have spoken without "question intonation"; #37 ("And then?") she might have phrased as "Tell me about the last one." These noninterrogative phrasings would not have altered Jill's information-seeking purposes.

Information-seeking utterances "turn to someone" to help the speaker do some sort of building work. Their *boundedness* is to say to the partner, "I need X." Their *completion* specifies, in some way, what the particular X is—the fact, clarification, explanation, justification, or confirmation that is being sought. And their *expressiveness* (evaluative accent) typically suggests work in progress. It is quite a different sound from that which characterizes wondering.

Wondering

If the expressive accent of wondering is different from that of infor-mation-seeking, it is (largely) because its purpose is different:

> Whereas information-seeking utterances incline toward *closure,* won-dering utterances attempt to hold the discourse *open.* The sound of trying to hold open is different from the sound of trying to close. Eliciting information sounds different from inviting con-jecture and speculation. Entertaining issues sounds different from trying to resolve them.
>
> Whereas information-seeking utterances tend to be *work-ful,* wonder-ing utterances tend to be *playful.* Working to find out something sounds different from playing with possibilities.
>
> Whereas in information-seeking utterances the goal is *product* (some-*thing* to be known, confirmed, explained), in wondering utter-ances the goal is engaging in the *process* itself—reflecting pri-marily for its own sake at that moment. The sound of going after something is different from the sound of reflecting on some-thing.
>
> Whereas information-seeking utterances most often live in *actual* worlds, the home territory of wondering utterances is *possible* worlds (Bruner, 1986). Dealing with the factual sounds different from dealing with the imagined, the uncertain, the ambiguous.

Clearly we are dealing with tendencies here, not with absolutes. Other aspects of communication events besides the speaker's purpose at a given moment contribute to the expressive intonation of a conversational turn. However, purpose is a major influence and in wondering utterances, the speaker's purpose is to engage another in playing with possibilities, reflecting, considering, exploring. Perhaps more than anything else, wondering is a stance we take toward topic and toward partner(s).

As with any language act, a wondering utterance provides the "possibility of responding to it." Therein lies its boundedness and completion. Also, like any language act, it suggests the kind of response it seeks. In contrast to information-seeking utterances, whose completeness is to specify the X being sought from the partner, the completeness of a wondering utterance is to offer an invitation for another to join the game. Wondering utterances turn to the partner in a way that indicates that uncertainty is the name of that game. Notice that Silca (#11) hands the floor over by trailing off in a very tentative way ("Like maybe, um . . ."), and what could more clearly indicate uncertainty than Miranda's relinquishing the floor with "I don't know" (#27).

A wondering utterance puts forward a possibility:

> "Maybe she was marrying him 'cause that was the only way that she could stay queen."
> "Like, did he ask her, 'Will you marry me?' and she said, 'Yes,' or was, was it kind of just planned?"
> "It seems that in that whole part where he, where he was talking to her about, um, setting a mirror up and all that, he seems to be, I don't know what it really is, um, really self-righteous or, or, I don't know."

These are contributions to possible interpretations. No certainties here. No "clos[ing] down the process of wondering by flat declarations of fixed factuality" (Bruner, 1986, p. 127). A wondering utterance says to the partner(s), "Consider this possibility"; an information-seeking utterance says, "Tell me X." The kind of response that is sought in the information-seeking utterance (an answer) would be the very response that would end a wondering dialogue. The two turn to a partner in quite different ways, each way carrying out its own kind of inquiry purpose.

It would be tempting to contrast information-seeking utterances and wondering utterances by saying that the former are goal oriented and the latter are not; that Jill had a goal but the 11th graders did not. Surely this would be a mistake. Wondering utterances have goals no less than information-seeking utterances do. It is only that their goals are different. Trying to engage a partner in helping you play with uncertainties is no less a goal than trying to engage a partner in helping you find out something that you want to know. Can we call goal-less the perseverance of the wonderers in the Gertrude discussion? Surely their goals are as compelling and as real as Jill's.

Margaret Donaldson (1979) seems to recognize the different goals of information-seeking inquiries and wondering inquiries. On the one hand, "We are beings who ask questions; . . . there is a fundamental human urge to . . . understand the world" (p. 118). Often it is "the realization of incongruity between our notion of the world and what it turns out to be like [that] lead[s] us to want to understand it better" (p. 117). This sounds like information-seeking. But, on the other hand, "Sometimes we positively seek [incongruities] out, as if we liked having to deal with things that we do not understand, things that challenge us intellectually" (p. 117). This sounds like wondering.

Acts of Going Beyond

As different as information-seeking and wondering are, they are both acts of inquiry, that is, acts in which the speaker engages another in her attempt to understand the actual or possible. Both are acts of going beyond. This means that they are necessarily acts of creativity.

Definitions of creativity abound. They also conflict. However, common to all of them is the notion of newness, which of course means doing something new with what is given. I have mentioned already Bakhtin's notion of utterances as unrepeatable (new) events that use repeatable (given) language elements. Thus all utterances are creative in that they use what is given to construct something new. But inquiry utterances go beyond this in that their essential purpose—their very reason for being—is to move into the new. They intentionally go beyond the present known. Even (seemingly) mundane inquiry utterances acknowledge the existence of a beyond that the speaker does not know and cannot see.[5] This is an act of imagination. Further, in an act of inquiry, the speaker positions herself to conceptualize in a new way, thus to engage in another act of imagination. Into-the-beyond is what inquiry utterances are. Their essence is a creative thrust. How easy it is to forget this in the busyness of classroom life—easy to forget that every inquiry act is an act of creativity and imagination.

And because inquiry acts intentionally move into the unknown, they are also acts of courage. Information-seeking seems a small foray into the unknown in comparison to wondering, which wallows in it. If indeed wondering takes greater confidence and courage, this may in part explain why we are all uncomfortable with it at least some of the time. It may also help to explain why we so often take another with us, rendering our private wonderings into social acts—utterances—rather than sitting by ourselves, reflecting in lonely silence.

INQUIRY DEVELOPMENT: THE BEGINNING

If it is the case that inquiry is universal—part of what it is to be human in the world—then we would expect to see signs of it in infancy. And we do. Obviously no child is born with the ability to verbalize inquiry acts, but the development of inquiry's precursors is clear during the child's 1st year, and during her 2nd year we begin to hear actual inquiry utterances.

In calling the developments of the first year precursors of inquiry, I do not mean to suggest that the reason for these developments (in some cosmic scheme of things) is to carry out this particular communication purpose. These early developments are the foundation of all aspects of the child's language acquisition, not just her development of inquiry. However, I do mean to suggest that these early developments are necessary to and continuous with subsequent inquiry development. Child language acquisition research of the past several decades indicates that during their first year, infants demonstrate (1) the "quality of turning to someone" (Bakhtin, 1986, p. 99), (2) the early expression of a dialogic (turn-taking) principle, and (3) the actualization of communication purpose. All three are essential in inquiry. (It is important to remember that the following discussion is based mainly on research carried out with mainstream subjects.)

Turning to Someone

In a literal sense, infants turn to someone. By 2 months, the child demonstrates a person-object distinction and a clear preference for person. Presented with a real (or even schematically represented) human face and a real (or represented) object, the infant chooses the human, physically turning to it and focusing on it (Trevarthen, 1977). Turning to another is the basis of communication, including acts of inquiry in which one intentionally draws another into her act of understanding. That turning has its roots in earliest infancy.

Expression of a Dialogic Principle

Researchers (Schaffer, Collis, & Parsons, 1977; Stern, Beebe, Jaffe, & Bennett, 1977; Trevarthen, 1977, 1992) have documented a pattern of alter-

nation between mother and child that is evident from birth. There is synchrony in their physical movements, with one partner moving and then
being more still while the other's movement increases. The pair's vocalizing shows synchrony too: the infant vocalizes more when the mother is
more quiet, and the mother tends to speak more in the pauses between
the infant's vocalizations. Though some overlaps occur, with both partners vocalizing at the same time, these are quite predictable (e.g., both
partners laughing at the same time, or mother soothing the child with
comforting talk while the child is making distressed sounds) (Schaffer,
Collis, & Parsons, 1977; Trevarthen, 1977, 1992). But apart from these predictable overlaps, the mother and child exhibit a clear pattern of alternating moves in synchrony with one another. Notice that this coordinated
alternation can be seen as an early version of the feature of *boundedness*
in Bakhtin's utterance, his "change of speaking subjects."

In mainstream families (the families in which the majority of this
research has been done), by the end of the child's first year, these turn-
taking patterns have become elaborated into extended game sequences
or routines, for example, peekaboo or give-and-take games (Bruner, 1978,
1981; Ratner & Bruner, 1978; Trevarthen, 1992). Thus it seems that well
before the child is conversing through conventional linguistic means, she
is engaged in turn-taking with a parner. This turn-taking is, of course,
essential in inquiry dialogue. The sophisticated dialogic expression we
saw in Jill as she conversed with her mother, began as simple turn-taking
exchanges when Jill was a tiny infant, years before she was able to ask
her mother about squirrels, rabbits, and ducks.[6]

Actualization of Communication Purpose

Recall that a defining feature of utterance is *completion*, "the speaker's
speech plan or *speech will*" (Bakhtin, 1986, p. 77). This "will" is the speaker's
purpose, and we see it early and continuously in language acquisition.
By 6 weeks of age, the infant is clearly attempting to connect with others.
Her gaze and smile have become social acts, not simply random movements. Attempting to connect with others is certainly a purposeful turning to someone. However, it is a global, undifferentiated purpose: I want
to connect with you. Over time the child's purposeful expression develops
in two major ways: (1) purposes become more differentiated and more
specific (e.g., the child connects with an adult in order to secure help in
performing a physical task [Bruner, Roy, & Ratner, 1982] or in order to
direct the adult's attention to some object of interest [Bates, 1976]); and
(2) expression becomes more diverse as the child develops a repertoire of
means for accomplishing her communication purposes (e.g., reaching or

pointing while looking toward an adult, vocalizing while gesturing toward an object, gazing alternately at adult and desired object, using wordlike vocalizations).

At what point does the infant's gesture or vocalization express specific communication purposes rather than simple attempts to connect with another person? It's hard to tell. Many child-language researchers have observed that mainstream adults often ascribe specific purposes to the infant's physical movements and vocalizations (probably) before these behaviors actually have such significance for the child.[7] The following example is typical. It comes from a conversation between a mother and her 7-month-old daughter, Sarah, who is sitting in her high chair in the kitchen while her mother fixes her breakfast.[8]

1. M: You can't wait? You can't wait to eat? Say, "Hurry, Mama, I'm hungry. Hurry, Mama."
2. S: (verbal noise)
3. M: (overlaps S) "Hurry, Mama. Hurry. Hurry, Mama." I'm hurrying, little girl. I'm hurrying, little girl.
4. S: (loud energetic squeal)
5. M: (overlaps S; quick) Oh, oh, oh, oh. You're mad at Mama? Are you mad at me? . . .

6. S: (vocalizes while looking at high chair tray)
7. M: You see yourself? Who's there? Who's in there? . . .

8. S: (verbal sound and mouth noises)
9. M: Oh tell Mama.

In this example, Sarah's behaviors are basically squeals, splutterings, and focused gazing, but her mother interprets these as Sarah's attempts to express impatience (#3, #5), to call Mother's attention to the reflection in the high chair tray (#7), and to tell Mother something (#9). Such examples make one wonder whether the infant's "purposeful expression" is, at the beginning, nothing more than a figment of the adult's imagination. But surely the child's move into increasingly differentiated purposeful expression is helped along by the adult *expecting* that the child will express purposefully (nonverbally, verbally, or both), and also by the adult *responding* to the child's early expression as if it is purposeful. In both the expectations and responses, the adult is assuming that the young child is a human being like herself, trying to carry out her own intentions in interaction with others.

Increasingly, during the first year, vocalizations accompany signaling gestures. Eventually these become conventional words and word combinations and are able to stand on their own, without the help of gesture and supporting context to convey their meaning and purpose. But what is so striking about vocalizations as they become wordlike is that the child uses them so purposefully. Inquiry is one of those early purposes for the child. Halliday (1977) identified seven distinct communication purposes that his son, Nigel, developed from 9 months to 18 months. One of these he called "heuristic," communication through which the child explores the environment. And Dore (1975) identified nine social purposes expressed in children's one-word speech, including "requesting an answer." How remarkable it is that the young child, using only single words, can create inquiry utterances that bring others into her acts of understanding.

Bringing It All Together

The three compelling urges that I have suggested are perfectly joined in acts of inquiry are all present in the child's first year: to connect with others (social), to understand the world (intellectual), to reveal oneself within it (personal). However, it takes awhile for the child to coordinate these three, as she must do in inquiry utterances.

I have mentioned already the early presence of the child's social orientation (e.g., her early preference for humans over objects and her initial global attempts to connect with others). As for the beginnings of personal expression—the revealing of individual self in the language act—research on individual differences (as well as abundant testimony from mothers and caregivers of infants) attests to distinct individuality in young children (Furrow & Nelson, 1984; Miller, 1982; Nelson, 1973, 1981; Wolf & Gardner, 1979). Much of this research has been done with children older than one year. However, since the behaviors investigated are complex ones (e.g., word use, early syntax) and the individual differences are well established at 12 months (the age of subjects at the outset of many of these studies), it is reasonable to assume that individual differences were present before the researchers arrived. Expressing oneself in unique individual ways seems inevitable, and these individual expressive ways are evident early.

And what about the intellectual? Does the infant behave in ways that demonstrate the presence of the intellectual, as well as the social and individual? Indeed. "The infant is intrinsically motivated to learn, recognize, and acquire knowledge and skills" (Papousek & Papousek, 1983, quoted in Rogoff, 1990, p. 38). H. Papousek's problem-solving experiments with infants only a few months old led Donaldson (1979) to conclude that "there is a fundamental human urge to make sense of the world" (p. 116). Britton (1973) concurs, suggesting that curiosity is innate, and that a child begins "with the drive to explore the world he is born into" (p. 93).

There is no doubt, then, that the personal, intellectual, and social urges are all present and expressed in infancy. But if the child is to develop inquiry (and every child does), the existence of these three is not enough. The child must coordinate them into acts in which she—as the individual she is (personal)—brings another (social) into whatever it is that she is focusing on and trying to understand (intellectual).

One line of research that is especially helpful at this point is that which focuses on the infant's development of requesting, the child's "insertion of the adult as a means to attaining objects or other goals" (Bates, 1976, p. 51). This development involves an understanding of ends (what you want) and also means (how to get it) and a coordination of the two. Inquiry acts can be viewed as a subcategory of requests, namely, requests for another's help (means) in understanding something (goal). Bates traces the infant's development of an understanding of means-end relations (and of the adult as a possible means) from the early establishment of a pattern in which the child's cry expresses a need (e.g., to be fed, to be held) and an adult meets that expressed need; to the child's use of her own body as a means of reaching her goals; to the child's use of a "tool," either an object (e.g., the infant pulls toward herself the blanket on which the desired toy is resting) or an adult (e.g., the infant looks toward the desired object and then looks intently at the adult as if to ask, "Will you get that for me?"). The child's use of single words to accomplish her inquiry purpose is simply the next step in turning to others (social means) to find out what she wants to know (intellectual goal). In her one-word inquiry utterances, she has coordinated the social and the intellectual.

Notice the continuity. From birth the child moves increasingly into intentional dialogic expression. Social, intellectual, and individual orientation are evident in the child's early physical behaviors and vocalizations. Over time the infant coordinates the social, intellectual, and individual and does so in the service of intentional expression—language (as) *act*, including acts of inquiry. The child's communicative development flows continuously as she tries to carry out her communication purposes, using whatever means she develops along the way—gesture, smile, gaze, vocalization, word. She marshals these expressive means early in her life to serve inquiry's purpose. As the Jill transcripts demonstrate, the child, over time, continues to refine and elaborate her repertoire of expressive means that serve to carry out her inquiry acts. And the 11th graders' transcript hints at the continuing development of inquiry expression across a wide range of social contexts, genres, discourses.

It seems quite extraordinary that the child so early in life is able to manage the complex coordination of social, intellectual, and personal impulses in communication acts that deliberately bring a partner into a personal act of understanding. It is well to remember that virtually every child we teach was, from her beginning, so oriented toward engaging others in helping her understand the world that in one short year she learned to join social and intellectual and personal expression in acts of inquiry.

LOOKING AHEAD

Child-language researchers are ultimately interested in answering a *how* question: How does the child build this complex purposeful communication system? This question seeks an explanation of the means by which this development occurs. We see a child do something new and we want to know what brought this about. But such explanations are hard to come by, especially when the focus of interest is something so complex as language. On the way toward answering the *how* question, researchers observe and painstakingly document and describe what children at various developmental stages do as they interact with others. They especially attempt to identify and describe patterns of development within individual children and across different children. This is a *what* answer to a *how* question: describing a developmental sequence (telling what happens) is not the same as explaining it (telling how it happens). Yet these descriptions of developmental sequences (especially the patterns within them) give hints about the *how*, the means by which the child is developing communicative abilities.

Our focus is the child's inquiry development, and in the coming chapters I will have more to say about this development beyond infancy. Much of this will be description, not explanation. I am a long way from being able to answer the *how* question and I will struggle with it in subsequent chapters. Basic to that struggle are two recurring notions that I believe are fundamental to a beginning understanding of how children develop inquiry: the notion of *emergent inquiry,* and the notion of *social context as demonstration and engagement* (F. Smith, 1983).

Emergent Inquiry

I have borrowed and adapted the term *emergent literacy* (Clay, 1966), a term designating "the period between birth and the time when children read and write conventionally" (Sulzby & Teale, 1991, p. 728). But emergent literacy not only labels a particular period of development; it also refers to a particular set of beliefs about the nature of children's literacy development during that period of time: that literacy development is a natural, continuous, and nearly universal process in which the child actively constructs concepts about print within a social environment that immerses her in a range of literacy activities (Sulzby & Teale, 1991; Teale, 1987).

The assumptions I make about the nature of inquiry development are similar. I mean to suggest that, from birth, virtually all children develop the ability to engage others in their attempts to make sense of the world, and that this process occurs naturally in children's daily interactions with others. This view sees the emergent inquirer as actively and continuously engaged in constructing her understanding of inquiry acts: purposes, expression, participants, contexts.

Emergent inquiry is an orientation that provides continuity for thinking about the child before and after her arrival at school, for inquiry's emergence—starting at birth—continues well into and beyond the school years and finds special opportunities in the school context that are not available at home.

Social Context as Demonstration and Engagement

The first central notion, emergent inquiry, especially spotlights the child and what she is doing. The second turns the spotlight on the social environment in which emergent inquiry occurs. Together, in absolute interdependence, the two notions provide our best hope of an answer to the question of how children develop inquiry.

Every child's social experience provides numerous demonstrations and engagements. By *demonstration* I mean "show[ing] how something is done" (F. Smith, 1983, p. 102) in the process of actually doing it for real purposes, not as a contrived "lesson." To *actually do* is often to (simultaneously) *show how to do*. When Jill's mother answers Jill's questions, she shows how an adult answers a child's questions (and many other things too, of course, for example, the completion of conversational turns, the expression of particular stance). The showing-how is in the doing itself. This is the way with demonstrations.[9]

Demonstration alone would be insufficient for the emergent inquirer. She must also, in some socially authentic way, participate. Sitting on the sidelines is not enough: she must *engage*.[10] As we will see, that engagement is not always verbal, but there must be some kind of involvement in inquiry events.

I assume that members of whatever community a child is born into will demonstrate its interactive ways and engage the child in these ways in activities that constitute daily life for that group (Rogoff, 1990). I assume, further, that the ways of demonstrating and engaging are culturally specific. Each community demonstrates and engages in its own ways—ways that it deems appropriate for helping the child become a socially competent member of the group. Rogoff's (1990) study of children's "apprenticeship in thinking" shows several different cultures' ways of providing "guided participation in cultural activity" (p. vii) for these children. This work attests to both the universality (*that* they occur) and the cultural specificity (*how* they occur) of societies' demonstrations and engagements involving children.

In subsequent chapters I will have more to say about demonstration and engagement. However, even at this early point you can see that demonstration and engagement are purpose-full. In interactions with and around the child, community members carry out language acts, that is, conversational turns that attempt to achieve communication purposes. These will necessarily include acts of inquiry (such as information-seeking and wondering). Every child, an emergent inquirer, is immersed in many daily demonstrations of and engagements in acts of inquiry. It is part of the child's—and the community's—humanness to connect with one another in their attempts to understand the world.

CHAPTER 3

Inquiry Purpose in the Classroom

Children's and teachers' inquiry acts inside the classroom are, like those outside, communication acts. They are conversational turns that *turn* toward the partner(s) for help in going beyond present understanding. Like all language acts, each inquiry utterance provides whatever the speaker deems sufficient for the partner(s) to respond to (completion), and each is nonneutral, resonating with mood and tone and feeling (expressiveness)—curiosity perhaps or puzzlement, reflectiveness or tentativeness. It is a stance, an "accent," that is familiar to all of us, for we not only hear our students' inquiry voices; we also hear our own. We are inquirers too, which matters a great deal if our intention in the classroom is to support children's emergent inquiry. In the classroom, as outside, demonstration and engagement are central.

This chapter focuses on authentic inquiry events in classrooms: first, by contrasting examples of authentic and inauthentic inquiry events; next, by examining one authentic classroom example closely; and finally, by considering factors that make it more difficult to provide authentic inquiry events in classrooms than one might expect.

RECOGNIZING AUTHENTIC INQUIRY

We begin with our own ability to hear the sounds that inquiry makes. Of course! How can we possibly support children's continuing development of something we cannot hear? Yet recognizing inquiry acts is not so easy as one might think. If it were, then the many earlier educational psychology research studies (mentioned previously) would not have missed it, for example, those studies in which researchers counted children's interrogative forms, mistakenly thinking that they were counting children's inquiry acts, though in fact the children were not trying to understand anything at all. Researchers are not the only ones to have problems identifying what is and what is not inquiry in the voices of children. My third-grade teacher, Mrs. McKenzie, had this problem too.

She would begin each social studies unit the same way: "We're going to be studying Eskimos[1] [or Indians or Mexicans or whomever]. Let's think of all the questions we have about Eskimos. You tell me the questions and I'll write them on the board." This may sound reasonable enough, possibly even like a way to invite children to inquire. But it wasn't. There was absolutely nothing that I and my eight-year old suburban Philadelphia classmates wanted to know about Eskimos.[2] But did this stop us? Not at all. Hands would fly up, Mrs. McKenzie would call on individual hand wavers, and the board would fill up with what I now recognize to be an extraordinary list of noninquiries:

What do Eskimos eat for breakfast?
What do Eskimos do for recreation?
What are Eskimos' hobbies?

Over time there came to be a sanctioned set, and the task was to think of a missing member and suggest it. I'd look up at the board and say to myself, "Let's see now. Which ones aren't up there yet? Hmm. We still don't have 'What are their customs?' or 'What's their religion?' " We gave Mrs. McKenzie the "questions" she was after. There was purpose in our utterances, but it was not inquiry's purpose. We were engaging in a teacher-pleasing exercise. It was only a game. We were not engaging in inquiry, for there was nothing we were curious about, no information or explanation we were seeking or trying to confirm, nothing we were wondering about. Our turns were complete, giving Mrs. McKenzie something to respond to, but they did not turn toward a partner in puzzlement or curiosity. As competent eight-year-olds, we were linguistically skilled enough to place the right kind of *sentence structures* into the spaces Mrs. McKenzie provided. However, we were not engaging in *communication acts* that carried out inquiry's purpose, although Mrs. McKenzie did not know this.

Here is another game that sometimes gets confused with inquiry in both classrooms and research studies. The teacher (or researcher) holds up a picture and says to the children, "Ask me any questions you can think of about this picture, something that begins with *where, when, why, what, who,* or *how.*" But there is nothing the children want to know about the picture, nothing they wonder about in regard to it. If there were, they would have asked. But this makes no difference. The questions come.

"Where were they before they came where they are in the picture?"
"What are they gonna do next?"
"Why does he have that thing in his hand?"

The teacher nods and smiles in response to each offering—may even say, "Good"—which isn't at all the way we respond to people's real acts of inquiry, of course. When people ask us something for real, we answer it or say we don't know or ask them for clarification or suggest a way to find out or ... But the teacher's response of smile, nod, "good" is OK with the children because they know this event is not inquiry at all and so they really do not expect the teacher to respond as she would if someone really had inquired. Worse yet, it could be that this strange teacher response gets no particular reaction from the children for, although the ritual makes no sense, the children have come to accept rituals that do not make sense as being part of school. And I cannot help thinking of my own inquiries that, more often than not, don't begin with *where, what, why* at all: "Help me understand X," I say to a student, or "Tell me about Y," or "I wonder if ..." And so it is with children's inquiries also: they do not necessarily announce themselves with where, what, when, why, how, who—which may partly explain why they are sometimes difficult to recognize in a classroom.

Twenty Questions is another classroom favorite that sometimes gets confused with inquiry. While visiting another university, I attended an undergraduate science methods course one day in which the instructor was demonstrating this game as one the students might want to use during their student teaching. The instructor produced a box and said, "Ask me twenty questions to see if you can find out what's in this box." I raised my hand, he called on me, and I did what any competent three-year-old would do: I asked, "What's in the box?" "Oh no, no, no," he said quickly. "You can only ask questions that can be answered yes or no." His response was the clearest possible indication that this activity was a guessing game, not an inquiry event (which he may have been fully aware of, I'm not sure). Now Twenty Questions is a great game and there may be some very good reasons to play it in a classroom. However, engaging children in an inquiry event is not one of them. When our children play Twenty Questions, they are not engaged in inquiry, just as they are not engaged in buying and selling real estate when they play Monopoly. If it is emergent inquiry that is our interest, then it must be inquiry acts, events, discourse that we engage the children in. And this means being able to hear in children's words the presence or the absence of inquiry's purpose.

For me that purpose is absent in these words: "What was uh, some

kings were uh, about the kings?" (Apparently this student was attempting to ask, "Why is it that kings did not always make the best judges?")
(Palincsar & Brown, 1984, p. 136). The words are spoken by Charles,
a 7th grader who has been identified as a poor reader, specifically
one who is an "adequate decoder" but a "poor comprehender" (though
he is "*not* labeled as learning disabled or mentally retarded") (p. 126).
Charles's words are puzzling. Why would a competent adolescent language user—a native speaker of English—produce such a "question"?
Remember four-year-old Jill. She asks lots of questions and they do not
sound anything like Charles's.

Context provides the answer to this puzzle. Charles was a subject in
a training study designed to help him (and other similar poor readers)
develop "comprehension-monitoring and comprehension-fostering" abilities. The training intervention, called reciprocal teaching, focused on
"four strategies that were deemed to be ideal comprehension-fostering
and comprehension-monitoring activities" (Palincsar & Brown, 1984,
p. 168), namely "*summarizing* (self-review), *questioning, clarifying*, and *pre-
dicting*" (p. 120). Pairs of subjects worked with the adult teacher (the investigator) every day for 15 days. The adult would introduce a new passage of expository text to the pair of students and assign one of them the
role of "teacher" for the first text segment (typically a paragraph), which
the pair would then read silently.

> Then the teacher [one of the two students] for that segment proceeded first
> to ask a question, then to summarize, and to offer a prediction or ask for a
> clarification when appropriate.
>
> The adult teacher provided the guidance necessary for the student
> teacher to complete the preceding activities through a variety of techniques:
> *prompting,* "What question did you think a teacher might ask?"; *instruction,*
> "Remember, a summary is a shortened version, it doesn't include detail" and
> *modifying the activity,* "If you're having a hard time thinking of a question,
> why don't you summarize first?" (p. 131, emphasis in original)

The students took turns being the teacher. Here are the results:

> Reciprocal teaching . . . led to a significant improvement in the quality of
> the summaries and questions . . . [and] to sizable gains on criterion tests of
> comprehension, reliable maintenance over time, generalization to classroom
> comprehension tests, transfer to novel tasks that tapped the trained skills of
> summarizing, questioning, and clarifying, and improvement in standardized
> comprehension scores. (p. 117)

And when, in a second study, the training procedure was carried out by two classroom teachers and two resource room teachers (instead of the investigator) working with their own "real" reading groups (of poor readers), the results were similar.

It is the "questioning" part of this procedure that is of special interest ... which brings us back to Charles. "Questioning was not practiced as an isolated activity, but as a continuing goal of the whole enterprise—what main idea question would a teacher or test ask about that section of the text?" (Palincsar & Brown, 1984, p. 122). Charles was considered "a success story" (p. 154). It is easy to see why. On the first day of this training intervention, after reading a passage about poisonous snakes in the southeastern United States (including water moccasins, copperheads, rattlesnakes, and pit vipers), Charles asked, "What is found in the southeastern snakes, also the copperhead, rattlesnakes, vipers—they have. I'm not doing this right" (p. 138). The conversation goes on (Adult Teacher [the investigator in this case] and Charles):

> TEACHER: All right. Do you want to know about the pit vipers?
> CHARLES: Yeah.
> TEACHER: What would be a good question about the pit vipers that starts with the word "why?"
> CHARLES: (No response)
> TEACHER: How about, "Why are the snakes called pit vipers?"
> CHARLES: Why do they want to know that they are called pit vipers?
> TEACHER: Try it again.
> CHARLES: Why do they, pit vipers in a pit?
> TEACHER: How about, "Why do they call the snakes pit vipers?"
> CHARLES: Why do they call the snakes pit vipers?
> TEACHER: There you go! Good for you. (p. 138)

But on Day 11, after Charles read a passage about the Venus Fly Trap, the conversation sounded very different:

> CHARLES: What is the most interesting of the insect eating plants, and where do the plants live at?
> TEACHER: Two excellent questions! They are both clear and important questions. Ask us one at a time now. (p. 139)

And on Day 15, after Charles read a passage about the Southern Lights at the South Pole, he and the investigator had this conversation:

CHARLES: Why do scientists come to the South Pole to study?
TEACHER: Excellent question. That is what this paragraph is all
    about.

There can be no doubt that Charles shows remarkable improvement. The
question for me is, *improvement in what*? I know it is not inquiry because
Charles did not want to know anything about pit vipers or Southern
Lights or Venus's flytraps. I know it is not inquiry because the teacher
responded to Charles' "questions" in a way we would never respond to
an act of inquiry. I know it is not inquiry because if it were, Charles would
have been able to formulate his utterances even at the outset of the study,
just as four-year-olds do when they inquire. I know it is not inquiry because of what the participating adolescents said later about the study:
"finding the good right question was the most difficult activity" (Palincsar & Brown, 1984, p. 167). Finding it? Inquiries come from within us,
we do not "find" them. "*The* good right question"? Just one? Both "good
and right"? Does an outsider judge the goodness and rightness of what
I am trying to make sense of and the way I am going about it?

Charles and his peers were increasing their ability to be successful
participants in an instructional event that occurs frequently in their classrooms. I think the researchers wanted to increase the students' success
in these classroom events. But did they also intend to help these students
do something more in their "questioning"? I think they did. My reading
of this study suggests that they wanted to help these students develop
as real readers, not just people who can play out a particular type of
scripted classroom ritual. The researchers suggest that the strategies they
focused on in their reciprocal teaching intervention "comprise a set
of knowledge-extending activities that apply in a wide range of situations. . . . Mature learners question and elaborate their own knowledge
and the content of the text" (Palincsar & Brown, 1984, p. 119).

> Reciprocal teaching . . . involves extensive modeling of the type of compre-
> hension-fostering and comprehension-monitoring activities that are usually
> difficult to detect in the expert reader, as they are executed covertly. The
> reciprocal teaching procedure is a relatively natural forum for the teacher
> . . . to provide a model of what it is that expert readers do when they try to
> understand and remember texts. (p. 168)

This suggestion prompted me to pull from my library shelf a text
that I had recently been working very hard to understand: Bakhtin's
(1986) *Speech Genres and Other Late Essays*. I knew that I had filled the
margins with my scrawled comments, questions, and emotings ("Ah!"

"Nice!" "What a wonderful way to say this!"). Compared with Charles, I am an "expert reader." And so I wondered, in the absence of reading partners, when I ask questions (of myself? of the author?) in the margins of the text I am trying to understand, do I ask "main idea questions that a teacher or test might ask?" If so, then reciprocal teaching would indeed demonstrate what an expert reader does covertly.

Here are a few of the questions that I had written in the margins on pages 86–92.

> Utterances are very intentional, in this view. Does this connect in any way with chap. 1 of *Acts of Meaning?*—Bruner's focus on intentionality?
>
> What IS inquiry (discourse) to Bakhtin? Is it a "plan" (i.e., purpose/ intention)? Is it a genre? (I don't think so, for it doesn't fit his examples, yet it does involve a relatively stable combination of forms).
>
> [Is there] Such a thing as individual inquiry style?
>
> Is there anything to be gained by trying to define "question" as a particular type of conversational turn that evokes particular type of action response position in listener? What happens if you try to define question from listener's (instead of speaker's) point of view? As what is *understood*, rather than what is intended?
>
> Is this why children's questions express what they DO know more than what they don't know?

These questions make very little sense even to me taken out of context this way, for they are contingent on Bakhtin's written text. (He and I were having quite a conversation here.) But the point is that they do not sound at all like main-idea questions that a teacher or test might ask. And that is because they are not such "questions": they are *inquiries*, my own attempts to go beyond my present understanding, and in the absence of a physically present partner, I addressed these questions to . . . well, I'm not sure really. To the author? To my "otherized" self? These are my own inquiries, my own wonderings. "Questions" like those in the reciprocal teaching dialogues can belong to someone else. They can be produced on demand to satisfy someone else's requirements. But inquiries can only belong to the inquirer. These questions of mine—but even more, my impression of my own general behavior as a reader trying to understand challenging text—make me skeptical of Palincsar and Brown's (1984) suggestion that the kinds of "questions" practiced in the reciprocal teaching intervention "model . . . what it is that expert readers do when they try to understand and remember texts" (p. 186). I think that expert readers engage in *acts of inquiry,* not in the production of "teacherlike questions." It makes sense to me that—if inquiry is what real readers do—then inquiry is what teachers will demonstrate and engage their students in. Which is exactly what Karen Smith does.

AN EXAMPLE OF AUTHENTIC INQUIRY

Karen Smith's students are fifth- and sixth-grade Mexican American children from low-income families. They are emergent readers, considered by some (though not, I think, by Karen) to be "at risk." In the following example, six of these students (three fifth-grade girls and three sixth-grade girls) join Karen in literature study discussion (K. Smith, 1990b). These six students have become a (temporary) group because they all chose to read and study the same book, *Dicey's Song,* by Cynthia Voigt (1982). They spent a week reading the book on their own, and the next week, on three successive days, they discussed the book together. The story, in brief, is this: Dicey, 12 years old, is the oldest of four (fatherless) children who find their way from Boston to their maternal grandmother's home in Maryland after their mother is hospitalized with what appears to be a complete mental breakdown. After some months, several letters come to the grandmother from the Boston hospital, informing her of the mother's worsening condition, information that the grandmother keeps from the children. One day the hospital notifies the grandmother that her daughter is dying, and Gram and Dicey go to Boston. Dicey's mother dies, and Gram has the body cremated. Dicey and her grandmother return home to Maryland with the ashes.

Text No. 4: *Dicey's Song*

(The following excerpts come from videotape transcripts of the students' three discussions. Student, below, is any one of the six students.)

1. STUDENT: There's a part I wanted to ask when, uh, you know when they said they buried the mom in the yard?
2. TEACHER: Uh-huh.
3. STUDENT: I'm trying to figure out is that right what I read, because you know how they bury people in like the cemetery.
4. TEACHER: Cemetery.
5. STUDENT: You know it's weird if when they buried her inside the yard.
6. STUDENT: It would be kinda scary.

7. STUDENT: I know, to go by—
8. TEACHER: To have it there?
9. STUDENT: Yeah. Like having everybody's dead body.
10. TEACHER: OK. Do you understand they cremated her? They burned her body? Maybe that's what was confusing you. What they did, you know, usually people—well not usually—there's two ways—you either put the body like in a casket and they bury the whole body, or they take them and they cremate them, which means they burn the body, so all you have left is like some ashes. So they cremated her mother and they put the ashes in that wooden box. So that's what she was carrying on the train—you know the wooden box on the train?
11. STUDENT: Uh-hm.
12. TEACHER: She was carrying her mother's ashes. From her being cremated. (pause) So it wasn't a body.
13. STUDENT: I thought it was a body.
14. TEACHER: No. . . .

15. STUDENT: This is the part—this is what I don't get when, remember when the mom died?
16. TEACHER: Uh-hm.
17. STUDENT: And then the grandma said, um, she didn't tell her nothing, they just kept on going on sitting and tell her nothing. Until she seen her mom.
18. TEACHER: That she was dying?
19. STUDENT: Uh-huh.
20. TEACHER: And that surprised you?
21. STUDENT: Yeah. I wonder why she didn't tell her.
22. STUDENT: I thought that that would have [inaudible] was hiding when those letters were coming and she asked her what did they say and she say, "Nothing."
23. TEACHER: Yeah, I wonder why the grandma was so secretive about that, 'cause she did that with the letters and then she did that on the bus, didn't tell her.
24. STUDENT: Sometimes I thought it was 'cause, um, she didn't want them to find about her mom's [inaudible] 'cause she, um, liked them, not so she could adopt them or something?
25. TEACHER: Well sometimes it's—I think she knew that Dicey knew a lot of that. Seems like she made it harder on Dicey by not telling her. 'Cause it seemed like Dicey'd handled a lot of hard things in her life, she could have handled what was in those letters.

26. STUDENT: Well maybe she, maybe the grandma couldn't handle it that her last daughter died.
27. TEACHER: So you think maybe it was the grandma feeling it more than worrying about Dicey's feelings. Hmmm. . . .

28. STUDENT: It was pretty sad.
29. TEACHER: It sure is sad. You know, there's some controversy about writing for adolescents or children, that a lot of people think you shouldn't put death in books like this. That you, kids your age can't deal with that or it's too hard. What do you, what do you think about that?
30. STUDENT: This book [*Homecoming*, the preceding book in the *Dicey* series] was real hard too, when the mom left them.
31. STUDENT: Uh-huh.
32. STUDENT: But basically you have to look at the way their struggle is, in this book. How they get to give Grandma—get to know her—
33. TEACHER: Do you think it was too much to ask you to cope with death and the hard things that they were doing?
34. STUDENT: I think we learn faster [inaudible].
35. TEACHER: In what ways?
36. STUDENT: 'Cause um, this shows how to deal with it in a much better way than just start crying crying, 'cause crying doesn't do much [inaudible].
37. STUDENT: I think, I think that if the author shows you that, that if you ever run away or something if you don't have nobody around you or something that shows you how the way their struggle is there, and like if you're on your own, they show you the way, like, what would you do and stuff.
38. TEACHER: It's not gonna be that easy, is it? Just show you that it is a struggle, that tension, and that death is hard. It's really hard.

I do not hear a scripted conversation here. I hear this group doing what expert readers do: engaging with one another and with text as they go beyond their present understanding. This is inquiry, and because this is the overarching purpose of this event, inquiry acts dominate the discussion.

The teacher's and children's inquiry utterances reflect and also further the exploratory purpose the participants are playing out as they construct this oral text together. Karen *demonstrates* inquiry, with comments such as:

"That surprised you?"

"I wonder why"
"So you think maybe"
"What do you think about that?
"In what ways [do you learn faster]?"

Notice Karen's tentative stance, a crucial part of her inquiry demonstration (maybe, I wonder, I think, seems like, could have). Karen is demonstrating the language of conjecture here, bringing a reflective cast to the discourse that she and the students are creating. Not that she is conscious of doing this necessarily. She is simply being who she is (an active inquirer) doing what she does (engaging with the author and with others to extend and deepen her understanding of the book). This is demonstration.

The participants have come together, understanding that they will share their responses to the book they have read, by way of deepening their understanding (as they have done before in similar literature discussions). Their discussion actualizes this going-beyond purpose, but not in a prescripted way: their discussion evolves as their probing evolves, going in directions and using expressive means that neither Karen nor the students could have anticipated. I think that Karen's demonstration "tells" these students much about ways of responding to others in collaboratively constructing inquiry events such as this one. In her responses, she works

> to signal her attention (#2, #16, #31)
> to understand the point the student is making (#18, #20, #27, #35)
> to grasp points of confusion—the problems the students are having
>   with the text (#8, #10)
> to clarify misunderstanding (#10, #12)
> to support students' observations (#29, #38)

Karen is working hard here, and this work may provide the most important demonstration of all: inquiry is important. She would not work this hard, marshaling this kind of focused attention, unless she valued the inquiry activity in which she and her students are engaged. And indeed, it is clear that inquiry *is* that activity for her students as well as herself:

"There's a part I wanted to ask . . . "
"I'm trying to figure out . . ."
"This is what I don't get . . ."
"I thought it was . . ."
"I wonder why . . ."

"Well maybe . . ."
"I think that . . . "

The students sound very like Karen in the tentativeness of their talk, in their closely connected responses to one another, and in their commitment to the work they are doing. I wonder what their talk was like before they were so experienced in literature discussion.

The talk in the reciprocal teaching event sounds very different from the talk in the literature discussion. Of course. The two events are different in a number of ways, such as in the number and roles and grade levels of the participants, and the kinds of text the participants are focusing on (efferent or aesthetic) (Rosenblatt, 1978). But the most important difference—the one that exerts the greatest influence on the nature of the utterances within the interaction—is, I think, the overarching purpose of each event. The participants in these two events understand themselves to be carrying out quite different purposes. In the reciprocal teaching event, I believe that the adult and students understand the purpose to be that the students will learn to manage challenging text in ways that demonstrate "comprehension" as this is defined and performed in their classroom. Demonstration and engagement happen toward this end, for example, explicit clarification of the strategies, guided practice toward formulating questions and summary statements, supportive and encouraging responses to students' attempts, commitment to the work being done in these episodes.

It is not surprising that the sound of working to perfect a skill will be very different from the sound of working to explore a text. And yet initially it may seem surprising that the talk of working to perfect a skill includes so many questions, whereas the talk of exploring text includes so few. Surprising initially, perhaps, but not on reflection. These two contrasting events bring into sharp focus the difference between Bakhtin's sentence (unit of grammar) and utterance (unit of communication). The reciprocal teaching event abounds in "questions," that is, sentence structures that we label *interrogative*. But these are not inquiry utterances, that is, they are not speakers' attempts to go beyond present understanding with the help of another. They are, rather, the practice of a particular skill. In contrast, the literature-discussion transcript includes relatively few interrogatives, but is heavy in inquiry utterances. In each event, the utterances (whatever their form) contribute to the framing purpose of the event.

Palincsar and Brown (1984) make an observation that underscores the interrogative form/inquiry utterance distinction. They point out that "documentation of students' difficulties generating questions on what they are reading is legion, and . . . the problem is particularly acute for the slower student" (p. 121). The contrast between this well-documented difficulty (evident in Charles's behavior) and the apparent ease with which Karen's students inquire in these discussions, underscores the difference between the two events and the utterances that comprise them: the first is not an inquiry event and the "questions" within it are not inquiries; the second is an inquiry event, inevitably dominated by inquiry acts (most of which are not in question form). It is indeed difficult to "generate questions" to satisfy someone else; but it is not difficult to generate your own inquiries.

Notice that the students' (and Karen's) utterances in the literature discussion are not perfectly formed. Neither were Charles's early questions. But Charles's early questions and the discussion group's utterances are ill formed in quite different ways: Charles's early questions are quite bizarre for a 12-year-old, whereas Karen's and her students' utterances retain imperfections that are characteristic of normal conversation (uh, like, I mean). Notice, too, that Charles's later questions are flawless in form, whereas the utterances of the discussion group remain imperfect in form. This is because Charles participates in a practiced script, whereas Karen and her students participate in creating an exploratory text that is ever in rough draft. It makes sense that inquiry utterances are often imperfectly formed—even downright messy sometimes, for they are acts of going beyond, not acts of having arrived. It is important to hear the difference.

CLASSROOM CHALLENGES

Obviously, inquiry is not all we need to be doing in classrooms. There are other important kinds of work (and play) to do also. But surely inquiry is central. To say this is only to recognize the depth of inquiry purposes in every human life, and to appreciate the child's early and continuing inquiry orientation, as well as his achievement of quite sophisticated linguistic means of carrying it out. How strange it would be if inquiry did not occupy a central place in classroom life.

It is fine for inquiry purposes and other purposes to coexist in a classroom. But it is not fine for noninquiry purposes and events to substitute for inquiry events. What about Twenty Questions? If we play this game with our students and recognize that we are playing a game—if we mark this event as a game, enjoy this event as a game—fine. But it is not so fine if we see and treat this event as one that supports inquiry's emergence.

More troubling for me is the substitution of classroom games that (unlike Twenty Questions) are themselves suspect. For me these include Mrs. McKenzie's "please-the-teacher-question-event," the "what-where-why-questions-about-the-picture game," or—possibly the most pervasive of all—the whole-group "discussion" that is actually a public perfor-mance ritual masquerading as an exploration of ideas. If such interactions stand in place of inquiry events, then we are telling our students, "*This* is inquiry." And this is to tell them something that is not so.

It is easier, I think, to recognize inquiry acts when they are in inter-rogative form than when they are in other forms. The student says, "I'm trying to figure out is that right what I read, because you know how they bury people on like the cemetery." She is trying to engage another in her attempt to understand. Thus her words voice inquiry's intention. But it would perhaps be easier to recognize this had she said, "Is it right that they buried her in the yard instead of in a cemetery?" Later in the discus-sion Karen says, "Seems like she made it harder on Dicey by not telling her." Another inquiry act, but one we might more readily recognize as an inquiry if she had said, "Didn't she make it harder on Dicey by not telling her?" The challenge is to hear through the words to the intention that lies behind them and gives birth to them. I am glad that this teacher and student said what they did, choosing expressive forms other than inter-rogative sentences, because the greater the range of inquiry expression that the participants incorporate in their discussion, the greater the possi-bilities for every participant's development of a rich repertoire of expres-sive possibilities—which is, after all, what emergent inquiry is about. The presence of these harder-to-hear (nonprototypic) inquiry utterances in this meaningful, meaning-making event enhances emergent inquiry for these students and their teacher.

It also seems to me that inquiry acts of wondering are more difficult to recognize than inquiry acts of information-seeking. Wondering acts: invitations to others to join in playing with possibilities.

"I wonder why she didn't tell her . . ."
"I wonder why the grandma was so secretive . . ."
"Maybe the grandma couldn't handle it . . ." (instead of "Was it be-
    cause the grandma couldn't handle it?")

These wondering acts contrast with the information-seeking utterances of the transcript:

"Do you understand they cremated her?"
"That surprised you?"
"Do you think it was too much to ask you to cope with death?"

How facile these participants are in moving back and forth between seeking information and wondering. With each type of inquiry act, the speaker turns to others differently, takes a different stance toward the topic and toward the participants, brings a different tone to the discourse. In their responses, the participants move to the speaker and take on her stance. In #1–14, the participants engage in clarifying a confusion. In #1 and #3, the confusion is identified, and in #5, #6, #7, and #9, several students elaborate the problem. In #10 and #12 Karen provides the clarification the students seek. The participants know that this is a clarification agenda, not a wondering agenda. The goal is to resolve an issue and they join in doing that. And when Karen poses her own inquiry in #29 and #33, the students work to provide an answer for her. But the agenda is different in #15–27. Here the purpose is not to clarify confusion or provide information, but rather to reflect, to play with possibilities, to wonder. Both the inquiry acts and others' responses to them indicate that these participants know what the agenda is and what kind of inquiry discourse they are in. They shift stances as appropriate, moving in and out of information-seeking and wondering orientations.

If acts of wondering are more difficult to recognize than are acts of information-seeking, would it help to actually name these acts in classroom discourse? What if we responded to students' wondering utterances (not always, of course, but sometimes) with a comment such as, "Hm. So you're wondering about . . ." or "I sometimes wonder about that too." Would our use of the word *wonder* help to make wondering acts more visible—to our students and to ourselves? Naming something has a way of doing that. We cannot have a word for something without there being something there for the word to represent. A word alerts us to the presence of a particular something and helps us form a concept. But beyond rendering wondering acts more visible (audible?), would our generous use of the word *wonder* also legitimize this type of language act as one that is valued in the classroom? I really don't know; I am of two minds here. Surely we would want to avoid substituting contrived talk for authentic talk. The point is not to sprinkle the word *wonder* through class discussion at regular and frequent intervals, reminiscent of the vocabulary control of basal readers. But perhaps as we ourselves become more aware of acts of wondering, the word that names these acts might naturally become more prominent in our talk. (See Copenhaver, 1993; Seifert, forthcoming; and Whitin & Whitin, 1997 for examples of teachers intentionally incorporating children's wondering into their curriculum.)

Not only are wondering acts more difficult to hear than are information-seeking acts; they are also more difficult to provide for in a classroom. In many schools, efficiency and accountability drive the educational endeavor. In such a school, wondering will not score any points: It takes time. It does not improve test scores. It does not meet sequenced curricular objectives. It does not result in a product—you have nothing to show for it. It gives students and teachers nothing helpful to say in response to another's question, "What did you do in school today?" The answer "We wondered a lot" is not helpful.

In such schools and classrooms, wondering may be especially difficult to recognize because there is so little of it.

Perhaps the inquiry acts that are the most difficult of all to hear are those that are expressed in ways culturally unfamiliar to us—when the sounds that inquiry makes are different from those we are used to hearing in our own social group. The group that nurtured us taught us its inquiry ways. So, too, did the social groups that nurtured the students we teach. It is unlikely that there exists a community in which children do not engage in inquiry. It is equally unlikely that there exists a community in which these ways are not culturally distinctive.

During the past several decades, we have increasingly come to recognize, to understand, and to value the culturally distinctive "ways with words" that children bring to the classroom. (See Baugh, 1983; Edelsky, 1991; Heath, 1982, 1983; Lindfors, 1986, 1987; Smitherman, 1977.) And increasingly we have responded by modifying our ways of instruction— how we incorporate, respond to, and build on children's various ways with oral and written language. (See Au, 1980; Hudelson, 1989, 1994; Rigg & Allen, 1989.) This culturally oriented interest has not focused specifically on children's ways of inquiry. And so the bad news is that we currently know far less about cultural variation in children's inquiry than we would like to. But there is good news too. We are perhaps more ready to listen for it than we have been at any time in the past. Being more aware of the presence of language variation in our classrooms, we may be more attuned to its presence in inquiry acts specifically. We can listen, knowing that we will hear it, believing that it is there. The question that orients our listening is not "How come this child doesn't express curiosity about anything?" but rather "How does this child express his curiosity? How does he engage others in his own going-beyond?" Researchers have described children from social groups that especially value listening (sometimes more than speaking) (Philips, 1972, 1983) or that expect deference from children as a sign of respect in adult-child interactions. Such children's interactive ways may pose special challenges for teachers from a mainstream background that tends to value overtly expressive, highly initiating behavior in children. We may need to hear the "sounds of silence," to recognize inquiry acts expressed nonverbally or in peer interaction.

Perhaps the best news of all is that classrooms have never been better places than they are today for hearing inquiry's many voices. This is because classrooms are increasingly about voice: about *having* it, about *using* it. We are no longer surprised to find many classroom events that resonate with student voices—interactive writing, learning logs, writing workshop, cross-age tutoring, literature discussions like Karen's, individual student projects, interactions with others beyond the classroom via the Internet . . . the list is long, but these kinds of classroom experiences no longer surprise us. All these activities share two features that should help us hear inquiry's different voices. First, they all empower students: there is power sharing between student and teacher. Mrs. McKenzie did not share power with me and my third-grade peers. She set the agenda, she gave the assignments, she provided the scripts; we carried them out and did so on her terms. Thus she did not hear *our* voices, but only her own played back in our "What do Eskimos eat for breakfast?" But in classroom events like those above, which increasingly characterize today's classrooms, students shape agendas, projects, discourse. Second, these classroom events all involve students in interaction that is abundant, diverse, and authentic. Student empowerment and student interaction in classrooms work well for culturally diverse inquiry, for in such classrooms inquiry can *speak* in many voices—voices both culturally and personally distinctive; and so, in such classrooms, inquiry's many voices can be *heard*.

Expression

In Part I we focused on inquiry purpose: its role in defining inquiry acts; its early emergence; and its presence (or absence) in classrooms. Now in Part II we turn to inquiry expression, considering the expressive forms we use (Chapter 4) and what it is that we express through these forms (Chapter 5).

People (including educators) tend to hear utterances expressed in question form as acts of inquiry. Sometimes they are, but often they are not. Then too, inquiry acts are often expressed in ways other than interrogative form. The challenge (especially in classrooms) is to hear inquiry acts whatever their expression. So we begin (Chapter 4) by trying to differentiate between question forms and inquiry purposes, and then by exploring their relationship. Both the distinction and the relationship are important to an understanding of inquiry expression and its development in children.

At first we may think of inquiry expression as a straightforward matter of conveying to someone what it is that you want to know. But, as we'll see in Chapter 5, it is much more than this. Our inquiry expression also conveys much about what we know already and how we are using that knowledge in our attempt to go beyond it. Inquiry's "favorite forms" (question words such as *where, when, why*) are important in this going-beyond work, and their acquisition by young children is a stunning accomplishment. Expression of stance is in the act as well: Our words convey our attitude toward the partner and toward the topic. We explore these matters of inquiry expression in Chapter 5.

Chapter 6 brings us to the classroom—especially it brings us to *teachers* in the classroom. We are only too familiar with the traditional role of teacher-as-*questioner*. We know how this one sounds; we recognize its expression. But the expressive ways of teacher-as-*inquirer* are very different. It is this role we focus on in Chapter 6, listening to the sounds that inquiry makes in teachers' inquiry demonstrations.

CHAPTER 4

Inquiry's Forms and Functions

In this chapter I have two goals: to separate inquiry purpose (function) and expressive form, and to put the two back together again. Inquiry purposes and expressive forms are *different*. They are also *related*. The goal is to better understand both their distinctiveness and their relationship. A transcript of a conversation between Justin (almost four years old) and his mother will help to clarify the difference; and a transcript of excerpts of conversation between Sarah (seven months old) and her mother will help to clarify the relationship.

DIFFERENTIATING LANGUAGE FORMS AND COMMUNICATION FUNCTIONS

It is not a new idea to you that language forms and communication purposes are different.[1] This difference was the basis of the decision to choose utterance (a unit of purposeful communication) rather than sentence (a unit of language form) as the basic unit in considering inquiry. But however easy this form/function distinction may be to state and even to recognize intellectually, it is a difficult distinction to really believe in when the focus is inquiry acts. The last chapter focused on distinguishing between those acts that are and those that are not inquiry, precisely because there is such a strong pull to equate *inquiry utterance* and *question form* (interrogative). It is often difficult to hear the difference between the two, especially in classroom language events. We will consider the reasons for this confounding of form and purpose in the next section of this chapter when we focus on the relationship between them, but in this section the purpose is to clearly distinguish the two. It is an important thing to do because failure to distinguish inquiry acts and interrogative forms results in two problems: (1) *including* as inquiry much that is not inquiry at all (i.e., interrogative forms that express other communication purposes but have nothing to do with trying to engage another in one's attempt to understand something), and (2) *excluding* from consideration much that is inquiry (i.e., utterances that do have this purpose but use noninterrogative forms to carry it out). The following are all in question form (i.e., interrogatives), but have nothing to do with inquiry:

> Ya wanna fight? (challenging)
> How do you do? (greeting)
> Won't you come over Friday evening? (inviting)
> Would you help me move this table? (requesting)
> Can't you do anything right? (criticizing)
> (Teacher to noisy third-grade class) Do you want to go out for recess or don't you? (threatening)
> (One adult to another at a bus stop) Looks like rain, doesn't it? (starting a conversation)
> (Mother to her 18-month-old) Where's your nose? (eliciting performance)
> (Teacher to class) What's the capital of Nebraska? (testing)

As listed here, these are sentences, not utterances, for they are not occurring in real conversations. Yet we can readily imagine real conversations in which each of these could occur as a speaker's conversational turn. And if they did occur in real conversations, they would not be inquiry utterances, because they are not seeking a partner's help in understanding anything.

On the other hand, in the earlier transcripts (Jill, 11th graders, literature discussion), we have seen examples of utterances that were inquiries but were not in interrogative form (e.g., Jill's challenges, connections, protests; the 11th graders' and 5th and 6th graders' wondering comments).

Research on Questioning

There was a substantial body of educational research in the 1960s and 1970s that confounded *inquiry* and *interrogative*. That research was intended to be about—indeed, thought it was about—children's inquiry development. It was not. It was, rather, about children's development and use of question forms in various contexts.

The impetus for much of this research was a concern that children were not questioning enough in school. It was thought that children would be more active and effective learners if they questioned more and teachers questioned less. And there was good reason to be concerned about the predominance of teacher questioning in classrooms. One study of questioning in fourth- and sixth-grade social studies classes found teachers asking an average of 47 questions per 20-minute period, whereas students asked an average of 6.9 (Davis, 1971). The same study found only 38.5% of the children asking any questions at all during social studies, whereas three children accounted for over 50% of all questions asked by children, and five children accounted for over 75%. Other studies echoed these teacher/student disparities in questioning. There was reason to be concerned.

However, the form/function ambiguity in the word *question* went unnoticed. And so concerned researchers carried out studies of various kinds aimed at increasing either the overall number of questions children would ask, or else the number of questions of particular types that children would ask. Experimental studies, comparing number of questions asked by children in experimental and control groups, varied such factors as whether the children received question-asking training (Blank & Covington, 1965), whether their questions received answers (Ross & Balzar, 1975), whether the child was praised for asking a question or whether the child received praise and modeling of question-asking (Zimmerman & Pike, 1972). The various "treatments" (training, answering, praising, modeling, etc.) increased the numbers of questions that participating children asked, but neither the questions nor the stimulus tasks (e.g., "What questions can you ask about this picture?") had anything to do with inquiry: Children were not trying to understand anything, and they were not seeking anyone's help.[2] Torrance's research linked various preschool "approaches" ("traditional," "creative aesthetic") to the asking of "mature" or "immature" questions (Torrance, 1972), and related group size to types of questions asked (Torrance, 1970). But the question-asking situation was contrived: the children were shown a picture of Old King Cole and told to think up questions about what was going on in the picture that they couldn't know by just looking. One might get questions from the children in this situation, but probably not acts of inquiry. Other studies explored ways of influencing children to ask more constraint-seeking questions in Twenty Questions games or more category questions in hidden pictures games, for example, by having children observe a model (Laughlin, 1968) with or without an accompanying verbalization of a constraint-seeking strategy (Denney & Connors, 1974) or by calling the children's attention to the categories involved (Nelson & Earl, 1973). These treatments resulted in more interrogatives of certain types, but did not relate to children's engagement in inquiry.

It is easy enough to look at this body of research from our present moment in history and see it as misguided. But it made sense in its own time. Actually, one finds intriguing bits scattered through this body of work, for example, Berlyne's (1965) notions of epistemic curiosity and the factors that foster it; Saxe and Stollak's (1971) finding of a strong positive correlation between curiosity measures of first-grade boys and those of their mothers (the more curious the one was, the more curious the other was also); Allender's (1969, 1970) explorations of children's problem-sensing, formulating, search, and resolution behaviors (Shulman, 1965) in a hands-on "I Am the Mayor" unit (Allender, 1969, 1970); and Kenzie's (1977) attempts to describe inquiry styles in individual children. But these intriguing bits could not carry the day. The overriding assumption that question form and inquiry act were one and the same, coupled with the contrived nature of the research tasks, offered little possibility of our learning much about children's inquiry acts.

Language acquisition research came into full flower in the 1970s and 1980s. It included substantial interest in children's development and use of interrogative forms, as well as interest in the use of these forms by adults who interacted with the language-acquiring child. Unlike the educational psychology research of the 1960s and 1970s on questioning, the language acquisition research did distinguish between language form and communication purpose. This research addressed two central questions: What is the course of the child's development of the syntax and semantics of interrogatives? (For an early study of syntactic development, see Klima & Bellugi, 1971; and for early studies of semantic development, see Bloom, Merkin, & Wooten, 1982; Brown, 1968; Cairns & Hsu, 1978; Ervin-Tripp, 1970; Savić, 1975; Tyack & Ingram, 1977). What are the communication purposes for which the child and those who interact with her use these forms? (See Holzman, 1972; Savić, 1975; Shatz, 1979; Snow, 1977; Tamir, 1980.) The form issue was primary. It was form—interrogative—that identified the body of relevant data for study. The researcher identified all interrogatives used in particular conversations involving children, and then considered what communication purposes the partners used these interrogatives for (e.g., testing, directing, maintaining contact, calling attention). Some of these uses had to do with inquiry, others did not. This research has contributed to our understanding of inquiry in that it has documented the course of development of inquiry's "favorite" form (interrogative), and it has explored those events—some of them inquiry events—in which the child (and her partners) used this particular form. However, the limitation of this work for an exploration of emergent inquiry is that it omits a lot of the child's inquiry acts, namely, those inquiry acts that are not in question form.

If emergent inquiry is what we are trying to understand, then it is inquiry act that must stand at the center. The researcher will select children's acts of inquiry as the relevant body of data, and the guiding question will be, How do children carry out inquiry acts over time? Given a steadily increasing interest throughout the 1980s and 1990s in children's development of competence in oral and written discourse, it is timely to replace interrogative form with inquiry act as the center.

Bakhtin's distinction between "sentence as a unit of language" and "utterance as a unit of communication" has significant implications for an understanding of how children develop their ability to engage others in their own attempts to understand the physical, personal, and social worlds in which they live. This, after all, is a matter that lies at the heart of human development, indeed, of "what it means to be human in the . . . world" (Wertsch, 1991).

I think of the interrogative-form-versus-inquiry-function issue as one of casting nets and catching fish. If the fish I want to catch and study are instances of inquiry acts, then I must cast a different net than I would if I wanted to catch fish that were instances of interrogative form. I need a net that will catch *all* instances of inquiry acts (whatever their form) and that will catch *only* those—will not let into my net interrogative forms that are doing other kinds of communication work (e.g., inviting, greeting, requesting, threatening, challenging, testing). This matter of casting nets and catching fish brings me to Justin and his mother.

Justin

The following conversation occurs a few weeks before Justin's fourth birthday. He and his mother are in the car on the way to nursery school. I include their conversation in its entirety because it is one of those rare occasions when life has handed us a well-made play. The conversation has a clear beginning (when Justin's mother turns on the tape recorder as they begin the ride to nursery school), and a clear end (their arrival at nursery school), and it offers a manageable amount of text to consider at one time. The conversation is heavy in inquiry. It is composed of seven segments (marked by pauses, topic shifts, or both), most of which have inquiry as their overarching purpose. The inquiry segments are good examples of what Tizard and Hughes (1984) call "passages of intellectual search," that is, "conversation in which the child is . . . puzzling over something she does not understand" (p. 114).

Inquiry is central to Mother's utterances as well as Justin's: she actively elicits his help as she tries to better understand his perspective. However, it is Justin's inquiry I focus on here by way of demonstrating the interrogative form/inquiry function distinction and its importance. Specifically the question is this: Which of Justin's inquiry acts would we miss if we focused on interrogative forms? Justin uses a variety of noninterrogative forms as he engages his mother's help in trying to understand how birds cry (Segment 2), how birds communicate with each other (Segment 4), how people and birds cry (Segment 5), and what heaven is like (Segment 6), and finally as he tries to recall a particular room at Grandmother's house (Segment 7).[3]

Text No. 5: Justin's Ride

Segment 1

1. JUSTIN: . . . a little birdie fell off a tree.
2. MOTHER: Is it laying on the ground?
3. JUSTIN: No, it's just standing there.
4. MOTHER: It's limping, right? 'Kay, let me buckle you in.
5. JUSTIN: No, maybe it fell off the garage.
6. MOTHER: Ooooo, is it OK?
7. JUSTIN: I think.

    (pause)

Segment 2

8. JUSTIN: Is *tweet-tweet* how they cry?
9. MOTHER: Is *tweet-tweet* how they cry?
10. JUSTIN: Yeah.
11. MOTHER: Aah, well, *tweet-tweet* is how they're usually singing. I don't know what sounds birds make when they cry.
12. JUSTIN: Maybe *tweet-tweet* is how they cry.
13. MOTHER: Well, *tweet-tweet* is how they sing and how they talk to each other. Maybe a sad *tweet-tweet* would be how they cry.
14. JUSTIN: 'Kay.
15. MOTHER: You think?
16. JUSTIN: Yeah, but sometime . . . yeah, but they do sad *tweet-tweet* all the day.
17. MOTHER: Oh, they do?
18. JUSTIN: Yeah.

    (pause)

Segment 3

19. JUSTIN: A beautiful birdie! Yeah, but some of the birdies are gross.
20. MOTHER: Oh, they are?

21. JUSTIN: Yeah. 'Cuz some of 'em are o-range.
22. MOTHER: Oh, you don't like the orange ones?
23. JUSTIN: No. 'Cuz they're gross. Orange ones are gross.
24. MOTHER: I think the red ones are pretty.
25. JUSTIN: I think the red ones are pretty too. Not the orange ones.
      Orange ones are gross.
26. MOTHER: Really. What are the black . . .
27. JUSTIN: Yeah, the black ones are pretty.

Segment 4

28. MOTHER: Why d'you think the orange ones are so gross?
29. JUSTIN: Because they're . . . because they fly in the air and I have
      very good eyes to see. And I have very good eyes to, um, hear
      them go *tweet-tweet*.
30. MOTHER: You have very good *ears* to hear them go *tweet-tweet*.
31. JUSTIN: Yeah.
32. MOTHER: It's your ears that you hear with.
33. JUSTIN: Yeah.
34. MOTHER: Right?
35. JUSTIN: Uh-huh. Yeah, but, do birds have ears?
36. MOTHER: Aah, well, yeah . . . they're not ears like our ears, but
      they *can* hear.
37. JUSTIN: Yeah, but birds can't really hear each other.
38. MOTHER: Yeah, they can. They talk to each other. When they're go-
      ing *tweet-tweet* they're talkin' to each other.
39. JUSTIN: Yeah, but we can't really hear 'em, um, go *tweet-tweet* talk-
      ing to each other.
40. MOTHER: We can't understand what they're saying, no.
41. JUSTIN: No.
42. MOTHER: Some people can who really study birds—have figured
      out what each little sound means and so some people under-
      stand what the birds are trying to say when they make differ-
      ent, different sounds. But I don't know . . . but I haven't studied
      birds.
43. JUSTIN: Oh, yeah. One time I understanded what two little birdies
      were saying . . . by a light and they were looking at each other.
44. MOTHER: Really?
45. JUSTIN: Yeah. That was talking.
46. MOTHER: Uh-huh. Sure.

      (pause)

Segment 5

47. JUSTIN: Oh, yeah . . . um, one little birdie . . . no, one little duck on
    . . . on "Tom and Jerry" . . . um, it was crying like *waaaaa*, with
    tears coming down.
48. MOTHER: Huh.
49. JUSTIN: That's how little birds cry, maybe.
50. MOTHER: Yeah.
51. JUSTIN: Maybe they cry like ducks do.
52. MOTHER: With tears?
53. JUSTIN: Yeah, maybe. Yeah, but *you* don't cry with tears, do you?
54. MOTHER: Yeah. All people cry with tears.
55. JUSTIN: Yeah, but Granddaddy didn't cry, did he? [The child's
    grandfather—mother's father—died shortly before this conver-
    sation.]
56. MOTHER: Aah, well . . . I guess sometimes he cried.
57. JUSTIN: When it was time to go to heaven?
58. MOTHER: I think Granddaddy was probably very happy when it
    was time to go to heaven. He was probably a little sad and a
    little happy. Sad 'cuz he was gonna miss us for a little while
    and also very happy to be with God and Jesus in heaven.
59. JUSTIN: Yeah, but he's always gonna miss us.
60. MOTHER: Yeah.

    (pause)

Segment 6

61. JUSTIN: But . . .
62. MOTHER: Heaven is a very nice place to be.
63. JUSTIN: Yeah, but, we're *never* gonna die.
64. MOTHER: We will *live* in heaven sometime.
65. JUSTIN: Yeah, but . . .
66. MOTHER: We'll still be alive.
67. JUSTIN: Yeah, we'll be alive.
68. MOTHER: Uh-huh.
69. JUSTIN: And we'll be standing up just like we are now.
70. MOTHER: Right . . . walking around, talking, jumping, playing,
    laughing.
71. JUSTIN: Watching . . . um . . . yeah, but, what will we be doing?
72. MOTHER: Just having fun and being *very* happy.
73. JUSTIN: Yeah, but will we see Granddaddy?
74. MOTHER: Yeah.

75. JUSTIN: Oh . . . in his room?
76. MOTHER: Mmmm, I'm not sure what his room looks like. But we'll see him.
77. JUSTIN: Well, maybe out in the hall.
78. MOTHER: Yeah, maybe out in the hall.

(pause)

Segment 7

79. JUSTIN: Yeah, Mom, remember when it was time to go see Grand-daddy? . . . he died . . . um. . . they took us to his room.
80. MOTHER: Uh-huh. . . oh, no, we won't be . . . we won't see him in that room.
81. JUSTIN: Yeah, but that was a long, long time ago.
82. MOTHER: Right.
83. JUSTIN: Well, I don't remember that.

(pause)

84. JUSTIN: Oh, that was at Grandmother's house.
85. MOTHER: No, that room was not at Grandmother's house.
86. JUSTIN: I know.
87. MOTHER: Granddaddy is not in that room anymore. Granddaddy is in heaven.

(pause)

88. JUSTIN: But that was at Grandmother's house when we went to see him.
89. MOTHER: Right. Here we are.

In Segment 2 it is clear that Justin likes his idea that *tweet-tweet* is how birds cry. When his mother does not confirm his idea, suggesting instead that *tweet-tweet* is how birds sing (#11), Justin repeats his idea in a softened ("maybe") form. His mother admits the possibility of a "sad *tweet-tweet*" (#13)—a modification that Justin seems to accept, although with the stipulation that birds "do sad *tweet-tweet* all the day" (#16). What is most striking in this segment—its very essence—is the negotiation between Justin and his mother around Justin's original idea. There is no doubt that Justin is engaged in inquiry here, working his way through to a better understanding of the significance of bird sounds. Hefty work it is, too, eliciting help from mother, considering, compromising, modifying. Yet there is only one interrogative from Justin, the one that initiates the topic (#8). If we were to consider only that one, we would see how

Justin gets a topic of interest onto the floor, but we would miss the inquiry work he engages in as he pursues it, pushing his way through to an altered understanding of that topic. We would also miss his ways of continuing to engage his mother's help with this intellectual task.

In Segment 4 Justin and his mother clear up two misunderstandings: that you hear birds with ears, not eyes, and that there is a difference between hearing and understanding (#35–#46). Justin seems to accept his mother's eye/ear correction—no negotiation of this point as there was in the earlier "sad *tweet-tweet*" segment. But the hear/understand clarification requires more work between these two. In #37 and #39, Justin counters his mother's suggestions, saying that we can't "really hear" birds talk and birds can't "really hear" each other. Apparently it is Justin's "really hear" that indicates to his mother that he means *understand*, not *hear*. In #43 and #45 Justin brings the notion of understanding birds' talk back to himself, relating it to his own experience. In Justin's nine turns in this segment, there is only one interrogative: "do birds have ears?" But throughout the segment Justin is, once again, carrying out quite demanding inquiry work—the work of grasping and accepting the correction, countering his partner's ideas persistently, and finally relating a new idea to his own experience. (Notice that the new idea is one that contradicts his original idea that we can't understand birds.) If we focused only on Justin's interrogatives in this segment, we would miss the intellectual-and-social work he is doing—the proposing and accepting and countering and applying of ideas. This is the work of trying to understand with the help of a partner. It is inquiry work.

In Segment 5 Justin's focus is on crying: the crying of a duck, of birds, of adults. (Notice in #49 how skillfully he returns his mother to his favorite idea—that *tweet-tweet* is how birds cry). Justin is doing a lot of relating of one thing to another in this segment, either because the two are similar or because they are different: perhaps birds cry like ducks do; ducks cry with tears, but adults don't; people cry but Granddaddy didn't. Notice the "yeah, buts" of #53, #55, and #59, in which he basically accepts his mother's idea, but in each case suggests an exception. In each of his three interrogatives (#53, #55, #57) Justin is putting forward his own idea for confirmation. He doesn't get it the first two times, but he takes what his mother gives (in #54 and #56) and goes further with it. Connecting, countering with exceptions, eliciting confirmation of his ideas and then, when he does not get it, going further with the partner's ideas—these are important ways of getting and using a partner's help in your own sense-making. They are far more diverse and substantial than the asking of three questions (#53, #55, #57). Every one of his utterances in this segment turns to his mother for something more as he works toward greater understanding. This is the work of inquiry.

In the "heaven" discussion (Segment 6) Justin begins by working through the apparently unsettling matter of whether he (and his mother) will die, first asserting ("we're *never* gonna die"), then accepting his mother's comforting modification. From #69 to #78 Justin's agenda is to try to imagine heaven—and himself in it: what he will be doing, who he will see, what it will look like (with rooms and halls). I interpret his interrogatives in #71, #73, and #75 to be requests for his mother to contribute more specifics for the mental picture he is creating. This is a powerful way to use a partner. But the power lies in the work that he is doing—getting his mother's participation in his act of imagination—rather than in the forms he is using to do that work.

If we considered only the interrogatives in Justin's talk on this short ride to nursery school, what acts of inquiry would we miss? We would miss his negotiating and compromising, his modifying and connecting, his accepting and countering, his applying and relating, his visualizing and imagining—all carried out in intentional partnership with mother, seeking her engagement in his attempts to understand. We would, in the end, catch most of Justin's initiation of topics, but little of the work that he was doing by way of pursuing his understanding of those topics. Chukovsky (1968) may be right about a language-acquiring child like Justin being "the hardest mental toiler on the planet" (p. 10), with the possible exception of Justin's mother.

RELATING LANGUAGE FORMS AND COMMUNICATION FUNCTIONS

For 20-some years I have been teaching a graduate seminar called "Children's Questioning." Though the title reflects the thinking at the time I started teaching this course, it is an unfortunate choice because the word *questioning* is ambiguous in regard to whether the course is about children's inquiry or about children's use of interrogative forms. In fact, the course focuses on children's emergent inquiry. In the very first class meeting, I begin to deal with the language form/inquiry purpose issue: the focus of the course will be children's expression of inquiry, whatever the syntactic form it happens to take. I give the students an exercise during that first class, requiring them to consider short scenarios in which children use interrogative forms both for inquiry purposes and for noninquiry purposes (challenges, threats, etc.); and also scenarios in which children use noninterrogative forms for both inquiry and noninquiry purposes. The typical student response is, "Oh yes. I see. We inquire using all kinds of language forms, and questions—interrogatives—aren't always inquiry acts. Sometimes they are requests or challenges or criticisms, threats or greetings and so on." I come away from the first class feeling that we have made a good start. It is only the first of many times that we will visit the form/function issue during the semester, for it invariably weaves its way through the entire course.

About a month into the semester, the students begin to work on their original, small-scale research studies, each student designing her research, discussing her plan with me, going off and gathering data (usually audio- or videotaping or both) and then transcribing her tapes in preparation for carrying out her analysis. Then, about two thirds of the way through the semester, when I am confident that the students grasp the difference between inquiry acts and interrogative forms, it happens. At least one student, her own tapes now transcribed, comes to me crestfallen.

"As I was taping, I was sure the kids were inquiring all over the place. But I've transcribed the tapes now and there are hardly any questions at all."

We look over the transcript together and indeed, the kids *are* "inquiring all over the place"; they just do not happen to be doing it in interrogative form. Year after year, despite my ever more "effective," "imaginative," "engaging" ways of hammering away at the interrogative/inquiry distinction, the same scene plays itself out in my office. And in each case, the student all along has said all the right words in class and in informal interactions with me when we discussed the form/purpose distinction. Yet when she turns to the real talk of real children, she does not hear inquiry when its sound is not that of question. She talks the distinction, but doesn't really know it—feel it—in that deep place where belief lives.

Because this has happened so many times, I have finally been forced to stop badgering and bludgeoning my students with this distinction, trying to convince them that inquiry acts occur in noninterrogative form, and instead ask myself *why:* Why is it that inquiry utterances and interrogative forms are so resistant to separation in our thinking? Why is it that, although we can quite rationally recognize that inquiry acts can be carried out by means of a variety of syntactic forms, we continue to cling to interrogatives as the real acts of inquiry, to feel at our deepest level that to inquire is to ask a question?

The answer lies in the relationship of the two. It is a relationship of close connection that gets played out in the many inquiry events we observe and participate in throughout our lives. It is possible to come at that interrogative/inquiry relationship either from the form side, or from the communication side.

A Form Perspective

Speakers of English have the sense that imperatives (commands) are the basic forms for requesting; that declaratives (statements) are the basic forms for informing; and that interrogatives (questions) are the basic forms for inquiring. We recognize that we often use other forms to carry out these communication purposes; yet we hold to these as canonical, that is, the most basic or fundamental. If I want you to open the window, I can request this using the imperative "Open the window," but I can also say, "Would you mind opening the window?" or "Could ya get that window?" or even, in some circumstances, "Boy, it sure is hot in here!" There lingers the sense that "Open the window" is basic to these other possibilities—that they are "dressed-up" versions of the basic imperative form. There's a tendency to think that if we stripped away the politeness trappings and interpersonal subtleties, we'd be left with "Open the window." That's what we are *really* saying.

The situation is comparable with inquiry: We take interrogative (question) to be its basic (canonical) form. We feel that questions are the real forms underneath noninterrogative expressions of inquiry. For example, we feel that underneath "Tell me about your day" lies the question "What did you do today?" and that underneath "Hmmm. I don't think I have the mileage between Rockford and Tyler" lies the question, "What is the mileage between Rockford and Tyler?"

The canonical interrogative forms in standard English are of three basic types:

1. Yes/no questions, which (formally, at least) seek an affirmative or negative response. They can be *reversed* (Will you be there?), *nonreversed* (sometimes called "intonation questions" because interrogativity is expressed by intonation rather than by reversal of subject and first verbal element, as in You will be there?), or *tags* (You will be there, won't you? You will be there, right? You won't be there, will you?).
2. Wh-questions, which begin with a "question word" (e.g., what, where, when, why, how, who).
3. Polar questions, which offer a choice (Do you want the big one or the small one? Are you going to Penney's or Sears first? Will Janet or Robert use the extra ticket?).

I am ignoring for now the complexities within these basic categories (e.g., the various types of questions that begin with *what*, the variety of why questions and how questions). This simplified picture of interrogative forms is enough to allow us to ask whether it is possible to paraphrase as interrogatives those inquiry utterances that are in noninterrogative form. If interrogative forms are canonical in inquiry—if they really are the basic, underlying forms for inquiry utterances—then we would expect to be able to take Justin's noninterrogative inquiries in the segments we considered above, and paraphrase them as these essential forms.[4]

In many of Justin's information-seeking inquiries he is seeking his mother's confirmation of an idea he puts forward. Two of these (#53, #55) are expressed as tag questions: "Yeah, but *you* don't cry with tears, do you?" "Yeah, but Granddaddy didn't cry, did he?" Another six are expressed in noninterrogative form, four of them beginning with "yeah, but," (as do #53 and #55):

birds can't really hear each other (#37)
we can't really hear 'em, um, go *tweet-tweet* talking to each other (#39)
he's always gonna miss us (#59)
we're *never* gonna die (#63)

The way of turning toward another (for confirmation of his idea) is explicit in #53 and #55, but surely implicit in the other four. It is very easy to paraphrase these as tag questions, similar to #53 and #55. In the two remaining noninterrogative confirmation-seeking utterances (#45 and #69), again the sense of tag question is strong:

"Yeah. That was talking [wasn't it?]." (#45)
"And we'll be standing up just like we are now [won't we?]." (#69)

Notice that with or without the tag that makes the confirmation-seeking explicit, Justin's mother provides what Justin seeks: feedback about the correctness of his idea. That is, she understands his purpose to be that of seeking confirmation, whether or not he uses an interrogative form (tag question). In either case he is engaging in the same kind of inquiry act, and his mother recognizes that.

Four more of Justin's noninterrogative inquiry utterances from the segments we considered above are "maybe" utterances (#12, #49, #51, #77). I hear these as Justin's "softened" requests for confirmation of his ideas. They could also be wondering acts, but I do not hear them this way, because Justin is so committed to the idea he has put forward. Entertaining uncertainty is not itself the activity for Justin, as is the case in acts of wondering. He wants closure. His mother apparently hears these utterances as confirmation requests also, for she provides confirmation in all but #51, where she tries to get clarification of what Justin means. (Presumably she would have gone on to confirm except that Justin asked a new question in #53.) So these softened versions, too, could be paraphrased as tag questions:

> *Tweet-tweet* is how they cry, isn't it? (#12)
> That's how little birds cry, isn't it? (#49)
> They cry like ducks, don't they? (#51)
> [We'll see him] out in the hall, won't we? (#77)

Notice that in paraphrasing these "maybe" utterances as tag questions, we lose the softening, the tentative stance that Justin is bringing into the discourse. But this is metamessage, expression of attitude, rather than content. The message "I want you to give me feedback on this idea" is retained in the interrogative paraphrase.

The remaining three noninterrogative inquiries are sense-making utterances (not information-seeking utterances or wondering utterances). The three include one "Yeah, but . . ." (#16), in which Justin counters his mother's idea, and two "Yeah, and" utterances (#43, #47) in which he connects the idea on the floor to his own experience. These are all important inquiries: Justin is in intentional partnership with his mother, trying to figure something out. However, I do not sense an interrogative paraphrase underlying these inquiry acts. The underlying paraphrase that works for inquiry acts of information-seeking and wondering types may not hold for other kinds of sense-making inquiry acts (a matter that begs to be explored in a book of its own).

The noninterrogative wondering utterances of the 11th graders in the "Gertrude" transcript are relatively easy to paraphrase as *I wonder + interrogative*, as in these two examples:

> "Maybe she was marrying him 'cause that was the only way she could stay queen" becomes *I wonder + was she marrying him because that was the only way she could stay queen?*
> "It seems that in that whole part where he, where he was talking to her about, um, setting a mirror up and all that, he seems to be, I don't know what it really is, um, really self-righteous or, or, I don't know" becomes *I wonder + was he being self-righteous when he was talking to her about setting a mirror up?*

It appears that canonical interrogative forms do underlie information-seeking and wondering acts of inquiry (though their linguistic relationship to other collaborative sense-making acts is less clear). It is a relationship that seems to be real in the minds of standard English speakers. No wonder my students keep looking for questions in their transcripts! No wonder children's noninterrogative inquiry acts in classrooms are difficult to hear.

A Communication Perspective

Canonical form is a mental notion we have of linguistic structure. It is *inner*. But Bakhtin (1986) comes at this interrogative/inquiry relationship from the *outer* side. His interest is not what lurks in the recesses of the speaker's mind, but rather, the actualities of social interaction. The central notion is *typicality*. The basic understanding is that humans engage in a variety of social events—*types* of interactions—each type having its own character. Here and there in his writing, Bakhtin gives examples of some of these types of interactive events such as "village sewing circles, urban carouses, workers' lunchtime chats" (Vološinov, 1973, p. 97).[5] Nowhere does Bakhtin attempt to specify some complete set of these event types; in fact, he throws up his hands in the face of such an impossible task. But he maintains that each type of social event has its typical utterances, that is, utterance types which frequently play out that kind of event.

These typical utterances "belonging" to various kinds of interaction events he calls "speech genres." This is problematic for several reasons. First, we are used to thinking of a genre as a type of literary work—narrative, poetry, essay, novel, and so on. But Bakhtin uses the term for both oral and written events. Thus the poem or novel, like the casual greeting, is an utterance, a turn in an ongoing dialogue:

- It is *bounded* by the contributions of others and thus stands as a single "turn" of one individual;
- It has *completion* in itself, being sufficient to elicit a response from another (e.g., a reader);
- It has *expressiveness*, conveying stance, attitude, orientation.

And so written genres are "typical utterances," possessing Bakhtin's defining characteristics of "utterance" (boundedness, completion, expressiveness).

Second, this view of genre or typical utterance is unsettling at first because it includes interactional turns of such varied length, everything from an "Oh" in conversation to *War and Peace.* To think of *War and Peace* as an utterance is something of a challenge. But the crucial notion is typicality in the utterances that constitute social life. It is within social interactions of various kinds that a child learns language. For Bakhtin, learning language is learning to be generic, that is, learning to participate in the interactive events of one's community. And this means learning the typical utterances of the community's social events. "To learn to speak," says Bakhtin, "means to learn to construct utterances (because we speak in utterances and not in individual sentences . . .) . . . . We learn to cast our speech in generic forms" (1986, pp. 78–79).

It is from this perspective of typical utterances and types of communication events that Bakhtin speaks of questions. They are not a topic of central focus in his work. Nevertheless, comments about questions are sprinkled through his work, and these provide a perspective that helps to illuminate the close connection we feel between interrogative form and inquiry act. We know that they are not the same thing, and yet . . .

Remember that Bakhtin is adamant about the distinction between sentence (form) and utterance (communication). Yet he sees interrogative as a special case, a type of sentence that "occup[ies] a special position" (Bakhtin, 1986, p. 90). For Bakhtin, interrogative is one of several "types of sentences that usually function as whole utterances belonging to particular generic types" (p. 89). In other words, in the case of interrogatives, sentence (form) and utterance (communication act) frequently coincide. In daily discourse, interrogatives frequently are conversational turns.

Does this mean that they are the same after all? No. We can think of numerous situations in which two distinct things often occur together in our experience. Age and size are different units, yet they often go together: the older the child, the larger the sneaker. And so it is with interrogative form and inquiry act. The social fact is that, in our daily experience, the two frequently go together. Remember again the properties of utterance: boundedness, completion, expressiveness. In the case of inquiry acts that are expressed as interrogatives, these properties seem to belong to the sentence as much as to the utterance:

- Often an interrogative sentence is a conversational turn, all by itself, *bounded* by the speech of others. (Jill's "Nest-es" transcript provides good examples.)
- Often *completion*—the sufficiency—is in just this single sentence; it is enough to be responded to.
- Often the single interrogative sentence *expresses* a tentative, reaching-out stance—turns toward the partner in uncertainty.

These are the defining characteristics of *utterance*, but they cling to interrogative *sentence* when utterance coincides with sentence and, as in the case of inquiry acts, does so frequently. Then these characteristics seem to belong to sentence, and we hear the sentence form (question) as the communication act (inquiry). Interrogative "knits together very stably with its generic [typical utterance] expression," says Bakhtin (1986, p. 90). In the daily discourses of our lives, question is inquiry's favorite form. And so our own social experience explains our tendency to hear—to feel—questions as acts of inquiry, whether or not they actually are.

This "knitting together" of interrogative forms and inquiry acts figures significantly in emergent inquiry. Much of language acquisition research has focused on the acquisition of language structure: the child's development of increasingly complex and conventional semantic, syntactic, and phonological structures. But Bakhtin (1986) does not see language acquisition this way. He views the child as engaged in the development of speech genres, the typical utterances of daily discourse.

> We know our native language . . . not from dictionaries and grammars but from concrete utterances that we hear and that we ourselves reproduce in live speech communication with people around us. We assimilate forms of language only in forms of utterances. . . . The forms of language and the typical forms of utterances, that is, speech genres, enter our experience and our consciousness together, and in close connection with one another (p. 78).

In emergent inquiry, is it the case that "forms of language . . . in forms of utterances" enter the young child's experience (and consciousness) together, as Bakhtin suggests? If we examine actual inquiry events involving very young children, do we find in the talk a knitting together of question form (interrogative sentence) and inquiry purpose? With these questions in mind, I examined transcripts involving Sarah, a child you met briefly in Chapter 2. I was in for some surprises.

EMERGENT INQUIRY: THE CASE OF SARAH

When she was 7 months old, Sarah seemed very curious about her reflection, gazing intently at it in her high chair tray, in mirrors, in the shiny faucet of the bathtub. Here is how her mother's talk sounded in their interactions when Sarah was focusing on her reflection.

Text No. 6: Sarah's Reflection

(Sarah is sitting in her high chair, her gaze focused on her high chair tray. Italicized questions are those in which Mother articulates Sarah's curiosity.)

1. SARAH: (verbal sound as if signaling)
2. MOTHER: You see yourself? *Who's there? Who's in there?* Hi Sarah. (pause) Can you see yourself? (pause) Can you see yourself in there?

(Sarah and her mother are looking in a mirror following Sarah's bath, during which she bumped her head.)

3. MOTHER: Hello. *Who's that?*
4. SARAH: (exertion sound)
5. MOTHER: *A pretty girl?* Hi. Hi, girl. *Who is there?*
6. SARAH: (exertion sound)
7. MOTHER: Hi, Sarah James.
8. SARAH: uuuuuuu
9. MOTHER: Hi. *Who is there? Is that you? Is that a girl that just bumped her head? Hm? Is that you?* (whispered) It is you. (whispered)

Mother's talk abounds in interrogatives. Notice that when she voices Sarah's curiosity, she does it from her point of view, not from Sarah's: She asks, "Is that *you*?" not "Is that *me*?" as if spoken by Sarah. Mother's questions seem to say, "You're wondering who's in there and is that you." In these questions, Mother gives words to Sarah's experience at that moment.

However, during this period, Sarah's mother used questions for a variety of other purposes as well, not just to give voice to Sarah's curiosity. One example, in the preceding excerpts, is her questions that seem to seek information from Sarah (e.g., "Can you see yourself in there?"). See Table 4.1 for a more complete list of communication purposes this mother's questions served during this period. Now, this situation presents a puzzle: If Sarah's mother uses questions to express a variety of purposes, then it seems that questions do not knit so stably with inquiry's purpose as Bakhtin (1986) suggested.

But a closer examination of transcripts from this pair reveals that whenever Mother's purpose is inquiry, she uses a question to express it. This is important because it means that the variability we find when we

FIGURE 4.1. Mother's Communication Purposes and Examples in Interrogative Form

Communication Purpose	Examples
Requesting repetition	What is it? Huh?
Requesting behavior	Can you sit still for <u>one</u> second? (Mother is dressing Sarah) Could you lay down so Mama could change you please?
Joining Sarah's focus of attention	What do you have? What's up? What are you doing?
Focusing Sarah's attention	See these trucks and stuff? Who's this? Your little doll?
Encoding present/past situation	Is it (an ice cube) cold? [i.e., It is cold.] Are you on your tippy toes? [i.e., You are on your tippy toes.] Did you hit your head with that spoon?
Inviting Sarah to do something	Can you do patty-cake? Can you whisper?
Joking	What are you doing? You doing the splits? Are you a daddy longlegs? A Sarah longlegs?
Implementing routines/games	Who's/What's this? and See X? (all book-sharing routines)
Sharing texts (stories, songs)	"Mr. Brown can moo. Can you?" (line from book)
Making conversational comments	Mama's gonna run you a bath, OK? Mama better check out our dinner, don't you think?
Greeting (after sleep or separation)	How are you doing, Bud? (getting Sarah up from nap)
Criticizing Sarah's behavior	Do you have to throw it? (food) Do you eat your books?
Expressing frustration	Oh, Sarah, is Mama going to have to change you? You're not in a very good mood today, you know it?
Expressing affection	Are you bright eyes? Are you my baby?
(Seeming to) seek information	You like my dress? Why are you so mad today? What are you smiling about?

begin with question form disappears when we begin with inquiry purpose: questions express many purposes, but inquiry is invariably expressed by questions. If the underlying question guiding the emergent inquirer were "How do people use question forms?" her experience would answer, "For a host of different purposes." But if, as I suspect, her guiding question is "How do people inquire?" her early experience will answer, "By asking questions."

It is not surprising that interrogative is Mother's choice for expressing inquiry in her conversation with Sarah. This is the canonical form of inquiry for her. Given that her purpose is to communicate with Sarah—to share a world with her through talk—it makes sense that she would select the simplest, clearest, most basic and unambiguous way to express what she is *doing* in the conversation.

If interrogatives work so well in conveying that we seek the partner's help with our intellectual task, why don't we just stick with them? Why do we go on (like Justin and the 5th and 6th and 11th graders) to develop more indirect, noncanonical expressive means of inquiring? One important reason must be that the noninterrogative forms often do special kinds of interpersonal work in our interactions. Perhaps we would always express our inquiries in interrogative form if we were not trying to do such things as conveying our stance toward content, context, or each other; expressing our own personalities; being friendly; being polite; trying to keep our partner's willing participation in the dialogue—on and on through a host of aspects of our personal relationship. When I talk to you, I convey message (content) but I also convey metamessage, telling you how I feel about you, me, our relationship, and the event we are engaged in. Recall Justin's "maybe" utterances. These convey that he is willing to negotiate, that he is open to what his mother has to say, that he is ready to adapt and modify his point of view if necessary, that his stance is reflective and tentative. These are metamessages, having more to do with interpersonal relationship, attitude, and stance than with heaven and birds' *tweet-tweets*, the content of his talk.

Like Justin, Sarah will go on to develop a range of expressive means of inquiry, for she will want to convey attitude and feeling and relationship as well as "content" in those acts. And like us, she will continually experience interrogative form and inquiry act "knitting together very stably" in the human mind (canonicity) and in social life (genre).

CHAPTER 5

Inquiry Expression

Several times I have shown undergraduate classes a film, *Shared Nomenclature* (Ohio State University), in which four pairs of individuals (kindergartners, second graders, sixth graders, adults) carry out a task where one partner knows the solution to a problem and the other partner is trying to figure it out. The two participants sit at a table facing each other. A partition separates them so that they cannot see each other, although they can talk to each other freely. On the table, in front of each participant, is a set of six blocks. Every block in the set bears a different abstract design. The two partners' sets are identical, but in addition to the blocks, one partner also has a picture showing a particular arrangement of them. It is his task to arrange his set of blocks according to the picture and to tell the partner on the other side of the partition how he should arrange his blocks so they will form a matching pattern.

Before showing the film each time, I have had several class members carry out the task while the rest of us watched, and then I have asked the students to make predictions about how they thought the four pairs they were going to see in the film would perform this task. Each time, I have listed the students' predictions on the board so that we could discuss them after viewing the film. In every class, one prediction was this: "The kindergartners will ask each other a lot of questions because they don't know as much as the older pairs. The child who is trying to make the arrangement will have to ask the direction-giver a lot of questions in order to find out how to do it." And, of course, the kindergartners—in contrast to all the other pairs—ask no questions at all. How could they? They lack sufficient understanding of the task to be aware of what it is they need to find out. They do not glimpse the possibilities beyond what they presently know.

My students apparently share that commonly held assumption that acts of inquiry arise in ignorance. They don't. They arise in what one knows, and in what one is doing with that knowledge. Certainly one's inquiry acts express awareness of an area of one's ignorance; indeed, they are deliberate attempts to reach into that area. But they surely do not arise there. No inquiry act was ever born in a vacuum. These acts arise in what we do know, including the fact that our knowledge is limited and something lies beyond it. Our inquiry act is the articulation of our sense of what may lie beyond what we presently know.

We need only reflect on our own acts of inquiry to recognize that we inquire most in those areas where our expertise is greatest, and least in those areas in which we are most ignorant. All I can ask about nuclear physics is, "What is it?" But my inquiries about children's language acquisition are endless. It is there that I have a sense of the possibilities that lie beyond what I know now. To inquire is literally to give voice to these possibilities that I sense, to render my sensing of possibilities a social act that we call inquiry.

The point is more powerfully made by considering children's inquiry than by reflecting on our own. Even the "simplest," most fleeting inquiry utterance, voiced in passing in the comings and goings of daily life, speaks loudly of the knowledge that gave birth to it, as well as of the way the inquirer is using that knowledge to go beyond it.

> My 9-year-old-son, having eaten the broth from his bowl of chicken-and-stars soup, stares at the pileup of stars at the bottom of the bowl and asks, "Are there more stars in the sky or in a million bowls of chicken and stars soup?"
> As a 6-year-old he tells me, "We see the moon at night and we also see it in the daytime. Does that mean there are two moons—one for us and one for the people in Japan? Or is there just one moon and we have it all the time and the people in Japan never get it?"
> "People say no two snowflakes are alike," he tells me one day. "How can they know that? How can anybody ever have looked at every snowflake?"

The knowledge in each case is partial and the inquiry act reaches beyond it, into the place where he is ignorant, but it does not—*could not*—arise there. It is his knowledge that makes his inquiry acts possible.

> There is clearly much that Erik does not know about amountness, about what a million is, about the endlessness of heavenly bodies in space. Indeed, his inquiry reaches out into these areas of his ignorance. But it is in what he does know of these—the sense he has of amountness, of million, of stars, of space—as well as in his sense of his own limited understanding—his vague

awareness of the more that is "out there" for him to know—it is
in this knowledge that his inquiry is born.

When he asks about the moon, he is clearly working from an understanding (however limited from the adult's perspective) of the
earth's rotation.

And in his snowflake inquiry, it is easy to identify the limitations
on his knowledge of natural phenomena and human ways of
exploring them. But his act of inquiry is born of his knowledge
that reliable information sources do not say things for which
they do not have good evidence, and that a likely way of getting
evidence is to systematically and comprehensively examine all
cases.

Notice that he is largely wrong in the thinking that initiates each of
these inquiry acts: *wrong* to think that the amount of stars in his bowl
and in the sky are remotely comparable; *wrong* to think that there might
be two moons or only one that stays put; *wrong* to think that scientific
certainty requires examining all instances of a phenomenon (rather than
invoking general principles). But thinking "wrong" attests to the presence
of activated knowledge no less than thinking "right" does. One cannot
think nothingness, ignorance; one thinks *something*. This is knowledge,
however "right" or "wrong," partial or profound it might be. Without it,
acts of inquiry would be impossible.

What do we express in our acts of inquiry? We express our present
knowledge, but also our *reaching* beyond it. The knowledge out of which
the inquiry utterance is born includes both meanings that we share with
others, and also meanings that are personally unique. And we express
the reaching through our stance—the attitude we convey toward partner
and toward topic. In this chapter, we focus on the child's development of
these aspects of inquiry expression.

After establishing the distinction between *meaning* (the socially
shared) and *sense* (the individual), we'll consider the child's development
of that crucial set of words that are inquiry's canonical forms and typical
utterances: question words and, necessarily, the world they represent.
These are socially shared meanings that are crucial to the child's inquiry
development. Then we'll move to the expression of feeling in inquiry—
the personally unique aspects of inquiry expression. And finally, we'll
consider stance, the inquirer's expression of attitude toward partner and
toward topic. Throughout, you'll hear the workings of demonstration and
engagement as the child develops these expressive aspects of inquiry.

MEANING AND SENSE

Inquiry utterances arise in knowledge. But what is knowledge? The question has fascinated the greatest human minds throughout recorded history. It is a question far too vast to treat extensively here. Yet Bakhtin and Vygotsky, each in his own way, make a point about knowledge (word knowledge specifically) that bears on our consideration of children's inquiry. Both men clearly differentiate between the stable and constant aspects of words and word meanings on the one hand, and their adaptable, flexible, changeable nature on the other hand. For Vygotsky (1986) the distinction is between *meaning* (the fixed and stable) and *sense* (the dynamic and changing):

> The sense of word . . . is the sum of all the psychological events aroused in our consciousness by the word. It is a dynamic, fluid, complex whole . . . which has several zones. . . . Meaning is only one of the zones of sense, the most stable and precise zone. A word acquires its sense from the context in which it appears; in different contexts, it changes its sense. Meaning remains stable throughout the changes of sense. The dictionary meaning of a word is no more than a stone in the edifice of sense, no more than a potentiality that finds diversified realization in speech. (pp. 244–245)

It is easy to see that, if we are to communicate with one another, we must share stable meanings of words: there must be some consensus as to what *stars* and *moon* and *millions* and *snowflakes* mean. Yet it is also easy to see that our sense of a word is individual, a unique composite of understandings and feelings—"psychological events"—born of our personal encounters with the word in many contexts. All those past encounters still resonate in the word for each of us. We do not take a word's meaning and leave behind the associations we have of the particular moments when we came to know it.

You have already encountered Bakhtin's distinction between the "repeatable," socially shared aspects of language, and the "unrepeatable," unique aspects of communication. You can see that this distinction parallels Vygotsky's meaning/sense contrast. When Bakhtin turns his attention away from sentences and utterances, and considers words and the understandings they convey, he again differentiates between socially shared meaning (words "from a dictionary") and unique communication experience (words from "other people's mouths").

> The word does not exist in a neutral and impersonal language (it is not, after all, out of a dictionary that the speaker gets his words!), but rather it exists

in other people's mouths, in other people's concrete contexts, serving other people's intentions: it is from there that one must take the word and make it one's own. (Bakhtin, 1981, pp. 293–294)

For both Vygotsky and Bakhtin, then, socially shared meaning is part of a larger whole—a "stone" in the "edifice" that is the "sum of all the psychological events aroused in . . . consciousness." This is the knowledge out of which inquiry is born. Meaning is crucial, of course. It is because Erik and I share the meanings of his words and of the relations among these meanings that we are able to talk with each other about moon, stars, and snowflakes. This stable semantic meaning is part of the knowledge that Erik brings to our encounter, and without it his inquiry acts would be impossible. But it is only part. He also brings his own unique understanding of *moon, stars, millions,* and *snowflakes,* forged out of his daily encounters with others—words spoken by particular individuals in particular contexts with particular expressive accents at particular moments. Always the particular.

Think again of Justin and Jill. We hear in their inquiry acts, as in Erik's, the coming together of the socially shared (meaning) and the personally unique (sense). Both children are concerned with crying:

". . . when I went to the hospital did I cry?" asks Jill.
"Maybe *tweet-tweet* is how [the birds] cry," suggests Justin.
". . . but *you* don't cry with tears, do you?"
". . . but Granddaddy didn't cry, did he?"

Their "crying" is not the one that comes "out of a dictionary," although it surely includes that as "one of the zones" of the word for them. But the dictionary knows nothing of Jill being frightened in the hospital, knows nothing of birds' *tweet-tweet*s, of Justin's mother or of Granddaddy. Yet these are part of "crying" for Jill and Justin, the experiential knowledge that clings to this word and is part of the "sum of all the psychological events aroused in [their] consciousness by the word."

Remember that an act of inquiry attempts to engage another in one's own act of understanding. Thus it is an act equally social and personal. If the child is to engage another, he must rely on those aspects of language that he and the partner share: the conventional, stable, constant, agreed-upon meanings and structures that language provides. But so must he rely on the unrepeatable, the unique—*his* particular task, *his* understanding, *his* background experience, *his* personal puzzlement, *his* caring in that moment, brought together in his act of inquiry.

EXPRESSION OF SOCIALLY SHARED MEANING

To learn one's first language (or languages) is to learn both words, and the world those words represent. As people in the child's community interact with him and with one another around him, their words necessarily represent their shared understanding of the world. This is not all their words do, but it is an important part of what they do, and without this shared understanding, communication would be impossible. The child encounters particular words in a range of specific situations, but however diverse this range, a stable core of meanings for these words remains constant: they continue to represent a socially shared understanding of the world.

Learning Question Words

In emergent inquiry, there is a particularly important set of words and word meanings, the so-called question words (where, when, why, how, who, etc.). Why is this particular set so important? After all, we know that a child's inquiry arises in knowledge of word-and-world far beyond this set—a world of animals' homes and hospital experience, of colors and sounds, of heaven and grandfather, of crying and dying, of amount and verification ... We know, too, that one can inquire about anything in the world without using these question words at all. And even when we use these words, we are not necessarily inquiring about anything: "How are ya?" "Why, how beautiful!" and "When will you ever learn manners?!" all include "question words," but if they occurred in conversations, one would be a greeting, one an emotional exclamation, and one a criticism—none an act of inquiry.

Yet for all these caveats, we recognize that question words are inquiry's canonical forms and typical utterances. Therein lies their special importance. These words indicate aspects of experience (such as time, place, agency, cause, means) that community members consider as they try to make sense of their world. Not surprisingly, these are words they use to name the emergent inquirer's sense-making too. Recall infant Sarah's mother in the reflection episodes; she gave these words to Sarah's puzzling experience of her world. And what a remarkable world this particular set of words conveys!

Consider what the child must understand about the world in order to competently use the words

What dis/dat?
Where X (go)?

Where . . . from?
Why?
Who/What? (as subject or object)
When?
How?

In order to be asking "What dis/dat?" (one of the child's earliest questions), the child must understand that the space he lives in is populated by things that are separate from one another. They share the space, but do so distinctly from one another. Each is an entity. And each has a name. Asking "What dis/dat?" expresses these socially shared understandings. Without them the child could not use this "typical utterance" in his own way, to carry out his own intentions to find out what he wants to know. But use it he does and in a remarkable way. It has been observed that, at around age 2, many children ask an abundance of "What dis/dat?" questions. The child's vocabulary shows a dramatic spurt at this time (Vygotsky, 1986). It seems as if, having discovered that things are separate entities and have names, the child also discovers that "What dis/dat?" can work to help him find out what those names are. What is important to the child is not the word combination per se, but the work that that particular word combination can do for him: Each time he asks the question, he gets another label. The child has hit on a speech genre (typical utterance) that very powerfully helps him do what he is trying to do: find out the labels for objects in his world. The child has discovered this in the many specific moments and contexts of daily interaction. Words—*these* words—out of people's mouths, in different contexts but always retaining a socially shared core of meaning. The child now imbues these words with his own intention: to find out the labels which are of interest to him. What power this simple utterance gives the very small child! But he could not use this question with others in his community if he did not, like them, recognize the separateness of things in space, understand that each has a name, and know that "What dis?" serves to elicit it. Asking "What dis?" is no small accomplishment.

Where questions also convey important knowledge that the child has built about the world he lives in. Object permanence (or object constancy) is the crucial understanding here, the realization that when an object is out of sight, it has not ceased to exist, but is simply displaced. Where questions encode this meaning. Object permanence is a major cognitive achievement of the child's first year. Picture an adult and a 6-month-old sitting on the floor facing each other. The adult has a ring of keys that the child wants. When the adult, in full view of the child, places the keys behind his own back, the child cries. The keys are gone; they no longer exist. But play the same game 6 months later and when the adult hides the keys behind him, the child does not cry, but instead crawls behind the adult to find the keys. Though the child cannot see them, he knows they still exist. A child could not ask, "Where Mommy?" or "Where ball go?" without this understanding that, although Mommy or the ball are out of sight at the moment, they continue to exist. Later where questions about where present objects have come from (where . . . from) entail the same understanding—and no small act of imagination, I think, to recognize that what is here at this moment was at some other place at some past moment. In order to share this word with others, the child must share the world it represents, a world in which objects are permanent though displaced.

Why questions have to do with causal relationships between antecedent and subsequent events. This seems a major assumption to make about the way the world is—that events are not simply random and arbitrary, but that they have (identifiable) precipitating causes. It is not surprising that the child comes to see the world in this way, of course, given that that is the way others in his community see it and the way that they "tell" him it is. Nor is it surprising that early why questions are typically the single-word "Why?" (and the early response to why questions is often the single-word "Because").

An intriguing pattern has been observed in many children at around the age of 3, in which there is a sudden spurt in the child's use of why questions. Then, after several months of highly inflated use, why questions drop down to a "normal" level and remain there. One assumption is that the child is trying to figure out how why questions work—what the causal relations are that they encode and how they are used in conversation (both of which turn out to be rather complex). This relating of word and world (causal relations in this case) is not easy. The child's behavior suggests that he is on something of a data-gathering mission. Each time he asks a why question, he gets yet another example of the phenomenon he is trying to understand. There is no suggestion here that this questioning behavior is conscious and deliberate on the child's part, but it is patterned in a way that suggests an unconscious language acquisition strategy at work. Again we see the child using his social world in his own ways, toward his own ends. It is easy enough to see that the particular instances of causal linkings in any child's experience will be very diverse, yet every unrepeatable specific instance of why will include that repeatable shared-meaning aspect of causal linking.

Piaget's (1955) work suggests the range of types of connections that why questions entail, including whys of causal explanation, whys of motivation, whys of justification (Piaget, 1955). And Bloom, Merkin, and

Wootten (1982) have pointed out the discourse complexities that why questions entail (especially their ways of connecting with others' previous utterances in a conversation). Thus both word and world are complex in the case of why. It is no wonder, then, that the development of why questions takes time. But it is clear that the course the child traverses toward fully competent use of why questions in various contexts and imbued with his own intentions rests on the fundamental understanding of the world as a place where causal relations obtain between events. This is an important aspect of the child's total sense of why, expressed in his inquiry acts.

To be asking both what and who questions is to distinguish between animate and inanimate entities in one's world. But if the child uses who and what as both sentence subjects (Who fell? What fell?) and as direct objects (Who did you see? What did you see?), then it can be assumed that the child also distinguishes between agents of actions—doers, causers—and "receivers" of actions—those "done to." The sensorimotor child seems well situated to make such discoveries, being himself often the agent acting on objects (throwing things, biting things, shaking things), and also being in constant contact with caregivers who are primary agents in his world. Many of the child's earliest two-word utterances suggest his grasp of agent and object relations (e.g., "Mommy fix" or "throw ball"). Clearly these understandings of animate and inanimate, and of agents and objects of action, underlie (and make possible) the child's use of what and who questions. Others in his experience have encoded the child's puzzlement about doers and done-tos as what and who.

Books have been written about the complexities of time concepts. Clearly the child's when question is rooted in some sort of time notion. His time notions develop over a substantial period, but what is especially important for us, I think, is that even the child's earliest when questions express an orientation to the world that sees events as ordered with respect to time. Part of the child's understanding of when is that time is a fundamental ordering principle. In order to ask when, the child must have some emergent sense of this relational dimension.[1]

The relation that is the basis of how questions is means-end. Some of our how questions ask about instrumentality (How did you fix that? With a hammer); some ask about a process (How did you get that answer?); some seek an explanation or justification (How did the jury reach such a verdict?), but they all recognize that there are means by which existing states of affairs have come about. The world that the word *how* indicates is one in which explicable processes bring about certain results. The child's how question is based on his understanding of the world as this kind of place, specifically a place in which ends are brought about through means. Using the word *how* conveys this understanding of the world.

This list of question words is not exhaustive. There is more—much more: whose, rooted in one's understanding of possession; which, rooted in one's understanding that categories have separate, individual members; what kind, rooted in one's understanding of hierarchical categories, and so on. The point is that it is out of the child's quite remarkable understanding of the world that his use of question words is possible. It is easy to take the child's acquisition of this set of words for granted because they are acquired so effortlessly, so universally, and so early. We expect children to be able to use these words in many situations (though certainly not all) when they come to kindergarten. But the development of question words and their socially shared meanings about the world we live in is an extraordinary accomplishment—not to be taken for granted at all.

Developmental Sequence

How does the child acquire these words and the socially shared meanings they encode? One way to approach this question is to sketch a general developmental sequence that has been observed in many children. This is not an altogether satisfying response to the question, of course. What we would like to do is climb into the child's mind and watch its processes. But the familiar developmental sketch, though far from perfect, gives some hints as to what might be going on in there.

The research on children's acquisition of question words assumes that the sequence of acquisition of these words will to some extent reflect the child's cognitive development sequence. Much of this research relies on a Piagetian orientation that sees the young child's direct interaction with the physical world as being particularly important in the child's cognitive development.[2] This expectation that there will be some recognizable correspondence between a sequence of cognitive development and a sequence of development of question words is fulfilled to some degree. We find that identification questions (What dis? What dat?) and where questions (along with yes/no questions) are early, being much in evidence around age 2. Why seems to be a favorite of many 3-year-olds. When and how questions typically come somewhat later. This general sequence is one we might expect, for it accords with our notion that location (where) is easier (e.g., more concrete and relating to the understandings built by the sensorimotor child) than the abstract notion of time (when); that eliciting names for concrete objects (What dis?) is easier than dealing with abstract causal relations (why), and so on. (See Bloom, Merkin, &

Wooten, 1982; Cairns & Hsu, 1978; Ervin-Tripp, 1970; Savić, 1975; and Tyack & Ingram, 1977, for studies that have attempted to identify this developmental sequence.)

Of course the situation is far more complex than this simple description suggests. We speak of *what* questions, but in fact there are different kinds of what questions:

1. What is that?
2. What are you doing?
3. What are you eating?
4. What kind do you want?
5. What fell?

These are all quite different. As canonical forms, (1) seeks a label, (2) seeks the verb phrase of a sentence ("eating a steak"), (3) seeks the direct object ("a steak"), (4) seeks a subcategory, (5) seeks the noun phrase ("subject" of sentence). Obviously, in actual conversation—if these were utterances instead of sentences—they could get all kinds of noncanonical responses (see Goffman, 1981):

1. What's that?
   So what do ya' think it is?!
2. What are you doing?
   Pardon me?
3. What are you eating?
   Beats me!
4. What kind do you want?
   What kind I want, you ain't got.
5. What fell?
   I didn't hear anything.

Not only are there various kinds of what questions, but there are various kinds of whys (Piaget, 1955) and hows and so on. Besides this, question types do not occur in a vacuum; they occur in conversations and are influenced by a host of discourse factors (Bloom, Merkin, & Wootten, 1982). Also, contexts differ, some being more supportive of certain kinds of questions than others: How familiar is the context? How routine is it? How self-explanatory is it? So a child can seem to "have" a particular question word in one context but not in another. And then there is the matter of research design. Our notions of developmental sequence are based on the ways that researchers have gathered and analyzed data.

Thus the sequence suggested on the basis of children's responses to some sort of contrived, unnatural lab task is often different from that derived from naturalistic observation. So the task of identifying a developmental sequence for these important words is a more difficult undertaking than one might suppose. Yet this work does suggest a general sequence in which the child's earliest questions tend to be identification questions and where questions (along with yes/no questions, typically expressed initially as single-word utterances spoken with rising intonation). Why questions typically are acquired somewhat later, developing in all their complexity over a substantial time period, and when and how questions—also developing over a significant time span—are among the later questions the child controls. It goes without saying that there is individual variation among children, that there is overlap in the development of these forms, and that the development of each is itself a developmental sequence and not an all-at-once phenomenon. Nevertheless, the general expectation is what dis? and where and yes/no before why, and why before when and how.

Demonstration and Engagement

Identifying a general developmental sequence is not the only way to examine the emergent inquirer's acquisition of question words. Also, as helpful as a Piagetian orientation may be in illuminating some important aspects of a child's cognitive development, Piaget's child often seems rather lonely as he sits and acts on physical objects in his environment. It is easy to forget that his cognitive development is deeply and continuously social. Word-and-world connections are built in the child's social encounters as those around him give voice—word—to experience. Again we invoke the social mechanisms of demonstration and engagement as the best hope of understanding the child's development of inquiry in a social and physical world. Recall the earlier description of language as a piece of paper: "Thought [meaning] is the front and sound [expression] the back . . . one can neither divide sound from thought nor thought from sound" (Tannen, 1989, p. 16). There is no way for a child's community to demonstrate inquiry and to engage him in it without this indivisibility of meaning and expression, of world and word. Members of the community, interacting with and around the child, demonstrate the way they view the world, what they perceive to be its basic nature and categories and relationships. Especially important to their expression of their worldview are inquiry's typical utterances and canonical forms. For English speakers, these forms encode a world

- of separate entities (identification questions) that continue to exist even when they are out of the range of sight and touch and hearing (where) and also have a "life" before now and after now (where . . . to; where . . . from);
- of properties of objects and actions, which differentiate members of a category from one another; and subdivision of larger categories into smaller subcategories (e.g., what color, what shape, what type);
- of time, space, and amount as basic properties and relationships in the world, that serve as organizers in terms of which we can consider experience in an orderly, anchored way (when, where, how much, how many);
- of events as causally related, and people themselves as "causers" (why);
- of end states that come about through the action of various means (how).

The point is that in those most typical inquiry utterances in everyday conversation, the words themselves alert the child to aspects of the world that the community attends to in organizing and understanding experience. Through these typical inquiry utterances, others "tell" the child the world as they *see* it and as they *say* it. It is their world and word that the child will share.

It seems remarkable that the child's development of such a complex worldview and language to encode it should occur in inconsequential events like looking at one's reflection in a mirror or sharing a bedtime story or conversing on the way to nursery school. But it is in the demonstrations and engagements provided in just such everyday events that the emergent inquirer comes to share his community's world and words of inquiry.

And these events are always particular. The myriad conversations the child observes and participates in each day play out the socially shared meanings of question words in terms of particular instances—the *identity* of particular entities (nests and eggs and fish; hepatitis and operations and rheumatic fever; Tom and Jerry, birds and heaven); consideration of particular *properties* of particular entities (birds that are red, black, orange . . . and "gross"; a heaven where people talk, play, jump, and laugh; a Granddaddy both happy and sad, who cries with tears); *location* of particular objects or events (rabbits' holes under the ground; squirrels' nests in trees; fish eggs in water; Granddaddy and Justin in heaven); *time* of particular events (of going to the hospital, of having a baby, of going to heaven); or *relations* of particular phenomena (of being sad and crying; of being in a hospital and feeling frightened; of a bird's sound and a message of crying or singing). There is no way to consider identity, properties, location, time, causal or means-end relations without considering these in terms of a specific someone or something of experience. In its social discourse, the community gives the child an interpretive framework and words to convey it, but always in the unrepeatable situation of the unrepeatable moment.

EXPRESSION OF FEELING

Meaning is not all. Vygotsky (1986) tells us that it is only a "stone" in an "edifice" of sense, "the sum of all the psychological events aroused in our consciousness by the word" (p. 244). Feelings are an important part of that totality of psychological associations. People can't talk about topics without conveying how they feel about them. It's easy to hear feeling in the talk of Jill and Justin and their mothers, especially when there is some contrast, for example, when two participants' feelings about a particular topic are different, or when one speaker's feelings toward a topic change over the course of discussion, or when speakers' topic changes (or shifts of focus within topics) are accompanied by corresponding changes in expressed feelings. The Jill and Justin transcripts include numerous examples:

Orange (at least as a color for birds) elicits expression of strong distaste in Justin; yet his mother's puzzlement at his strongly negative reaction suggests that she finds nothing distasteful about orange (birds). And Justin seems to feel that crying is inappropriate for adults, but his mother holds no such view.

Initially Justin's feeling about death is apprehensive, but his mother's feeling is happy—even excited. Justin warms to her excitement about heaven, changing his feelings in relation to this particular topic (from apprehensive to excited).

Initially Jill feels anxious about any hospital experience, whereas her mother's attitude seems calm and secure. But as the conversation proceeds, Jill becomes less fearful, possibly in part because of her mother's calm manner and in part because of her own focus on the "resting" category of hospital experience (her "favorite part in the hospital") as opposed to operations (which are "yuk").

In some instances, as topics shift, Jill's feelings shift too. The topic is animals that lay eggs. Jill very matter-of-factly elicits members

for this category from her mother. Birds, OK; ducks, OK; fish—
"Uhn uhn!" Turtles are even more unacceptable as egg-layers.

The feelings expressed in these conversations toward birds' colors, crying, death, hospital experience, egg-laying, become part of the sense of
the words for these children and their mothers. And there is no contradiction in the fact that, though Justin's meaning of "death" remains constant,
his sense of "death" includes both the possibility of feeling apprehensive
and of feeling excited about it; or that Jill's sense of "hospital" includes
both the possibility of feeling frightened and of feeling secure. Their
sense of "death" and "hospital" includes an aggregate of possible feelings
and attitudes. Social meanings and personal feelings live together in
speakers' talk about the topics they are trying to understand. Conversation is not a cool exchange of socially shared dictionary meanings.

EXPRESSION OF INQUIRY STANCE

Here is a problem. If it is the case that all language acts involve expression of meaning and of feeling, then what is it that makes inquiry
acts different from other language acts? What sets these acts apart? We
know it is not linguistic *forms* that identify inquiry acts, for although inquiry has its canonical forms and typical utterances (e.g., question words,
interrogative sentences), there are no words or sentence types that belong
exclusively to inquiry expression. We know it is not the expression of
feelings that identifies inquiry acts, for feelings of all kinds are expressed
in language acts of all kinds. Inquiry acts have no monopoly here. We
know it is not the *content* of the talk that identifies inquiry acts, for animal
homes, hospital experience, bird sounds, death, crying could be the content of any language acts, not just acts of inquiry.

So, if it is not the form or feeling or content of our talk that identifies
it as inquiry, then what *is* it in the expression that "says" to a partner,
"Inquiry is the purpose of this language act"?

The answer is *stance*. We hear the inquirer's special way of turning
toward the partner and toward the topic. It's a two-way turning because
it expresses inquiry's two-way purpose: a social purpose of engaging another's assistance, and an intellectual purpose of increasing one's understanding. It is a sound of reaching—of two-way reaching, in fact, for the
inquirer reaches beyond self to the partner in anticipation of verbal response, and reaches beyond what he already knows to what lies beyond
it. The inquirer expresses an orientation toward partner and topic that is
uncertain and invitational.

- An act of inquiry is one's articulation of *uncertainty* regarding the territory one senses beyond one's present known world. It may sound timid, it may sound bold, but in either case, it is a venturing forth from known to new territory.
- An act of inquiry is the articulation of an *invitation* to the partner to join in a helping way. It may sound gentle, it may sound insistent, but in either case it is an attempt to bring the partner in in a helping role.

The uncertain stance that is the essence of inquiry's expression inevitably gets expressed in the demonstrations and engagements of the focal mother-child transcripts we have considered so far. Sarah's mother interprets and treats Sarah's gazing as expressive of uncertainty. She assumes that Sarah is not simply looking at her high chair tray, but that she perceives and is trying to figure out her reflection. Mother provides the language that gives voice to that uncertainty ("Who is that? Is that you?"). Jill's and Justin's mothers also respond to their children's expressions of uncertainty as being exactly that: uncertainty. They confirm, inform, explain, question further, correct, assert, but in each response, they acknowledge the child's inquiry utterance as an act of turning to the partner in uncertainty and invitation.

Initially it may be difficult to hear uncertainty and invitation in Jill's conversation with her mother. There doesn't seem to be anything very invitational or uncertain about "Yuk!" or "Nuh-unh!" But this is to consider the words themselves, and in communication events, there is no such thing as "words themselves." There are only words in communication contexts—utterances, not words per se. The overarching purpose that holds Jill's bedtime-conversation event is inquiry, and it is in terms of that overarching purpose that the participants grasp the thrust of the individual utterances. As I suggested in Chapter 1, within *this* pair's context and within their own shared history of bedtime-story events, both partners know to take Jill's utterances as acts of inquiry. However certain and final her utterances may sound to the ears of competent adult inquirers who are outsiders to this event, Jill and her mother, the insiders, know that Jill's "Nuh-uhn!" and "Yuk!" are not utterances intended to close down their collaborative exploration. They both know that these are part of her attempt to figure out some puzzling phenomena and to retain her mother's help as she does so.

Some of Justin's utterances, too, sound more certain and less invitational than the adult inquirer might expect.

". . . yeah, but they do sad *tweet-tweet* all the day."

"... birds can't really hear each other."
"... we're *never* gonna die."

But again, it is clear from the transcript itself that Justin and his mother hear—pick up and respond to—an uncertain and invitational accent that conveys this orientation toward partner and topic. To understand what is going on in these interactions, we must listen with participants' ears, not with our own—a very difficult thing to do.

Notice how the sounds of inquiry's invitational and uncertain turning change over time. The older inquirers in our focal transcripts—the 5th and 6th and 11th graders—convey an uncertain and invitational orientation in accents we are more accustomed to. Over time, Jill's and Justin's inquiry accents will sound more like these older students'. Ultimately we would expect Jill and Justin to include in their inquiry expression, more tentativeness markers (perhaps, might, possible, if, maybe), more expressions of politeness that help retain the partner's willing participation, a more moderate style of expression that sounds less blunt and demanding. Emergent inquirers like Jill and Justin have much to learn about how to use available expressive resources for conveying inquiry's purpose in their turning toward topic and partner. And learn it they will, in the continuing inquiry demonstrations and engagements provided by their communities. One particularly important community for these emergent inquirers will be the classroom.

The Ultimate Demonstration

Inquiry expression conveys something else too, something that may be the most important of all, yet the very thing we are most likely to miss altogether: *The world we live in is comprehensible and people try to understand it.* This one holds all the rest. If we did not take it as a given that the world is a rational, orderly place—if we saw it, rather, as random, chaotic, and unpredictable—how could there be any inquiry at all? I wonder how come ... ? Why is it that ... ? What would happen if ... ? would be devoid of meaning. Inquiry would be impossible, for asking about reasons and causes, means and relationships, can only occur if we assume that these exist. And if we did not assume that humans, by their very nature, are oriented toward trying to understand the world they live in, then we would be without our major way of interpreting human behavior. Again think of Sarah's mother in the reflection episodes. She treats it as "given" both that Sarah's reflection has an explanation and that Sarah is trying to figure out what it is. Notice that Sarah's actual behavior is only that of looking steadily in a particular direction. It is an act of interpretation on Mother's part (in accordance with an expectation she may not even be consciously aware of) that this behavior signals puzzlement, curiosity, an attempt to figure something out. Mother does not assume that Sarah is gazing aimlessly at the high chair tray or mirror, but rather that she is trying to figure out the reflection she sees. Mother assumes that Sarah is focusing on something that she herself would perceive (reflection) and find interesting were she in Sarah's place. She assumes that Sarah is a person like herself, and thus is trying to figure out an interesting aspect of her world. She assumes, in short, that Sarah is a "member of the club" of humans who live in a comprehensible world and try to understand it.[3]

Justin's mother conveys the same expectations in their conversation on the way to nursery school. Notice that her response to Justin's first comment, "a little bird fell off a tree," is to try to find out more about it: "Is it laying on the ground?" "It's limping, right?" "Oooo, is it OK?" She is giving a clear demonstration here that the world is a place we can understand and that we try to do that. She takes Justin seriously as just such a person in just such a world:

> She tries to be sure she understands what he is focusing on (e.g., #9, #52, the "gross" segment);
> She commits to extended, working-through sequences (e.g., #8–18);
> She corrects Justin's erroneous notions (e.g., eyes/ears; hear/understand);
> She answers and explains in response to his inquiries;
> She listens to and offers support for his reflections ("You think?" "Yeah." "Really?" "Oh, they do?")

And of course she explicitly mentions that some people study birds to "figure out what each little sound means." This is to take sense-making seriously, to legitimize it as important and expected human work. In all these ways Mother "tells" Justin that inquiry is expected behavior in humans. Humans just like *him*.

Jill's mother, too, plays out her implicit expectations that the world is a comprehensible place and that people, including Jill, try to understand it. It is Jill who directs both the "Nest-es" and "Hospital" conversations. Mother hangs in there with her, turn after turn, answering Jill's every question, responding to her every challenge. She would not invest herself in this way if she found Jill's inquiry behavior strange or unwarranted. Her investment reinforces Jill's inquiry as expected human behavior.

Surely all adults interacting with young children are not as patient as the three mothers in the inquiry episodes we've considered. Inquiry acts are imposing acts and adults (and others) sometimes become irritated by children's attempts to engage them in these acts, especially if the child's inquiry utterances are not carried out in ways that the community deems appropriate (e.g., if the child is too insistent, fails to observe politeness behavior that acknowledges the adult's superior status, or inquires about topics that are embarrassing to the adult). But to view the child's inquiry behavior as irritating is quite different from viewing it as alien or abnormal, a view that the adults in our focal transcripts do not hold.

It is remarkable that inquiry demonstrations and engagements should reveal so much about inquiry expression, enabling the emergent inquirer to learn that inquiry utterances:

- enact the assumption that the world is comprehensible and that people try to understand it;
- include inquiry's "typical utterances" (wh-question forms) that signal important dimensions of experience (categories, relationships), providing a helpful framework for constructing understanding;
- bring together socially shared meaning and personal feeling, as one tries to comprehend experience;
- voice inquiry's uncertain and invitational stance toward partner and toward topic. A reaching stance.

This is the expressive world of inquiry that the child is part of. It is the world the child makes his own.

CHAPTER 6

Inquiry Expression in the Classroom

Jerome Bruner (1986) remembers his fifth-grade teacher.

> I recall a teacher, her name was Miss Orcutt, who made the statement in class, "It is a very puzzling thing not that water turns to ice at 32 degrees Fahrenheit, but that it should change from a liquid into a solid." She then went on to give us an intuitive account of Brownian movement and of molecules, expressing a sense of wonder that matched, indeed bettered, the sense of wonder I felt at that age (around ten) about everything I turned my mind to, including at the far reach such matters as light from extinguished stars still traveling toward us though their sources had been snuffed out. In effect, she was inviting me to extend *my* world of wonder to encompass *hers*. She was not just *informing* me. She was, rather, negotiating the world of wonder and possibility. Molecules, solids, liquids, movement were not facts; they were to be used in pondering and imagining. Miss Orcutt was the rarity. She was a human event, not a transmission device. (p. 126)

Bruner's description suggests the power of Miss Orcutt's inquiry *demonstration* and his own *engagement* as an emergent inquirer. The two go hand in hand, of course. But in this chapter, it is teacher demonstration that takes center stage. Though we will not ignore students, it is the teacher who will stand in the spotlight, teachers like—and not like—Miss Orcutt. In this chapter, I consider two different views of teaching and learning, each of which gives rise to its own teacher demonstration: teacher-as-questioner, and teacher-as-inquirer. Then, relying on the already familiar literature discussion from Karen's classroom, I focus on teacher demonstration of inquiry and finally consider a special type of teacher inquiry.

The Miss Orcutts have ever been in short supply. She was not typical of her own time; she is not typical of ours. Because she was herself an inquirer, inquiry was what she demonstrated. Bruner (1986) contrasts her with a different version of teacher, one that he calls teacher as "transmission device." This teacher's demonstration (unlike Miss Orcutt's) will have much to do with *questioning*, but little (if anything) to do with *inquiry*. Sometimes her talk will have the sound of "gentle inquisition" (Eeds & Wells, 1989), sometimes the stronger sound of interrogation. But inquiry's sound—Miss Orcutt's sound of "negotiating the world of wonder and possibililty"—is different from both.

If questioning dominates one teacher's classroom interaction and inquiry dominates another's, it is because the two teachers have different notions of what teaching and learning are in school. Thus they play out different ways of being a teacher, one who helps students learn. A teacher's conception of who she and her students are and what they are doing together in "the place called school" (Goodlad, 1984) shapes the demonstration she provides as she and her students interact with one another.

It turns out that the distinction that was central in Chapter 4 between questioning forms and inquiry acts has significant classroom implications in the demonstrations of the two markedly different versions of teacher that I have just mentioned: teacher-as-questioner and teacher-as-inquirer.

TEACHER-AS-QUESTIONER

People are fond of talking about "typical" elementary classrooms. Given the absolute uniqueness of every classroom, it is likely that the notions that individuals label "typical classroom" are all somewhat different. But it is also likely that many of them include the sound of a teacher's voice (probably female), and more likely than not, the voice is asking a question.

Teachers' questioning has drawn a great deal of attention over the years. (For an introduction see Dillon, 1984, 1988; Gall, 1970, 1984; Hunkins, 1995; Morgan & Saxton, 1991; Redfield & Rousseau, 1981; Wilen, 1991.) The implicit assumption in this body of work is that asking questions is basic to the teacher's trade. This literature describes the kinds of questions that teachers ask, examines the effect of these questions, and offers advice about how the teacher might question "more effectively."[1] However, the presence of teacher questions as a fundamental reality of classroom life is taken for granted.

Much of this writing about teachers' questioning starts with interrogative form as the unit of interest and then asks, "What purposes do the teacher's questions serve?" (e.g., Cazden, 1988; Christenbury & Kelly, 1983; Heath, 1982a; Morgan & Saxton, 1991). It turns out that teachers use their questions to serve a wide variety of purposes, among them

• to manage student behavior, for example, to criticize ("Why can't

you sit still?"), to praise ("I just can't fool you today, can I?"), to
threaten ("Do you want to go outside today or don't you?") (Dillon,
1983; Heath, 1982, 1983; Morgan & Saxton, 1991)

- to manage group recitation and discussion events (Cazden, 1988;
  Dillon, 1983, 1984; Gall, 1984; Hunkins, 1995; Mehan, 1979; Morgan & Saxton, 1991)
- to direct students' thinking to significant and engaging issues (Cazden, 1988; Christenbury & Kelly, 1983; Dillon, 1983, 1994; Hunkins, 1995)
- to invite a student to reflect (Christenbury & Kelly, 1983; Dillon,
  1994; Hunkins, 1995; Morgan & Saxton, 1991)
- to invite students to evaluate or to provide explanations (Dillon,
  1994; Guszak, 1967; Hunkins, 1995; Morgan & Saxton, 1991)
- to assess student recall or understanding (Cazden, 1988; Christenbury & Kelly, 1983; Dillon, 1983)

In addition to describing teachers' questioning, the literature gives
quite a bit of advice about it. Teachers have been advised

- to ask fewer questions (Dillon, 1983, 1994; Morgan & Saxton, 1991)
- to direct their questions to a wider range of students (Dillon, 1988;
  Wilen, 1991)
- to wait longer for a response after asking a question (Morgan &
  Saxton, 1991; Rowe, 1974; Wilen, 1991)
- to plan their questions carefully ahead of time (Christenbury &
  Kelly, 1983; Dillon, 1983, 1984, 1988, 1994; Hunkins, 1995; Wilen,
  1991)
- to place their questions appropriately (Andre, 1987; Christenbury & Kelly, 1983; Dillon, 1983)
- to ask more "open" questions (Dillon, 1988, 1994; Hunkins, 1995)
- to ask more "high level" questions (Dillon, 1994; Gall, 1984; Hunkins 1995)[2]
- to sequence their questions so as to lead children to more complex
  understandings (Hunkins, 1995; Wilen, 1991)
- to balance convergent and divergent questions/"open" and "closed"
  questions/higher and lower level questions (Christenbury & Kelly,
  1983; Wilen, 1991),
- to ask particular types of questions in particular events (Palinscar &
  Brown, 1984)

Until fairly recently, the one bit of advice that was rarely given was "Ask
real questions, questions you yourself wonder about," what Albritton

(1992) calls "honest questions," and what I call acts of inquiry. (See also Dillon, 1983, 1984, 1988b, 1994; Hunkins, 1995.)

There were reasons for this state of affairs. The view that teacher questioning should live at the heart of classroom interaction does not occur in a vacuum. It is an integral part of a belief, held by many, that a student's goal at a given grade level is to master a body of knowledge and set of skills deemed appropriate for that grade level. Clearly if this is the goal for the student, then the teacher's job is to assist the student in achieving it. And so the teacher who holds this view will *question* (i.e., use interrogative forms) toward that end. It is no coincidence that interrogative is the form of choice if managing behavior toward a particular end is the goal. The person who asks questions is, more often than not, the one who controls the discourse, for interrogative forms pull for a verbal response from the partner and also determine to a considerable extent the type and domain of the response. The teacher's questioning works effectively to manage 1) student behavior, 2) content focus and processes of discussion/recitation, 3) sequences of steps in attaining skills, and 4) assessment of student achievement.[3]

Metaphors offer a helpful way of thinking about this mastery notion of teaching and learning which teacher questioning reflects and promotes. "Teacher as transmission device" is the one Bruner (1986) provides. It is a metaphor that captures the thing-ness of knowledge in this view. Knowledge is an object—a thing to be moved (transmitted) from teacher to student. Think of the verbs we often hear in relation to teaching and learning: *give* the idea, *get* it, *possess* it, *pass* information, *give* information, *have* it. In my state it is usual for educators to use the word *deliver* as in "deliver instruction" or "delivery system." Knowledge as things to be delivered, given, received. The teacher is seen as giver; the student is seen as receiver.[4]

I find it interesting that questioning and informing are so inseparable. You would think that these would be opposites—that the teacher would be either questioner (eliciting from the students) or informer (giving to the students). But these turn out not to be opposites at all. Question names a *form*, inform names a *purpose*. We can, and do, use question *forms* to serve an informing *purpose*. We say to the students, "So do you see that X?" or "Don't you think that Y?" or "And they X-ed, didn't they?"—all question forms that serve to inform (to provide information or to confirm it). And so teacher-as-knower/informer and teacher-as-questioner go hand in hand. If the teacher understands her role to be that of knowledge-giver, then she uses question forms to help her manage the classroom discourse toward that end. It is easy to see that questioning as information management has nothing to do with inquiry.

I often find myself thinking about this teacher-as-knower/questioner orientation as if it were part of a bygone era that has been replaced by a different version of teaching and learning (We used to . . . but now we . . .). Not so. For one thing, that orientation is not bygone. It is alive and well in many corners today. But this simplistic then/now contrast fails for another reason also. There has ever been a strong contrasting minority voice. It was present "then," as it is now. Miss Orcutt may have been a "rarity," but she was not alone.

One important earlier (1960s) minority voice—a real teacher-inquirer/learner voice—was that of John Holt. It was in the early 1970s, after I had stopped teaching second grade, that I first encountered Holt's (1970) suggestions for introducing a new camera to children.

> Let's imagine that we have our camera, and an instruction book, and that we are going to work with it in a class of young children. . . . It will be tempting to practice enough with it beforehand, so that we come to the class as an expert, but it is better not to. As much as possible, we should ourselves learn to use the camera before the eyes of the children. . . . if we have not used a camera before, or the one we will be using, then we should let the children see us doing the kinds of things we all have to do when we learn to use something new. . . .
>
> If we find that we cannot figure out how to run the camera, it will not be bad, but good, because it will give the children a chance to see us coping with a human problem. (pp. 204, 206)

A simple example. But Holt's words became neon lights on the page for me as I read, bringing into sharp and sudden focus two contrasting notions of teacher: teacher-as-knower/questioner, and teacher-as-inquirer/learner. I knew only too well which of these I had been.

I thought of how I would have handled the event of a new camera with my second graders. I would have examined the camera carefully, *at home*. I would have read the instructions over carefully, *at home*. I would have practiced using the camera, *at home*. I would have prepared an explanation using "appropriate vocabulary," *at home*.

And when I came to school the next day, I would have performed my explanation for the children. It would have been a clear explanation, well organized, effectively expressed. Questions would have been abundant in my presentation. They would have been well planned ahead of time and well placed in the explanation I gave, so as to move the children from not knowing how to use the camera to knowing how to use it. By means of these questions, I would have tried to transmit my knowledge to my students.

There were good reasons that I would have taken a knower stance rather than the learner stance that Holt recommended. I would have been doing what I had learned to do very well in my teacher education program—indeed, what I had been complimented on in those early teaching years for doing well. Also, I wanted the children, parents, principal to respect me as a teacher.

Commanding the children's *respect* was important. How can children respect a person who doesn't know how to use a camera? A teacher could lose face here, and I wasn't about to. *Efficiency* was important. We had lots of work to do each day, many behavioral objectives to meet. If the goal was that children be able to use the camera, then my responsibility was to teach them how to do just that. And so I needed to plan and carry out a clear, orderly presentation of simple-to-complex steps and then check to see that they could do it (i.e., that they had "reached 70% criterion level"). *Control* was perhaps most important of all. Twenty-four of them and only one of me. Surely one is asking for trouble if all 25 of you are going to be working to figure something out at the same time, with nobody already knowing how to do it. This way lies madness.

So I thought. Had I introduced a new camera in my way, my students would have learned to use it. The camera session would have been orderly, focused, controlled and efficient and the children might even have thought I was smart to know so much about cameras. My talk would have been information-passing talk, and my questions would have worked effectively toward this goal. They would have been interspersed at "appropriate" intervals and phrased in "appropriate" ways—would have informed and would have checked to see that the students "had it." Performance talk: me performing my camera expertise, the children performing theirs. No exploratory talk (Barnes, 1986), no inquiry demonstration. Holt's words did not tell me about introducing cameras; they told me about two visions of teaching, the teacher-as-questioner/knower vision that I had held, and the vision of teacher-as-inquirer/learner that I could only wish had been mine.

TEACHER-AS-INQUIRER

Teacher inquirer voices are currently gaining strength. Classrooms cannot contain them. We hear these voices in teacher-researcher articles in professional journals and books; in teachers' conference presentations; and in the ongoing dialogues of teacher groups. These are demonstrations that move beyond the classroom, but the stories they tell are *of* the classroom. Increasingly these are stories—demonstrations—of teacher-as-inquirer.

Over the past several decades, as we have watched children learn effectively in the absence of "delivery" of sequenced curriculum, we have come to understand and appreciate children's learning processes in a new way. Language acquisition offers the most powerful example I know. Abundant, rich descriptions of young children in widely different communities learning the world and a language to represent it, have forced us to reconceptualize what it means for children to learn in school: what it means for children to learn to read and write, to develop understanding in social studies, science, mathematics. It is a reconceptualization that places at the center of the educational endeavor the characteristics we value most in the very young: their curiosity about all aspects of the world, and their creativity in constructing and conveying their developing understanding of it.

And if we now see children's learning differently, then we must now see ourselves, these children's teachers, differently as well. If the child is not a receiver of delivered curriculum, then we cannot be deliverers of it. It is no accident that we see a move from teacher as transmission device to teacher as learning partner. It is a move from teacher-questioner to teacher-inquirer. It is a move in which *doing* follows from *being:*

- the teacher *is* a writer, and her "teaching" of writing follows from that;
- the teacher *is* a reader, and the interactions with and around text that she engages her students in follow from her insider experience;
- the teacher *is* social scientist, mathematician, scientist, and the explorations she invites and supports follow from her own active curiosity and engagement.

Above all, the teacher *is* inquirer, inevitably providing—living—a demonstration of inquiry's way of turning toward puzzling phenomena and toward one another in exploring them.[5]

DICEY'S SONG DISCUSSION

I showed the videotape of the first of Karen Smith's three *Dicey's Song* discussions with her fifth/sixth grades (see Chapter 3) to my "Children's Questioning" graduate class. I turned off the VCR and asked the class, "Reactions? Responses to what you've just seen?"

"Well," said one student. "It's not really inquiry, is it? I mean, they're just sort of chatting about the book."

An Inquiry Event

Surely the group's talk has an easy conversational flow that we might very well call "chatting." But unlike the student, I think this literature discussion *is* really inquiry, and I think so because inquiry's purpose frames this event (Bateson, 1972; Goffman, 1974).

The *frame* for any interaction is the participants' answer to the question, "What is it that's going on here?" (Goffman, 1974, p. 8). Karen and her six students understand that what is going on in their literature discussion is exploration of text. They share this framing purpose and it resonates in their individual utterances within the discussion. This is not a new idea to you. Recall the earlier inquiry episodes between Jill and Justin and their mothers. Jill was attempting to understand more about animals' habits and hospital experience, and Justin was attempting to do the same with birds' talk and heaven. Probing purposes framed these mother-child interactions, and the individual utterances within them both reflected and furthered those going-beyond purposes. So, too, in the literature discussions. The participants' awareness of inquiry's purpose—to go beyond, to deepen individual understanding of the text with one another's help—this purpose resounds in the conversational turns that comprise the event. Admittedly the participants' utterances are informal. Inquiry in a chat mode, if you like, but inquiry nonetheless. And because literature discussions are a staple in Karen's classroom, the participants come to this event with shared understanding of how to position themselves in relation to text and to each other, and how to express these relationships. Theirs is an inquiry stance: They turn toward one another and toward their topics in uncertainty and invitation.

One way to bring the inquiry frame of this literature discussion into sharp focus is to contrast it with literature discussion that is framed differently. Recall that in Chapter 3 we "listened" to the contrasting sounds of Karen's literature discussion and the reciprocal teaching sessions. Although both events involve teachers and students talking about written text together, they are different in a number of important ways: the number of participants involved, the length of the texts under consideration, the kind of text being considered (efferent, aesthetic [Rosenblatt, 1978]) and so on. But most of all, they are different in their framing, the participants' understanding of what is going on in these events, what the purpose is that they are carrying out. The reciprocal-teaching participants understand themselves to be practicing a strategy that will increase the students' ability to comprehend and to demonstrate their comprehension of passages of informational text, as comprehension is defined and demonstrated in their classrooms. As we saw in Chapter 3, questioning (not inquiry) figured prominently in moving the students toward this goal—indeed, moved them along quite successfully. In reciprocal-teaching events, it was questioning that was demonstrated. Question forms belonged to this strategy-developing frame, serving to help the children perfect their ability to carry out the comprehension scripts of their classroom.

In Karen's literature discussions, the scripts are of a different type. One major difference is that the adult's demonstration is of inquiry acts, not question forms. Consider Karen's talk, her inquiry demonstration. We would expect to find inquiry's canonical forms—interrogatives that turn to partners and pull for their assistance in the inquirer's sense-making. And indeed, as we saw in the excerpts in Chapter 3, Karen both poses her own questions and responds to the questions of the students in ways that demonstrate the usefulness of such forms in exploratory discourse. She seeks information from the students about their understanding ("Do you understand they cremated her? They burned her body?" "... you know the wooden box on the train?"), about their reactions to the text ("And that surprised you?"), about their opinion regarding "appropriate" topics for children's literature ("Do you think it was too much to ask you to cope with death ... ?")—all these in question form. In Karen's talk (and also that of the students) there is surely no lack of interrogatives, those canonical forms that "knit together stably" with inquiry's purpose.

However, the talk goes well beyond these canonical forms to include a variety of expressions of uncertainty that serve to invite others' reflections. Karen's talk abounds in tentativeness: "I wonder ..." "Maybe ..." "If ..." "I think ..." These expressions, no less than the canonical ones, reveal and further reinforce this interaction as an inquiry event. Given Karen's status as teacher and as the most expert participant, her tentative and invitational expression must contribute in a major way to framing literature discussion as exploration. (See Townsend, 1991, for an example of a teacher whose expression during literature discussion was sometimes tentative even when she was actually quite certain of the point she was making.)

But notice how the exploratory purpose of this discussion is expressed through utterances which, in a differently framed event, would bear no hint of inquiry. A student asks, "... you know when they said they buried the mom in the yard?" "Uh-huh," is Karen's response. Taken out of context "uh-huh" would be an unlikely candidate for "inquiry utterance." But taken out of context it would not be an utterance at all. It is an utterance *only* within its own real communication context, and within that context, it contributes to the inquiry purpose that frames this event. In a different conversation "uh-huh" might convey agreement or closure or evaluation. ("That's right.") But in *this* conversation it says, "Go on. I'm listening. I'm here with you as you work to clarify a matter that puzzles you." Karen's explanation of cremation provides another example. "So they cremated her mother and they put the ashes in that wooden box," Karen explains. "She was carrying her mother's ashes." In a differently framed event, this could be heard as the simple provision of information. But not in *this* event. Here it attempts to clarify a student's confusion, to help a student work through her puzzlement. "It was pretty sad," says a student. "It sure is sad," says Karen. Within a different frame, Karen's response could be heard as confirmation ("You're right about that") or as a pronouncement. But in this discussion it is neither. Rather, Karen is coming to the student's place, joining her there in an expression of empathy. Each of these three examples (like the other utterances of this literature discussion) belongs to an exploratory frame and thus is an inquiry act within this conversation. And so, when Karen encourages a student to go on (and stands with her as she does it), or clarifies a puzzling situation, or expresses her sharing of a student's feeling of sadness, we hear the echo of inquiry's essential characteristics: the sound of tentativeness and uncertainty; the sound of invitation and close connection of partners working through issues; and the sound of going beyond.

Just "chatting about the book?" I don't think so.

Karen's Demonstration

Karen is an inquirer in this literature discussion. Thus it is inevitable that she demonstrates expression of inquiry. What demonstrations are present here?

Inquiry arises in knowledge. Every time I read the *Dicey's Song* discussion transcripts, I am struck by the depth and extent of the participants' knowledge, and also by the use they make of it in going beyond it. Karen's demonstration that inquiry arises in present, activated knowledge is evident both as she poses her own inquiries and as she responds to those of her students.

The third segment (#28–38) offers a good example of Karen introducing her own inquiry into the discussion: "You know, there's some controversy about writing for adolescents or children, that a lot of people think you shouldn't put death in books like this. That you, kids your age can't deal with it or that it's too hard. What do you, what do you think about that? . . . Do you think it was too much to ask you to cope with death and the hard things that they were doing?" This inquiry of Karen's, like those of her students, arises in her knowledge, specifically, her awareness of an ongoing controversy about appropriate material for inclusion in adolescent literature, and also her knowledge that her students may have particularly relevant opinions about this matter. Her inquiry act draws on her knowledge in order to go beyond it—with her students' help.

In the second excerpt (#15–27) Karen's demonstration is in her response to the students' inquiry. They are perplexed about why, when Grandma kept getting letters from the Boston hospital informing her of her daughter's worsening condition, she did not tell Dicey: ". . . this is what I don't get . . . the grandma said, um, she didn't tell her nothing . . . I wonder why she didn't tell her. . . . those letters were coming and she [Dicey] asked her [Grandma] what did they say and she [Grandma] say, 'Nothing.'" To be puzzled by this behavior, the students must recognize it as being out of character, inconsistent with their expectations for how Grandma "should" behave. Their expectations are rooted in their deep knowledge of the character of Dicey and Grandma, as well as in their knowledge of how family members behave in sad and stressful situations. Their experiential knowledge and text knowledge come together here and give rise to their perplexity. Karen's response validates their present knowledge as well as supporting their further reflection on this perplexing matter. Indeed, she, too, is perplexed ("Yeah, I wonder why . . ." "I think . . ." "Seems like . . .").

Thus, Karen's contributions to this discussion, whether as inquirer or responder, enact her recognition that one's present knowledge offers the possibility of going beyond it.

Inquiry draws on various perspectives on experience. In the *Dicey's Song* transcript, the students are working with the dimensions (discussed in Chapter 5) that we often encode as where, when, why, how, who, and so on. With or without these question words, the participants' ways of going beyond their present understanding of the text involve consideration of time, of place, of causes and motivations, of properties and characteristics, of actions and of people as actors, of means-end relationships, of processes, and so on. Of course. These are the dimensions we use every day in trying to make sense of our world, and they are dimensions that authors use in creating text worlds such as that of *Dicey's Song*. It is not surprising that these dimensions would provide the discussion participants with various possible takes on the text they are exploring—the text they are *bringing sense to* and *making sense of.*

The world is comprehensible and people try to understand it. In Karen's interactions with her students during literature study, she conveys that the text world, like the real world, is sensible (on its own terms). Indeed, if this were not so, why would she provide literature discussions at all, events whose main purpose is to engage participants in making (further, deeper) sense of text? Surely the presence of literature discussion as a staple in Karen's classroom tells the students, also, that inquiring (about the world of life and the world of text) is important work that people do.

But it is not only the *presence* of literature explorations that tells the students that actual and created worlds are comprehensible and that people are oriented toward making sense of them through language. Her *talk* within these episodes also tells them this. In the first excerpt, "trying to figure out" about burying someone in the yard gets an extended clarification from Karen. Her "Maybe that's what was confusing you" says to the students that it is important to try to understand and that others will help you work through confusion. Karen's talk is quite different when the students are reflecting on why the grandma didn't tell what was in the letters from the hospital. Her talk takes on the tentative quality of the students' talk: "I wonder . . ." "I think . . ." "Seems like . . ." and finally her own wondering about a student's suggestion: "So you think maybe it was the grandma feeling it more than worrying about Dicey's feelings. Hmmmm." Surely there is no stronger way to demonstrate the validity of wondering inquiry than to follow the students' lead in doing it. This is to say in the clearest possible way, "Wondering is an important way to go beyond present understanding (of text)." But whether wondering with the students or working to clarify confusion, Karen's moves legitimize the activity of trying to make sense of the world (and of text).

Various language acts support inquiry's sense-making. As mentioned already, the talk in the literature discussions ranges widely across dimensions as the participants consider causes, means-end relationships, time and place, characteristics and motivations, actions and actors, all fundamental dimensions of exploration. But beyond this, the language acts vary too, as participants agree, disagree, encourage, empathize, express confusion, clarify, wonder, compare, offer evidence, express opinions, generalize, and so on. Karen's demonstration—her participation—supports this variety, telling the students that all these kinds of communication work can be enlisted in the service of furthering one's understanding.

Inquiry involves knowledge in action. In her own inquiry and in her support of the students' inquiry, Karen demonstrates the knowledge-in-action that is inquiry's hallmark. Across all the selected excerpts, I do not find a single instance of information dropping into the conversation as an end in itself. Knowledge here is not facts, but possibilities—potentials. In virtually every utterance, information is drawn on by way of doing something with it—making a connection, providing support, empathizing, generalizing, clarifying. In no conversational turn does the speaker say, "I know X": Rather, in every conversational turn the speaker is doing something with X. The knowledge in this discussion, its depth and its range, is stunning; but more stunning still is its active nature.

Sense in inquiry involves feeling as well as thought. Notice that the knowledge that is relevant comes from the heart as well as from the head. Karen demonstrates that feeling knowledge and factual knowledge both belong in the students' attempts to further their understanding.

STUDENT: It was pretty sad.
TEACHER: It sure is sad.

TEACHER: . . . death is hard. It's really hard.

This recalls the sense that Vygotsky distinguished from meaning.

Inquiry stands at the intersection of know/not-know. I am left wondering about an assumed dichotomy that we often take for granted: that a person either knows and is in a position to inform others, or else that she does not know and is therefore in a position to be informed by others. I have already mentioned the metaphor that represents knowledge as a kind of object that gets moved from place to place and from person to person: One person "has it" and "gives it" to another; and someone else "doesn't have it," tries to "get it," "receives it" and so on. But clearly this moving-about metaphor—locating and relocating knowledge—does not at all capture what is happening in the literature discussion. All participants both know and don't know; all both inform and inquire. Knowing and wondering, informing and inquiring are so interdependent that they seem like two aspects of one thing (two sides of a piece of paper again?) rather than like oppositions or dichotomies. Indeed, it seems that very connection of know/not know—that very moment, that very place—is an act of inquiry. It is the exact moment of standing on tiptoe in one's present known, reaching—reaching—toward what one senses just beyond it.

I find this know/not-know intersection played out in Karen's behavior. In her own inquiries and in her responses to student inquiries, she enacts the bringing together of the two that is inquiry's orientation.

Inquiry's stance is uncertain and invitational. As I was working on this chapter, I received a letter from Vivian Paley that included the following:

> Lynn [a mutual friend] has been curious for some time about *my* questions to the children. How, she wants to know, do I choose a question with which to begin a discussion after reading a book? I tell her that my initial question *always* involves something that *truly* perplexes or disturbs me. "Why must Tico give up his golden wings? It's not fair"; "I wonder why the family keeps telling the boy his carrot seed won't come up. Aren't they worried about hurting his feelings?"; "I like curiosity in children," I might say, "but Goldilocks seems almost too curious to me."

Vivian's "questions" here are clearly acts of inquiry. Hers is a stance of perplexity and also one of invitation: Join me in making sense of this puzzling matter.

It is precisely this stance I hear in Karen's interactions with her students. Her perplexity, like Vivian's, is genuine. She wonders about the text and issues related to it: "I wonder why the grandma was so secretive . . ." ". . . what do you think about that?" And she supports the wondering of others in the group: "And that surprised you?" "So you think maybe it was . . ." In both her own inquiry acts and her responses to students' inquiries, she demonstrates inquiry's orientation toward topic—an orientation that inclines toward possibility rather than toward "fixed factuality" (Bruner, 1986, p. 127).

Karen's stance toward partner(s) is, again like Vivian's, invitational. She invites others to join and help her understand, and she responds to the implicit invitation of others, joining them in their probing. In both, she demonstrates inquiry's invitational turning toward others.

It is Karen's stance toward topic and partners that—more than any other aspect of this event—tells me that she is not leading these students in "just chatting about the book." She is leading them in collaborative inquiry.

HOW MANY TEETH DOES A FOX HAVE? A SPECIAL CASE

Quite by coincidence, when he was about nine or so, my son alerted me to a special kind of teacher inquiry (or maybe, question?). I had read an article in our local paper in which a public librarian was describing the questions that people phone in to ask. Discussion of this article made its way into our family conversation.

"You mean," said Erik, a hint of disbelief in his voice, "if ya just call up the library and ask a question, they answer it?"—which, after all, *is* amazing when you stop and think about it, although I hadn't done so until that moment.

The following Friday, Erik stayed overnight with his friend next door. Saturday evening at dinner, he told us about his morning at his friend's house. It went something like this:

> I woke up before anybody else. The house was all quiet and I didn't have anything to do. So I decided to call the library and ask a question. But first I had to think of a question. So I thought and I thought till I finally thought of the question, "How many teeth does a fox have?" I called the library and somebody answered and I asked my question. The guy asked me my name and phone number and said he'd find out an answer and call me back. About 15 minutes later, he called and said, "Erik, a fox has 42 teeth. We have a lot of interesting books here about foxes and I can hold some out for you if you'd like to come by and look at them." "No," I said, "that's OK. All I wanna know about foxes is how many teeth they have."

At first, his question seems disingenuous, for he cared nothing at all about foxes' teeth. It was a pretender inquiry, a "foxy" question, you might say. Do we as teachers ask this kind of question sometimes? That is, do we ask questions that sound like inquiry acts but do not really seek the information they specify? I think we do, and this makes me wonder whether these questions are inquiry acts or just pretenders.

I have come to think that many such moves *are* inquiry acts, though (as in Erik's case) the information we seek is not that which our words denote. Think again of Erik. He was indeed inquiring. His *question* was about foxes' teeth; his *inquiry* was about librarians (Do librarians answer questions?). He asked the one in order to find out about the other. How often we do this.

In his dialogue journal, a sixth-grade Zulu student writes to me, "I am talking about this clentis wood I am crazy about that man who play films and it was the dangerous man in the world." In my response I ask several questions: "You must tell me more about Clentis Wood. Who is he? What does he do that makes him the most dangerous man in the world?"[6] Now do I really care about "Clentis Wood"? No, actually I don't, but I care very much about getting to know this student—making sense of him. My *question* asks the student to reveal himself to me, serving my *inquiry:* Who are you? What do you care about? What is your life like? How does your writing relate to these things? And above all, what opportunities might this interactive writing afford for me to help you?

For Vivian Paley (1981), the continuing inquiry is "How do the children think?" Her search is "for the child's point of view with which [she] can help him take a step further" (p. 213). And so she asks the children, "How do you know if somebody likes you?" (p. 150) or "Should a child receive money for a tooth?" (p. 43) or "What causes wishes to come true?" (p. 32), questions that are not ends in themselves, but serve that ultimate inquiry, "How do you make sense of your world?" Whether these on-the-way-to-something-else questions are or are not acts of inquiry matters a great deal because it has to do with what we are demonstrating: questioner or inquirer?

For me, these moves are inquiry acts because they enact inquiry's purpose: These acts are the teacher's attempts to engage students' help in going beyond her own present understanding. Never mind that there is not a one-to-one correspondence between word and act. This is often the case in language. Words, those repeatable structural aspects of language, exist to serve the unrepeatable in language—actual communication acts we carry out at particular moments among particular people. The inquiry act is not the words themselves (semantics) but lives *behind* the words and expresses itself *through* the words, living in the intention that prompts them. We have seen repeatedly how words *mean* only within the communication events that frame them. Again that framing question: What is it that is going on here? Well, what is going on here is that we, in essence, are saying to the student, "Show me your world. Show me how you understand it. Help me understand, and so help me help you."

FINAL REFLECTIONS

What a long road we have traveled from teacher-as-questioner to teacher-as-inquirer, a long road both in this chapter and in time. Twenty years ago, concerns about how teachers should ask questions dominated the professional literature. Today it is the word *inquiry* that dominates. I rarely pick up a new issue of our standard language education journals these days without being greeted with the word *inquiry*. This is a major shift and a most welcome one. I worry, though, whether this word is bandied about so freely that, rather than indicating a serious trend, it threatens to become merely trendy, something we thoughtlessly say we are doing because it is the thing to say, rather like saying, "I am a facilitator," or "I meet the needs of the individual child," or "I teach the whole child"— all of which easily become vacuous, windy rhetoric.

There is no windy rhetoric in Karen's inquiry demonstration. It's the real thing (inquiry) because she is the real thing (inquirer). And yet my student missed it. She didn't hear inquiry demonstration, only the sound of chatting. Perhaps this is not surprising, for although demonstration may be huge in its import, it can be inconspicuous in its sound.

Can it really be the case that by simply participating in a literature discussion with a group of students for 20 minutes, a teacher demonstrates that inquiry's various purposes are served by various language forms and by various language acts, that inquiry arises in knowledge and is knowledge-in-action, that it draws on various perspectives on experience and involves feeling as well as thought, that it voices a stance both tentative and invitational . . . on and on? Is it possible that teachers are doing such hefty work in events that often feel so pleasant, more like play than work? It is a bit terrifying to think of our own talk as being so weighty. But, mercifully perhaps, we rarely do think of it. We might find ourselves struck dumb if we thought too much about the inquiry selves we share with our students. Remember the centipede that would find itself unable to walk if it ever stopped to think about how it moves all those legs. But the centipede doesn't think about it. It just keeps on being a centipede. And so with us. We just keep on being what we are: individuals who wonder about the world we live in and try to engage others in our own attempts to ponder it further. This inquiry orientation (and the inevitable demonstration of it) lives within a philosophy that frames our teaching. The frame question again: What is it that is going on here?

Our teaching is the answer to that question. Our own inquiry acts and our supportive response to those of our students will occupy a central place in our teaching if we believe that "what is going on" is that curious, creative meaning-makers are engaging one another in their attempts to further their probing into the workings of the world.

PART III

Participants

Hands clapping. That's what comes to my mind when I think about participants in inquiry acts and events. One hand alone cannot clap; it takes two. But it is not enough that two hands be present—not even enough that they both be active. They must act in close coordination. Only then do the hands create clapping.

Dialogue is like this—all dialogue, probably, but especially inquiry dialogue, for inquiry acts and responses are the most tightly interconnected of all. One person's talk does not make an act of inquiry. Without response, without the active coordinated participation of another, an inquiry act seems but half an act.

Notice that although hands can only clap together, they must remain distinct entities. If they were to come together so perfectly that they merged, there could be no clapping. The separateness of each hand is no less essential to the act of clapping than their togetherness is. The distinctiveness of each partner in inquiry dialogue is *style*—the characteristic inquiry ways of the individual participant in the dialogue. The question of whether individuals have distinctive inquiry styles (comparable to their distinctive ways of walking or talking) is a compelling one, especially when the individuals in question are child inquirers in classrooms. Does it make sense to speak of an individual child's *inquiry style*? Is it helpful to do so?

In the chapters of Part III, we focus on participants in inquiry acts and events, considering both the togetherness of the participants (inquiry *dialogue*, Chapters 7 and 8), and their individual distinctiveness (inquiry *style*, Chapters 9 and 10). The togetherness and the distinctiveness of participants are present in all language acts and events, of course, but we focus on these specifically in relation to inquiry. There is no better place, for both the dialogic and the stylistic aspects of discourse are particularly evident in inquiry:

- inquiry acts and events are the most interconnected and dialogic of all;

- inquiry acts reveal "the speaking personality" (Bakhtin, 1981) in a particularly striking way.

It is no wonder that exploratory discourse in classrooms supports emergent inquiry as children participate *together* with others, as their own distinctive, unique *selves*.

CHAPTER 7

Inquiry Dialogue

> Once upon a time there was a little girl and her name was Irma-
> gold and she lived all by herself in the middle of the Cherry Tree
> Forest with only her father and her flying horse whose name was
> Spot because he was all red.

So begins every Irmagold story, the stories Jack creates for his four-and-
a-half year old daughter Susan, as they lie on her bed in the dark together,
before she goes to sleep. Irmagold stories are a family tradition, for Jack
used to tell them to Susan's brother and sister, now 13 and 14 years old.
In this chapter the focal transcripts come from the Irmagold story events
between Jack and Susan, and will help us examine inquiry acts within dialogue.[1]

We begin with a brief introduction to Jack and Susan's storytelling
interactions and then move on to consider three basic characteristics of
inquiry dialogue which the storytelling events bring into sharp focus.
Next we shift our attention to the role of the addressee in inquiry dialogue—the active, listener/responder without whom there can be no inquiry dialogue at all. Finally we'll reflect on the changed consciousness
that is possible through inquiry dialogue.

ONCE UPON A TIME

The central interactive event of this chapter is bedtime storytelling.
Telling, not reading. Like the events in previous focal transcripts, each of
these bedtime storytelling events is comprised of episodes, that is,
stretches of talk on a particular topic. Some of these dialogic episodes are
inquiry episodes (i.e., episodes in which one partner is engaging the other's participation in her sense-making); others are not.

For this chapter, I have deliberately chosen a focal event that is
framed differently from Karen's literature discussions: *exploration* of story
frames Karen's literature discussions; *experiencing* of story frames the bed-

time events of this chapter. The essence of these storytelling events is shared, pleasurable aesthetic experience. Inquiry acts (which develop into inquiry episodes) insert themselves into the bedtime-story dialogue. Inquiry has a way of doing that: it does not confine itself to exploratory frames, but contributes to other frames as well. Jack and Susan's shared bedtime-story events move back and forth between (noninquiry) story-presentation episodes and inquiry episodes, and it is precisely the contrast between the two that brings into sharp focus the special characteristics of inquiry dialogue.

Text No. 7: Irmagold and the Pixies

(Irmagold is walking in the Cherry Tree Forest at night and meets the pixie queen. The inquiry episodes are set off from the narrative portions of the transcript by line spaces.)

1. JACK: And the pixie queen took her hand and Irmagold walked with—Irmagold had to kind of bend over because she was so much taller than the pixie queen and she went right in the middle of the fairy ring. The pixie queen pulled something right out of her pocket. It was a ring just the size for a pixie queen and she put it on Irmagold's finger which was unusual because the pixie ring was much smaller in diameter than Irmagold's finger. But it went on and Irmagold was so surprised that the tiny ring got on her finger, but all of a sudden she realized she was just the size of the pixie queen.

2. SUSAN: Was the pixie queen this tall? (demonstrates)
3. JACK: Just about. Just about four inches tall.
4. SUSAN: Draw a picture of her so I can know what she looks like.
5. JACK: Alright. I'll draw a picture and you can draw a picture. She was very well proportioned and she had blond hair and black eyes.
6. SUSAN: I thought she had golden hair.
7. JACK: Golden hair, yes, golden hair. Beautiful golden hair and black eyes.

   Well, Irmagold and the pixie queen danced and they danced into the wee hours of the morning. Round and round they went, Irmagold's long green hair flowing out behind her and the pixie queen's long golden hair flowing out behind her. (Hums dancing music)

8. SUSAN: Were they going twirl, twirl, twirl?
9. JACK: Twirling. They were twirling around faster and faster and faster and faster.
10. SUSAN: And were getting dizzy?
11. JACK: Somehow, they didn't get dizzy, but it was very exciting dancing and the pixie music was very entrancing.

     But soon, it seemed to Irmagold, it seemed like very soon, it started to get light and the pixie queen said, "Irmagold, we must go. We do not dance when the sun comes up. You can keep this ring and whenever you put it on you will be just the size of a pixie.". . . And all of a sudden quick as you could blink an eye, the pixies all disappeared.

12. SUSAN: Why?
13. JACK: Because daylight was coming.
14. SUSAN: And why do they disappear?
15. JACK: Well, they just disappear in the daytime.
16. SUSAN: Because they have to go to sleep at daytime? They have to go to sleep?
17. JACK: I guess so. I think they can stay up in the daytime, but they only like to come out at night, pixies. . . .

This storytelling event, moving back and forth as it does between story narrative and inquiry conversation about that narrative, highlights three important ways that inquiry utterances influence the dialogues in which they occur.

THE ACTIVE NATURE OF INQUIRY UTTERANCES IN DIALOGUE

To Energize Discourse

There seems to be a universal burst-pause rhythm pervading human life. We find it in the biological functioning of living organisms as they alternate periods of activity and periods of rest. But we also find burst-pause rhythms in human interaction.

Language acquisition researchers have documented this burst-pause rhythm in early interactions (often called "protoconversations") between mothers and their infants (Schaffer, Collis, & Parsons, 1977; Trevarthen, 1977, 1992). Both mother and infant alternate periods of activity (e.g., physical movement, vocalization) and periods of inactivity. You may re-

member from Chapter 2 that mother and infant synchronize these alternation patterns so that when the one partner is active, the other "pauses."
We see this synchronization played out in the pair's physical movements,
a pattern in which one moves and then becomes more still while the
partner's movement increases. Sucking is a prime example: The infant
sucks, pauses, sucks, pauses; and the mother's movement and vocalizing
increase during the infant's pauses and decrease during the periods of
active sucking. The vocalizing of mother and infant shows a similar synchronization.[2] Mother and infant tend to take turns in vocalizing: When
the infant is more quiet, mother's vocalizing increases, and when the infant vocalizes, mother is more quiet. This research (Schaffer, Collis, &
Parsons, 1977; Stern et al., 1977; Trevarthen, 1977, 1992) attests to the early
presence of burst-pause rhythms in individuals' expressive behaviors,
and to the synchronization of these rhythms among interaction partners.
In calling these early synchronized events protoconversations, researchers are suggesting both that burst-pause (and its synchronization among
partners) is an essential rhythm in conversation, and that the child's early
(physical) burst-pause synchronization with others is continuous with
later conversational behavior.

   Inquiry utterances seem to be burst moves in the continual burst-
pause rhythm of interaction. They are moves that energize, activate, even
destabilize conversation. The preceding transcript demonstrates this in
a particularly dramatic way because two rhythms are juxtaposed: the
rhythm of Jack's flowing narrative, and the rhythm of the inquiry episodes that Susan initiates. Each time Susan introduces a new episode
with her inquiry utterance, she abruptly changes the rhythm of the event,
disrupting the steady flow of Jack's narrative. Each inquiry utterance is a
burst, an interruption, a move that momentarily jars the discourse, throwing it off-balance. We can think of dialogue as a continual balancing act in
which participants move between being *in balance* and *off-balance*. Inquiry
utterances are the quintessential off-balance moves in dialogue. They disrupt; they destabilize.

   It is interesting how variously this matter of balance has been
viewed. Is it better to be in balance (in a state of rest or resolution) or off
balance (destabilized, aroused, energized in our thought and expression
of it)? Well, it depends who you ask. Berlyne (1965), writing in a behavior-
ist era, characterized as "aversive" those situations in which one is off-
balance, situations which are "novel, surprising, complex, incongruous,
or ambiguous" (p. 72)—situations that give rise to "conceptual conflict"
(p. 77). One way to end the aversive state of conceptual conflict or uncertainty is to ask questions. Thus Berlyne's "questions" (our information-

seeking inquiries) are attempts to restore balance, to move the discourse (and thought) toward resolution—from burst into pause.

In contrast to Berlyne, the psychologist Frank Smith (1975) is quite comfortable with the off-balance of uncertainty. Writing about visual perception (in the act of reading), he defines uncertainty as "the range of questions that the brain might ask" (p. 28).

> Attention is perhaps best conceptualized as questions being asked by the brain, and our perceptions are what the brain decides must be the answers. . . . The question we are asking in effect constitutes the attention we are paying. (p. 28)

Smith calls the kind of questions he is talking about here *"cognitive questions* to make it clear that they function at the level of cognitive structure and are not questions of which we are aware; we could not actually put them into words" (p. 28). The internal, out-of-awareness character of these questions makes them very different from Berlyne's expressed questions. However, what is especially interesting is that Smith takes it as inevitable that the brain is in a constant state of questioning, not by way of getting out of a situation that is "aversive," but simply because it is the nature of the brain to be ever attending, noticing the world around and trying to make sense of it. In Smith's view, this is simply the way the brain is and what the brain does. Constantly. Inevitably. Thus Smith's human is ever a bit off-balance, ever wakeful, ever oriented not toward sense already *made,* but toward sense ever in the *making.* The off-balance state that Berlyne finds aversive Smith seems to welcome as both inevitable and good.

Margaret Donaldson (1979) moves us from cognitive, out-of-awareness questions back to the social (expressed) questions of everyday interaction. "We are beings who ask questions," writes Donaldson (p. 118). She deals with the in-balance/off-balance issue by characterizing humans as beings who sometimes seek the one state and sometimes the other. Sometimes our questions are attempts to end cognitive conflict that we find "unacceptable"—"something we try to get rid of" (p. 117). This sounds like Berlyne. But there are other times when "we positively seek [puzzling situations] out, as if we liked having to deal with things that we do not understand, things that challenge us intellectually" (p. 117). This duality echoes our earlier distinction between acts of information-seeking and acts of wondering: Both are inquiry acts in that they pull another into one's attempt to understand something further: but the first orients toward ending uncertainty, the second toward maintaining it.

Unlike Smith's "cognitive questions," Bakhtin's "questions" (our inquiry acts) reside squarely and necessarily in social dialogue. Though inquiry can be internalized, it remains dialogic: the presence of *other* is there. Unlike Smith's sense-maker, Bakhtin's human is never alone. His mental life is inhabited by the social dialogue that gave rise to it and that sustains it. Questions are the very essence of dialogue for Bakhtin: "If an answer does not give rise to a new question from itself, it falls out of the dialogue" (1986, p. 168). And for Bakhtin, that ongoing dialogue in which "question" is central, is written, as well as oral, and spans time and space.[3] How different are Berlyne's and Bakhtin's conceptions of the human inquirer: Berlyne's inquirer is attempting to be in-balance, while Bakhtin's thrives on being off-balance.

In quite different ways, these four (Berlyne, Smith, Donaldson, Bakhtin) deal with the matter of balance and the role inquiry acts play within it. For Berlyne, in-balance is the desired state and one's "questions" help to achieve it. For Smith, off-balance is good and also inevitable, and "questions" guide one's constant (though often unconscious) meaning-making activity. Donaldson's human chooses sometimes to be in-balance and sometimes off-balance, and Bakhtin's human participates in an ongoing dialogue that ends when questioning ends. Yet as different as the views of these four are, for all of them uncertainty is where inquiry acts reside, and they are acts that *act*-ivate, that energize the discourse.

To Shape Text

In the preceding transcript, Susan's inquiry acts not only provide bursts in the dialogue; they also contribute in a major way to structuring it. Her inquiry acts introduce a different text pattern.

The idea of language events being structured in somewhat predictable patterns is one that sociolinguists have captured in various ways. In the research literature, we find descriptions of various discourse events or types, each with its own distinctive structure, for example, convergent communication events in which one partner knows the solution to a problem and must convey it to the partner who must act on the information (as when one gives someone instructions for how to get somewhere) (Garvey & Baldwin, 1970); argument (Brenneis & Lein, 1977; Eisenberg & Garvey, 1981; Genishi & Di Paolo, 1982); sharing time (Michaels, 1981; Michaels & Collins, 1984); instruction giving (Cook-Gumperz, 1977); therapeutic discourse (Labov & Fanshel, 1977); joke telling (Sacks, 1974); teacher-led discussions (Au, 1980; Dillon, 1988a, 1988b; Erickson, 1982; Erickson & Mohatt, 1982; Mehan, 1979; Sinclair & Coulthard, 1975); children's speech play rituals (Kirshenblatt-Gimblett, 1976); adult-child book-sharing events (Heath, 1982b; Ninio & Bruner, 1978); hymn raising (Heath, 1983); and so on. Some linguists have likened dialogue to a game, the object of which is not to win, but to keep the ball in play. Each type of interaction event, like each type of game, has its own rules that guide (but never dictate) the players' moves.

Some researchers have described dialogic text as a hierarchical structure in which larger units are composed of smaller ones (Garvey, Baldwin, & Dickstein, 1971). I have done something similar, considering transcripts at the hierarchical levels of utterance (conversational turn), episode (clusters of conversational turns on one topic), and events (e.g., literature discussion, reciprocal teaching, bedtime story). For Bakhtin (1986), word/answering-word seems a fundamental structuring principle, akin to linguists' adjacency pairs (e.g., question and answer). Bakhtin sees communication as involving "forms of combinations of forms" (Emerson & Holquist, 1986, p. xvi), that is, text patterns beyond the single utterance. And Nelson and Gruendel (1979) describe young children's language *scripts*, adapting Schank and Abelson's (1977) definition to children: "A script is made up of slots and requirements about what can fill those slots. The structure is an interconnected whole, and what is in one slot affects what can be in another" (p. 41). Nelson and Gruendel are suggesting that even very young children have a sensitivity to discourse structure.[4] Some discourse events are more flexibly structured (e.g., informal conversations between friends) and others less so (e.g., jokes, word games, greeting and leave-taking rituals, some religious rituals). The point is that there is consensus among sociolinguists that partners in a communication event join in weaving a texture, a cloth; they do not produce a tangle of threads. Participants share expectations about the overall pattern of the piece they are creating—the kind of threads it can include and the ways they can be interwoven. The final piece will be unique, but it will be of a recognizable type; it will be *one*, but one of a *kind*.

Susan and Jack know a great deal about how to make an Irmagold story event. In the focal transcript above, two contrasting text patterns occur: narrative, and inquiry dialogue. The contrast between them brings the pattern of dialogic inquiry text into sharp focus. The narrative portions are stretches of talk belonging to one partner, enacting a structure in which imagined characters are presented, engage in some chronological sequence of activities that include some sort of problem and (in this type of narrative) a resolution. Its typical utterance is monologic performance.[5] When Susan initiates inquiry episodes, she clicks the partners into a different type of text structure, a dialogic, back-and-forth structure in which the inquirer (Susan in this case) "announces" her topic and does so in a way that pulls the partner in in a helping role. Inquiry utterances constrain the moves that immediately follow; thus they are quite controlling. For example, when Susan asks, "Was the pixie queen this tall?" the possibilities for Jack's next move are somewhat limited, and it is Susan's act of inquiry that has set those limits. Not that the limits are absolute, of course. There are still many types of responses Jack can appropriately give, but both partners expect that Jack's next utterance will in some way move them toward establishing the height of the pixie queen.

Also, inquiry utterances that initiate an inquiry episode set up structural expectations for moves beyond the one immediately following. These initiating inquiries project their influence over a larger domain than "next turn." The two partners expect that they will contribute to resolving Susan's issue and will do so through a series of turns in which Susan initiates and father helps until Susan is satisfied. Her satisfaction will end the episode. The kind of episode Susan initiates with her inquiry act is one that, though somewhat flexible, is not completely free. Susan and Jack share expectations about how inquiry dialogue should proceed, and they are able to implement them appropriately on a given occasion. This attests to the reality of "forms of combinations of forms" in inquiry dialogue.

With her inquiry acts, Susan not only clicks the participants into a different type of discourse structure; she also clicks them into different roles within the discourse. As narrator, Jack's role is performer; Susan's role is audience. But her inquiry acts change this, repositioning the partners so that Jack's role becomes that of supporter-of-Susan's-agenda. In taking a different role herself, changing from audience to inquirer, Susan casts Jack in a different role also. To introduce a new episode with a new purpose (inquiry dialogue vs. narrative) is to redefine participation roles within the event.

In addition to influencing text shape and participant roles, inquiry utterances influence topic in dialogue. Susan's inquiry acts provide good examples. Her inquiry in #2 shifts the focus from the story line to a consideration of the size of the pixie queen; in #8 the shift is to type of dancing movement; in #12 she shifts them to reasons that pixies disappear. None of these totally breaks with Jack's narrative text, but each one does shift it, taking the discourse topic where the inquirer wants it to go.

Is it any surprise that inquiry acts are not always welcome, given that they are typically acts that (1) destabilize discourse, (2) strongly influence the structure of the conversation, (3) determine the respective roles of the partners, and (4) give the topic control to the inquirer? How could utterances be more imposing than this? It is surely not surprising that a conversational participant should not always wish to be so controlled by the partner. The inquirer seems to hold all the cards.[6]

To Pull the Partner Into Text Constructing

Inquiry utterances are imposing acts in many ways, but the greatest of all may be the pull that these acts exert on the partner, not only to join the inquirer's agenda, but to do so in a verbally active way. It is not enough for the partner to acknowledge the inquiry act or to pay attention to it or to pretend to pay attention to it. "Enough" is to become an active participant, as you will see in the following transcript about Albert the Abalone.

Albert is a familiar member of the cast of characters in Irmagold stories, but apparently Susan has come to know Albert the Abalone without thinking about what an abalone looks like. The next text (including excerpts from two successive story sessions) presents Susan's attempts to understand what an abalone is. Notice the pull that Susan's inquiry acts exert on Jack, a pull that is absent or reduced in her other types of utterances in this text.

Text No. 8: Irmagold and Albert the Abalone

1. JACK: Irmagold was going for a walk and she was looking at the birds and she wasn't watching where she was going and she stubbed her toe on a rock.
2. SUSAN: That's really Albo, Alba, Albert, the Abalone.
3. JACK: You're right because the rock said, "Is that you, Irmagold?" and she looked down and it was Albert, the giant abalone. He kind of looked like a big stone if you didn't pay close attention. . . . he walked very slowly, Susan.
4. SUSAN: He had because he only had one . . . (pause)
5. JACK: One foot and no legs, 'cause that's what abalones have. So they went for a walk and as they walked, Albert told the story about how he had once been a handsome prince, but an evil witch had cast a spell on him and changed him into an abalone. And now that he was happy as a clam, he always carefully avoided witches because he did not want to get changed back into a handsome prince. . . .
6. SUSAN: Does Albert the Abalone have any toes?
7. JACK: No. Abalones do not have toes, just a foot. . . .

(In the next Irmagold story, Irmagold is again walking through the Cherry Tree Forest, this time to have lunch with Fernando the Bear.)

8. JACK: ... Well, as Irmagold was walking down the pine needle paths of the Cherry Tree Forest, she stubbed her toe on a rock.

9. SUSAN: It was really Albert the Abalone.

10. JACK: "Is that you, Irmagold?" said the rock. "Yes, it is, Albert. I knew it was you. I'm going to Fernando the Bear's house. Would you like to go with me?" asked Irmagold. "Certainly," said Albert. "Let me tell you a story about how I was once a handsome prince." So they walked very slowly to Fernando the Bear's house.

11. SUSAN: What if Irmagold had to carry him (inaudible)?

12. JACK: He'd be real heavy. I think he was a real heavy abalone.

13. SUSAN: Did he look like a hot dog?

14. JACK: No. He looks more like a large stone—the top half of a large stone. (pause) Well, it took them a long, long time to get to Fernando the Bear's house. . . . [They find Fernando stuck in a crack in the ground and try unsuccessfully to pull him out.] "I've got to go get help," she [Irmagold] said. "You stay here, Albert and keep Fernando company." "I'll be happy to," said Albert. And Irmagold went out—

15. SUSAN: (unintelligible) sit down?

16. JACK: No. He [Albert] kind of squats right there.

17. SUSAN: Like this? (squats)

18. JACK: Just kind of like this. (demonstrates)

19. SUSAN: You mean he—

20. JACK: He looks like an upside-down bowl.

21. SUSAN: (noise)

22. JACK: And he has a lot of eyes, pretty blue eyes, but he has more than two, he has a number of eyes. They just kind of peek out from under the bowl. Well, anyhow, so Irmagold went . . . to get help and Albert stayed and kept Fernando the Bear company and told him about how he had once been a handsome prince, but he had kind of liked being an abalone, in fact he said he was happy as a clam, and never wanted to get changed back into a handsome prince.

23. SUSAN: Why?

24. JACK: Because he was so happy being a clam. An abalone is like a clam—one shell. Isn't that silly?

25. SUSAN: Yes.

26. JACK: Irmagold went to the moat and . . .

27. SUSAN: Can you stick Albert the Abalone's foot out?

28. JACK: He's got one big foot. It's under his shell.

29. SUSAN: So you can't see it?

30. JACK: Only if you turn his shell over. Well—
31. SUSAN: Um, can, does Albert the Abalone have any arms?
32. JACK: Nope.
33. SUSAN: Why?
34. JACK: 'Cause abalones don't have any arms. They just have a foot.

Again it is contrast that helps to make the point: Inquiry utterances exert an especially strong pull on the partner for verbal response (and one that is on the inquirer's topic). In the preceding transcript, three of Susan's utterances are not inquiry acts—#2, #4, and #9. All three go with the flow of Jack's narrative. These three do not disrupt the narrative, and they do not shift the partners to different text structure, to different participant roles, or to a new topic focus. They do not pull Jack onto her agenda as her other utterances do (all inquiry acts). Number 2 and #4 get incorporated into Jack's narrative flow; #9 gets ignored. When Susan announces, "It was really Albert the Abalone," Jack can go right on with his story; but when she asks, "Did he look like a hot dog?", he can't.[7] This has to do with what Bakhtin calls "addressivity"—the ways of turning to a partner. Each "way of turning" conveys its own kind of expectations for response from the partner. Inquiry utterances in dialogue do more than "turn to" a partner. They *pull*. When Susan is audience for Jack's narrative, she is, of course, an active participant, but the kind of participation that is called for (attentive listening) is very different from that which she "requires" of Jack when she injects an inquiry utterance into his narrative. Her inquiry utterance pulls for a verbal response.

It is a puzzling paradox that the addressivity of inquiry utterances— their way of turning to a partner—is, at one and the same time, opening and constraining. The turning is open in that the speaker says to the partner, "I don't know but you do. I turn to you in my uncertainty. I open myself to your knowledgeable response." Yet at the same time, the turning is constraining, for it says, "You must come to this topic that I have specified, respond to the particular aspect I am focused on, select from a limited set of acceptable types of moves (e.g., give answer, ask for clarification, admit ignorance, refer me to someone else), and slot your move into the dialogic text structure that I have introduced." This is to hand the partner a particular slot in a particular type of text and a particular aspect of a particular topic. Very constraining indeed. And yet there is the openness toward being informed by the partner. And so the addressivity is both a relinquishing of control (you decide) and also a retaining of control (do what I want you to). Such an intriguing paradox. But then, such is the way of language.

So far our focus has been on the speaker, specifically on the contribution that his inquiry utterances make to the dialogue. What about the other(s) in the dialogue—the addressee(s)? The listeners? How does inquiry dialogue engage their participation? It's an especially important question in classroom contexts, given that the children may spend at least as much time listening as speaking during the school day. Bakhtin (and Albert the Abalone) can help us consider this important question about the addressee's role in inquiry dialogue.

THE ADDRESSEE IN INQUIRY DIALOGUE

Active Listening in Dialogue

Dialogue is not about speakers. If it were, dialogue would be simultaneous or sequential monologues. It isn't. Dialogue is about two or more partners interacting. In conversations between two individuals, both partners are speakers; both are listeners; both are responders. And in dialogic events involving more than two individuals (class discussions, church services, dinner conversations), listeners may participate fully even if they do not speak at all, vicariously "speaking," interpreting, raising objections, agreeing or disagreeing, and so on.

Yet in spite of this possibility of active (though silent) participation on the listener's part, we tend to see the speaker's (addressor's) role as a more active one than that of other participants. Frequently, speaking and writing are called "productive language skills," whereas listening and reading are called "receptive." Also, it is a familiar practice for instructors to give their students "class participation" grades for speaking in class. Apparently these instructors do not consider listening to be participation. And surely a preponderance of language acquisition studies have focused on children's development of speech, as if language development were *speaking* development, not the development of understanding. Of course, it is easier to study what a child says than to study what a child understands, and the younger the child, the truer this is. However, although this may be one contributing factor, it is not the only one. I believe that the privileging of speaking over listening in research studies has also been influenced by the pervasive notion that language is talk and therefore acquisition of language is development of speech. Talking is doing language; listening is just being there.[8]

Fortunately, over the past several decades, the study of children's listening/comprehending has increased, and the findings from this research invite a reconsideration of the role of addressee/listener in inquiry dialogue. Several factors have contributed to this change, among them the development of more sophisticated technology (especially videotape) that has enhanced our capacity to observe a wider range of relevant expressive behaviors, and the development of more sophisticated (often downright ingenious) procedures for eliciting the child's expression of understanding as he makes sense of speech (Eimas, Sigueland, Jusczyk, & Vigorito, 1971). But perhaps an even more important factor is an increasing appreciation of the *active*, constructive, interpretive process that listening entails. For example, Nelson (1973) identified and described a "comprehension strategy" in first-language acquisition, a strategy of talking less and observing language more; and Fillmore (1983) has identified and described a similar strategy for second-language learners who spoke very little but were "inclined to be attentive listeners and quite observant" (p. 164). Listening is not "just being there."

Bakhtin (1986) comes to the matter of active listening in a particularly powerful way, bringing into sharp focus the extremely active role of the addressee in everyday communication events.[9] Nowhere is that active listener role more apparent than in inquiry episodes. Bakhtin's key notion is that to listen is to *act*. Listening is doing something. To listen is to interpret, that is, to construct meaning out of speakers' words. Understanding text is, in a sense, creating it. "The only way that words can mean is to be understood" (Clark & Holquist, 1984, p. 213). Without the listener's active, interpretive understanding, the speaker's words are simply vibrations of air waves impinging on ear drums.[10] And so, in inquiry episodes, listening becomes an act of inquiry, for the listener creates from the speaker's words a meaningful inquiry act. He imbues the speaker's words with inquiry's intention. "The one who understands . . . becomes *himself* a participant in the dialogue" (Clark & Holquist, 1984, p. 1, quoting Bakhtin).

Active Listening in Jack and Susan's Dialogue

If Bakhtin is right, then in the preceding transcripts, Susan's speaking act is an act of inquiry *if Jack understands it to be so*. The transcripts offer good evidence that he does. Jack's acts of interpreting Susan's inquiry utterances are acts of constructing her utterances in his mind—their purpose, their focus, their place in the text that he and Susan are constructing. And the understanding itself is dialogic:

> To understand another person's utterance means to orient oneself with respect to it, to find the proper place for it in the corresponding context. For each word of the utterance that we are in the process of understanding, we, as it were, lay down a set of our own answering words .... *any true under-*

> *standing is dialogic in nature.* Understanding is to utterance as one line of a dialogue is to the next. Understanding strives to match the speaker's word with a *counter word.* (Vološinov, 1973, p. 102)

The active, constructing, other-orienting and context-orienting listening described here is evident in Jack's responses, for these could only be fashioned out of such listening. Indeed, Jack's responses to Susan's inquiry utterances demonstrate Bakhtin's notion of the close and (for him) inevitable connection between understanding and response:

> Any act of understanding is a response, i.e., it translates what is being understood into a new context from which a response can be made. (Bakhtin, 1986, p. 69 n. 2)

> . . . all real and integral understanding is actively responsive and constitutes nothing other than the initial preparatory stage of a response. (Bakhtin, 1986, p. 69)

Jack's verbal responses to Susan's inquiry utterances show his listening to be the "preparatory stage of a response" that, in fact, makes such response possible. He listens in the way that sensitive teachers do. His responses are tightly contingent on Susan's inquiries. They orient to Susan's syntax, to her purpose, to her topic. Jack's listening is an act; his response is another act. We hear only the second of these acts, the verbal response, but we hear *in* it the necessary preverbal response that is Jack's act of listening, without which his contingent response would be impossible.

Susan is a listener too. Indeed, she is the same kind of active, constructing listener that Jack is. When he responds to her inquiry utterances, she mentally "lay[s] down" her own "answering words." She verbalizes these as subsequent inquiry utterances.

> S: Were they going twirl, twirl, twirl?
> J: Twirling. They were twirling around faster and faster and faster and faster.
> S: And were getting dizzy?
>
> S: And why do they [the pixies] disappear?
> J: Well, they just disappear in the daytime.
> S: Because they have to go to sleep at daytime?[11]

Susan's inquiry utterances arise in her active listening, her interpreting, and her acts of understanding, as well as in the knowledge she brings to

FIGURE 7.1. Susan's Drawing of Albert the Abalone

this interaction. In order to inquire about Albert's (possible) appendages (arms, foot), weight (heavy to carry), movement (sit down), and appearance (look like a hot dog), Susan must not only have a considerable base of knowledge about these characteristics as they apply to organisms generally, but she also must have specific knowledge of Albert in order to apply her background knowledge to this new instance: Albert the Abalone. She has gained this Albert-related knowledge base through her active listening.

Susan's talk is not the only evidence of her active listening in the Irmagold transcripts. As luck would have it, several days after the two Irmagold stories from which these Albert excerpts come, Susan created her own Irmagold story, which she dictated to her mother, who wrote it down for her. Then Susan drew illustrations for her story, including a picture of Albert the Abalone—see Figure 7.1. (Note that the viewer is looking down at Albert from above in Susan's illustration.)

Here is what she told her mother about her picture of Albert:

> Albert the Abalone doesn't only have two eyes. He has a whole pack of eyes. He has a round body that looks like a bowl even when it's turned over you can see his one foot with no leg and no toe. He has a crown on with ribbons sticking out. When the evil witch turned him into a abalone he was happy as a clam. Because

he has that crown on when the evil witch turned him into an abalone it popped right back on his head.

Susan had never seen a picture of an abalone before—except for the one
in her "mind's eye," created as she listened to Jack's description of Albert.
It is impossible to look at Susan's illustration and read her description
without hearing Jack's voice: "Abalones do not have toes, just a foot,"
"he had once been a handsome prince," "now that he was happy as a
clam . . ." "He looks like an upside-down bowl."

Susan provides a dramatic demonstration here—graphic as well as
verbal—of the powerful act of listening in inquiry dialogue. Yet perhaps,
in the end, it's only a matter of common sense that Susan, the inquirer,
should listen intently in her turn. Why, after all, would she inquire—
elicit assistance in her sense-making act—and then shut down when the
partner responds to that deliberate elicitation? Would I ask you something and then clap my hands over my ears when you answered? Surely
not. Your response is what I actively seek; it is what I am waiting for. In
two-person dialogue, the inquirer's listening must surely be heightened
by the fact that the response was intentionally solicited.

The (answering) partner's listening in inquiry episodes must be particularly intense also. If the (answering) partner joins the inquiry act, he
does so knowing that he will subsequently be expected to provide a verbal response that is appropriate to the inquiry. This response can come
from only one place: that "initial preparatory stage of a response," that
is, listening.

Active Listening in Inquiry Dialogue

Again I find myself in the strange position of suggesting that although a particular aspect of language is important in all discourse, it is
especially so in inquiry dialogue. The aspect in question here is listening.
But how can one claim that listening is somehow more important in inquiry dialogue than it is in other kinds of dialogue? Earlier I made a
similar suggestion about the pull that inquiry utterances exert for verbal
response from the partner, that is, that the pull is especially strong in
inquiry acts. This way of arguing seems rather like asserting that inquiry
utterances are more powerfully *language* than other kinds of utterances
are. Obviously such an assertion would be unreasonable.

However, it isn't unreasonable to suggest that different kinds of discourse—different kinds of utterances, of genres, of events, of episodes—
draw differentially on the various resources that language affords. Indeed, we characterize different types of discourse by citing the aspects

of language that are particularly prevalent in each. When Smitherman (1977) defines *signification* as "the verbal art of insult in which a speaker humorously puts down . . . the listener" (p. 118), or Mehan (1979) cites initiate-respond-evaluate (IRE) sequences as prototypical in whole group discussion in classrooms, (Mehan 1979), they are not suggesting that artful insults or IRE sequences do not occur in other types of discourse. Rather, they are claiming that these features are especially prominent in the type of discourse they are attempting to characterize. My claim is similar. It is not that active listening is unimportant when the purpose is something other than inquiry. Indeed, Susan's listening to Jack's narrative was quite attentive and would offer a good counter example to such an absurd claim. The claim is, rather, that an especially prevalent characteristic of inquiry discourse may be a heightened listening. In any two-person dialogue, we expect each participant to be both speaker and listener/responder. But in inquiry dialogue, one partner explicitly *seeks* verbal response of a particular kind and thus he acutely tunes in to that response; whereas the other partner is one from whom the verbal response is being *sought* and thus he is accutely attuned to the elicitation.

This focus on the listener role brings us to something of a problem. Earlier I specified "*expression* of meaning" as a defining characteristic of language acts (including acts of inquiry). Yet now I am suggesting that the addressee's participation in inquiry dialogue is participation in language acts and thus, by definition, participation in "*expressing* meaning." In what sense is the addressee—in listener role—engaged in "expressing meaning"?

Initially, speaking and listening seem to be opposite and mutually exclusive: You're either speaking or listening at any given moment, but you can't do both at the same time. But as is so often the case with opposites, "They're not really opposites, just two sides of the same thing" (Pat Carini quoting a child's comment in response to "day" and "night" as a test item on opposites). Relating meaning and expression is the essence of both speaking and listening. The speaker expresses his meaning out loud; the listener doesn't. The speaker goes from idea to expression (word), the listener from (the speaker's) expression (word) to idea. Thus the two simply proceed in different directions, but the act for both participants is to relate meaning and expression, to render "word" meaningful. Looked at in this way, speaking and listening are not so different. "A word is territory *shared* by both addresser and addressee" (Vološinov, 1973, p. 86). The "word," the expression itself, belongs to both the speaker who articulates it and the listener who interprets it.

What's more, in Bakhtin's view, speaking and listening are not mutually exclusive acts. We don't do one *or* the other at a given moment.

Rather, we engage in both at once: "When people use language, they do so . . . as consciousnesses engaging in simultaneous understanding: the speaker listens and the listener speaks" (Clark & Holquist, 1984, pp. 216–217). The word *simultaneous* is important, for the assertion is not that speaker and listener alternate both roles *sequentially* (my turn, your turn, my turn, your turn), but rather that they are in both roles *simultaneously*. The listener "shares" "the territory" that is the speaker's utterance. Thus, the listener speaks.

No less does the speaker listen. The speaker puts himself in the place of the listener while in the physical act of speaking.

> When a speaker is creating an utterance, . . . from the very beginning, the utterance is constructed while taking into account possible responsive reactions, for whose sake, in essence, it is actually created . . . the role of the *others* for whom the utterance is constructed is extremely great. . . . From the very beginning, the speaker expects a response from them, an active responsive understanding. The entire utterance is constructed, as it were, in anticipation of encountering this response. (Bakhtin, 1986, pp. 94–95)[12]

Vygotsky (1986) provides the following example of a speaker's words reflecting the partner's presence.

> I am sitting at my desk talking to a person who is behind me and whom I cannot see; he leaves the room without my noticing it, and I continue to talk, under the illusion that he listens and understands. Outwardly, I am talking with myself and for myself, but psychologically my speech is social. (p. 234)

Vygotsky's example reminds me of the familiar experience of being in a room where someone is talking on the telephone. We hear only the one partner speaking, yet from the sound—the expressivity—of his utterances we know who is on the other end of the line. We hear the partner's presence in the speaker's words, for the speaker is acutely aware of the partner and shapes his own utterances toward him. "The speaker listens" in the very act of speaking, trying even at that very moment to stand in the partner's place.

INQUIRY DIALOGUE AND CHANGED CONSCIOUSNESS

Whose consciousness is potentially changed in inquiry episodes? We probably think first of the speaker. After all, the very purpose of his inquiry act is to go beyond his present understanding. But clearly if the inquiry utterance belongs to all participants in the dialogue—if it is territory shared—then the consciousness-changing possibility within it is also shared. That possibility, too, belongs to both the addressor and the addressee(s). Bakhtin (1986) focuses explicitly on the addressee in inquiry dialogue when he writes of "Questions . . . that change the consciousness of the individual being questioned" (p. 136). We have seen this played out repeatedly in our focal transcripts:

In Jill's inquiry acts, her mother encounters categories of and relationships among animal habits and habitats that are different from her own categories. In Jill's outright rejection of her mother's conventional categories and relationships we hear a distinct clash of perspectives. In each partner's stubborn refusal to accept the other's categories, we can hear that each partner has had to take the other's perspective into account. Thus both consciousnesses, Jill's and her mother's, have been extended, for each has encountered and responded to a new (for her) way of construing the miniworld of selected animals' behaviors.

On the ride to her son's nursery school, Justin's mother encounters his view of bird sounds, of people crying, of heaven. Justin's view of each of these is different from hers. It is Justin's inquiry acts that reveal his perspective—his present understanding of these domains. His mother's response to their conflicting views is one of negotiation. She and Justin work toward consensus and compromise. She also attempts to understand further Justin's perspective ("Why do you think the orange ones are gross?") and in some instances, to elaborate it (e.g., providing additional details to their mutual picture of heaven). As with Jill's mother, her responses to the (for her) new perspectives that her son reveals in his inquiry acts demonstrate that her world has expanded to include these possible views. These have entered, and thus changed, her consciousness.

In order for Jack to respond to Susan's inquiries as he does—correcting, providing new details, conjecturing ("I think he was . . ."), demonstrating (". . . like this")—he must come to where she is as revealed in her inquiry utterances, and that place is clearly a new one for him. It is not likely that Jack has thought about Albert's weight or about whether Albert might look like a hot dog or about how Albert sits or whether he might have arms. But these become possibilities in his thought when Susan's inquiry acts bring these into the conversation. In their inquiry dialogue, two conscious-nesses meet and both change.

Placing himself in the role of speaker, Bakhtin (1986) writes of "oth-ers" in a dialogue "for whom my thought becomes actual thought for the first time (and thus also for my own self as well)" (p. 94). He may very well have had inquiry dialogue in mind, for nowhere is there greater potential for changed consciousness of all participants. I doubt that he was thinking of classrooms. Yet it is classrooms I think of first as the most promising place of all for inquiry dialogue that has the potential to change the consciousness of all participants.

CHAPTER 8

Inquiry Dialogue in the Classroom

"Put your things away now and join me over on the rug for story-
time."
"That would make a good discussion."
"Do we get to do Show-and-Tell today?"
"If you're ready for an editing conference, put your piece in the box."
"We'll have literature study right after lunch."
"Can me and Jeremy do an investigation?"
"Would you like to share your writing in Author's Chair today, Jesse?"
"I have something special to tell you in my dialogue journal today."

Storytime, editing conference, dialogue journal—each label signals a type
of interaction event. Classrooms abound with such events, and teachers
and children shift from one to another throughout the day. Inquiry demonstrations and engagements occur within these dialogic events or classroom *genres*.

We begin this chapter with an introduction to *genre* and then move
into the classroom, there to focus first on the relationship of inquiry and
power, and then on collaborative inquiry events, a classroom genre that
can provide strong support for emergent inquiry. After considering three
actual examples of collaborative inquiry events in classrooms, we'll be
in a position, finally, to reconsider two issues that are important to this
classroom genre: the "sharing of territory" (Bakhtin, 1986), and the relationship of inquiry and power.

GENRE: AN INTRODUCTION

Surely every classroom has its own particular set of recurring interaction events, and even an event that goes by the same name in different
classrooms (e.g., show-and-tell, literature study, author's chair) gets en-

acted differently in each one. To be a member of a classroom community is to know how to participate in that group's interaction events.

The word *interaction* is especially apt. The events are *inter* in that they are social events in which individuals communicate with one another, and they are *actions*—doings. Notice how often children use the word *do* in talking about these events, as in "do show-and-tell," "do literature study," "do author's chair," "do dialogue journals," and so on. Each event has its characteristic ways for participants to create text together: its own possible text structures, topics, composition, style; its own stances toward topic and partner(s). Teacher and children step into one type of interactive event and then another, again and again throughout each day: Now I'm peer conferencing, now I'm in my problem-solving math group, now I'm having a fight, now I'm playing in the housekeeping center, now I'm listening to a literature tape, now I'm doing my interview, now I'm writing in my reading response journal/learning log . . . And within each classroom genre, inquiry has its own ways.

Tannen's (1993) term *structures of expectation* is a helpful one in thinking about the types of interactive events that occur in classrooms—not that Tannen was thinking about classrooms when she proposed this term. She coined it as an umbrella term to bring together various researchers' "takes" (e.g., *scripts, frames, schemas*) on the basic assumptions that everyday interactive events are patterned and that they are language-action composites. Doing a science experiment, having a lunchroom conversation, doing literature study group all involve different structures of expectation. Participants come to these different events—step into these distinctive frames—with shared expectations of how to construct text together in each one.

Genre is Bakhtin's term for these structures of expectation. Recall his characterization of genre as types of utterances: "Each separate utterance is individual, of course, but each sphere in which language is used develops its own *relatively stable types* of these utterances. These we may call *speech genres*" (1986, p. 60). But "genre" also refers to types of talk (or writing) beyond the single utterance (conversational turn), *"forms of combinations of forms"* (1986, p. xvi). Though there is some ambiguity here as to the domain of genre for Bakhtin—whether a type of utterance or a type of combination of utterances—there is no ambiguity whatsoever as to the typicality. Nor is there any ambiguity about the inseparability of talk (or writing) and action in genre:

> Language is realized in the form of individual concrete utterances (oral and written) by participants in the various areas of human activity. The wealth and diversity of speech genres are boundless because the various possibili-

ties of human activity are inexhaustible and because each sphere of activity
contains an entire repertoire of speech genres. (1986, p. 60)

This talk/action unity is easy to recognize in the genres of the classroom:
Students talk in certain ways because they are doing certain things (e.g.,
doing show-and-tell, doing science experiments, doing dialogue journal
writing).

Recall that Bakhtin (1986) characterizes language acquisition as genre
acquisition: "We are given these speech genres in almost the same way
that we are given our native language (p. 78). . . . We learn to cast our
speech in generic forms" (p. 79). The suggestion is that over time one
learns ways of talking within (and appropriate to) recurring interactive
events. It's a view that informed our consideration of Sarah's early language in Chapter 4 as she and her mother looked at and talked about her
reflection. And the four-year-olds' conversations with their parents were
generic too, conversation in storyreading, on the drive to school, during
bedtime storytelling. Thinking of language acquisition as genre acquisition enables us to link the child's emergent inquiry before she comes to
school, with her continuing development after she gets there. Participating in a range of genres is the essence of the child's day in a classroom.
And so it was before she came to school.

Both at home and at school, some of the genres the child participates
in are themselves inquiry events, that is, events that are framed as exploration, and in which the utterances resonate with this overarching purpose. Others are not themselves inquiry events, although (as in the Susan
bedtime-story interactions) inquiry acts may figure prominently in them.
It seems to me, however, that part of the expectation in these structures
of expectation at home and at school, has to do with inquiry. We can ask
of each genre:

- What is the place of inquiry acts within it?
- How welcome are acts of inquiry? (Are they the essence of the
  event? Are they tolerated? Are they irrelevant? Are they counter-
  productive? etc.)
- How do these acts enter the discourse?
- Who introduces them?
- How are they carried out?
- What kinds are considered appropriate (e.g., does the event incline
  more toward information-seeking inquiry or wondering inquiry)?

Participants' expectations are "answers" to these questions, and they will
be different in show-and-tell, author's chair, peer conference, dialogue

journal writing, storytime, math group time, science experiment and so on. However, one thing is certain: the child who participates in these classroom genres has all along been participating in various genres at home and elsewhere, and in those dialogic events, she has come to understand that inquiry is empowering.

INQUIRY AND POWER

Power is a word that triggers some ambivalance. We may feel a certain unease with the notion of power, being acutely aware of its double edge. We are confronted daily with images of those who are more powerful exerting their control over those who are less powerful. Thoughts of bullies, of politicians, of gatekeepers, of despots, of child abusers come quickly to mind.

"Power is not an issue in my classroom," we say, "not in the caring, supportive community that my students and I have created together." But it is not so. Power is a real presence within classrooms—indeed, within all human interaction—though not necessarily power of the abusing, strong-arm kind.

You may have felt the shadowy presence of power in earlier chapters focusing on inquiry's purpose and expression: Whose purposes? Whose expressive ways? Whose content? Whose stance? Who has the right to decide what participants shall talk about? Whose agenda is to be honored? Whose knowledge is relevant? Whose is central? And who has the right to set the tone, the way of turning toward the topic and toward each other? These are power questions.

Now as we move from a focus on inquiry purpose (Part I) and expression (Part II) to a focus on inquiry dialogue in classrooms, power can no longer remain a shadowy presence. It now takes center stage. *Dialogue:* self and other(s) in a relationship, territory shared, text collaboratively constructed—now power questions necessarily come to the fore. The inquirer's positioning of herself is an act that positions others as well. Thus, it is when we turn our attention to dialogue—the relationship of partners to one another in communication events—that we feel the presence of power issues most keenly, for it is here that one participant's actions affect others or, to put it another way, it is here that one participant's rights bump up against another's. Recall inquiry's destabilizing, shaping, pulling qualities discussed in the last chapter. Who has the right to destabilize the discourse? Who has the right to influence the shape of the dialogue? Who has the right to pull for another's verbal participation of a specified type? These are all questions about imposition and that is just what an inquiry act is: an act of imposition. Who has the right to impose on others in dialogic events? Power and inquiry really do go hand in hand in the classroom.

My dictionary offers two definitions of power that may shed light on our ambivalence. The first is "possession of control or command over others." This stirs some unease. But power can also have to do with command over ourselves: the "ability to do something," "ability to do or act; capability of doing or accomplishing something." It is this sense of power we seem to be drawing on when we say that we want education to empower students. We mean that we want them to be able to "do or act" so as to fulfill those continuing urges to connect with others, to understand their world, and to reveal themselves within it, the very three that come together in inquiry acts.

Recall from Chapter 4 that a large body of educational research since the 1960s has been concerned with student "questioning." A major goal of that research has been to find ways of increasing children's classroom "questioning" in amount and in quality. Many studies have explored possible ways of getting students to ask more questions in the classroom, and other studies have tried to get students to ask "better" ones. Although this work often confounded interrogative form with inquiry act, it was prompted by a desire to empower students. Zahorik (1971) bemoaned the fact that "for far too long schooling has been a matter of answering questions that children never asked" (p. 360). The unasked questions he was speaking of were children's attempts to elicit the help of others in their sense-making. He was, I believe, speaking of inquiry acts, though he used the label of his time: "question." He understood that inquiry is empowering. Surely we are even more fully aware of that inquiry-power connection today. And if we are ambivalent in our feelings about power, and if inquiry acts and events are about empowerment, then it stands to reason that some of the ambivalence we feel toward power may cling to our attitudes toward inquiry as well. We say that we want students to inquire actively, and we do; yet we may have the sense that insofar as they do, we are giving something up. There lingers the uneasy sense that the measure of one person's gain in power is the measure of another's loss of it. What teacher can't identify with Caryl Crowell and Karen Gallas:

> The quiet and easy cooperation of that first day are never seen again during the year. Once the students accept the power and responsibility to control discussion and learning in the classroom, I will never get it back, even when I think I would like to have it, if only for a moment. (Whitmore & Crowell, 1994, p. 67)

> It is the teacher's way to want to facilitate discussion; to moderate who talks and for how long; to discourage what I call bird walks, or digressions that seem to be off the topic; to make sure that children finally get the right answer . . . The act of giving up overt control of the talks takes time and determination, and is almost painful. (Gallas, 1995, pp. 18, 19)

When we encourage children's inquiry in classroom discourse, we may feel that we have "turned something over" to them—that something has moved from us to them. That something is power.

I look to a central metaphor to help untangle this ambivalent relationship we have with power and, by implication, with children's (empowering) inquiry in the classroom. Lakoff and Johnson (1980) remind us of how pervasive metaphor is in our daily lives, not as poetry, but as thought. Metaphors reflect and also shape the ways we conceptualize. They have consequences.

> Metaphor is pervasive in everyday life, not just in language but in thought and action. Our ordinary conceptual system, in terms of which we both think and act, is fundamentally metaphorical in nature. . . . [If] our conceptual system is largely metaphorical, then the way we think, what we experience, and what we do every day is very much a matter of metaphor. . . . human *thought processes* are largely metaphorical. (pp. 3, 6)

Earlier we considered the metaphor of knowledge as thing (something we have or give, possess or pass). Well, we seem to conceptualize power as a thing also. Think of the verbs we use in talking about power: One *holds* it, *gives* it, *takes* it, *shares* it, *has* it, *confers* it, *wrests* it (from another), *relinquishes* it, *retains* it, *distributes* it, *invests* (someone with) it, *wields* it, *bestows* it.[1] One of the consequences of conceptualizing power as an entity is that we see it as being a fixed amount. It is rather like a deck of cards. There are only 52 and I can deal them out in various ways but I cannot increase the number in the deck. If you have 40, then I have 12, and if I have 12, then you have 40; we can't both have 40. Garnering more for one means a corresponding loss for another. Those engaged in classroom questioning research, in an attempt to increase and improve student questions, were well aware that what their research was about was shifting the balance of power away from teachers and toward students. This was to realign teacher and student power relationships. Changing the total available to all was not a possibility. No more is it possible today, so long as we remain trapped within a power-as-thing metaphor. We will necessarily stay within notions of teacher "sharing" her power with students or "redistributing" power within classrooms.

I challenge that fixed-amount metaphor as it relates to inquiry discourse in classrooms. Inquiry acts do empower. I mean to suggest, however, that inquiry acts and events in classrooms can be empowering in a generative way, and that inquiry *of* itself creates *beyond* itself. I challenge the fixed-amount metaphor by turning to actual inquiry events in classrooms, specifically, genres of exploration. These dialogues urge us to find a different metaphor to help us understand the generative power of inquiry.

It is, of course, impossible to consider all classroom genres and the role of inquiry in each, not only because the number of these is large, but also because each classroom community creates its own. If a teacher were to sit down and list the repertoire of genres in her own classroom, her list would be different from every other teacher's list. But although we can't identify and examine all possible genres, we can examine specific examples from particular classrooms to gain a better understanding of the generative power of inquiry in some classroom genres.

COLLABORATIVE INQUIRY

My examples come from Vivian Paley's kindergarten (two examples) and Karen Gallas's first-second grade (one example), classrooms such as Jill, Justin, and Susan might enter. All three examples illustrate a classroom genre that is framed as collaborative inquiry (i.e., group exploration): *discussion* in Vivian's case, and *science talk* in Karen's.[2] You will notice once again that the framing expectation of the discourse in each example—what it is that the participants understand themselves to be doing—resonates in the individual utterances within it. Those utterances are inquiry acts, understood by the participants to be contributing to inquiry's overarching purpose. Once again, inquiry *event* (group exploration, in this case) holds within it inquiry *episodes* (conversation on a topic) and finally, inquiry *utterances* (individual conversational turns). Again we look to the *event* in order to understand the *utterances* within it. Bakhtin (1986) makes a similar point about utterance and word: "The utterance . . . radiates its expression . . . to the word we have selected, which is to say, invests the word with the expression of the whole" (p. 86). And so it is with generic events in classrooms. The framing purpose of the whole "radiates" its expression to the utterances within it.

"If You Were in Charge of the World"

The genre discussion occurs frequently in Vivian Paley's (1981) class-room. So does the label: "That'll be a good discussion for you," Wally tells Vivian (p. 38). "Shall we do the story after the discussion?" Vivian asks a child (p. 222). The easy, casual use of the label belies the seri-ousness of the event itself: "Discussions are the *lifeline* of our social fab-ric," Vivian tells me. "We take them seriously and expect that *every* idea or behavior during a discussion tells us something important about us" (personal letter, April 26, 1996). Attempting to discover these participants' structures of expectation for discussions, I asked Vivian, "What sort of event [do] you and the children understand 'discussion' to be?" Her an-swer provides a helpful basis for our consideration of the first two ex-amples (both from her classroom).

> Most discussions in my classroom originate in some sort of inquiry.
> "Here's something I don't understand . . ." would be a familiar
> stance of mine after reading a book . . . or a child might begin with
> "Charlie wasn't fair to me on the playground, you know what he
> did . . . ?" In other words: does this puzzle you as it does me; does
> this event seem as unfair to you as it does to me; can you match
> the idea under discussion with an example of your own?
>   Discussions, then, as differentiated from conversations, chats,
> or storytelling, are issue focused, try-not-to-interrupt activities in
> which one person at a time speaks, the teacher frequently repeats
> in some form what the speaker has said or connects one contribu-
> tion to others just made, and the children continually ponder a
> question . . . in a fairly open-ended manner. Sometimes a discus-
> sion is meant to lead to a decision; more often, not. It is understood
> that the act of discussing some problem in the formal, full-class re-
> view is, in and of itself, helpful and rewarding. The point is to get
> at many ideas as possible on a given topic with the expectation
> that one question or comment will lead to another and, in this
> manner, *better thinking* will result. . . .
>   It is understood that, in a discussion, there is no single ques-
> tion that is most relevant, nor is there a single answer which closes
> the topic. . . . Most discussions are expected to:
>
> 1. examine the human condition
> 2. figure out ways to bring more happiness to more children in
>   our classroom
> 3. bring out individual points of view and differences

4. gain knowledge or interesting ideas from each other. (personal letter, April 26, 1996; emphasis in the original)

The following discussion, like most in this classroom, begins with an inquiry: "If you were in charge of the world would you make only one language or many languages, the way it is now?" (Paley, 1981, p. 119). The inquiry is Vivian's. Clearly she is interested in the children's ideas on this topic, and in this regard, it's a how-many-teeth-does-a-fox-have type: I am asking this not in order to find out how languages should be distributed in the world, but rather to find out how you think about this issue (and to engage you in doing it because it is "in and of itself rewarding" and *better thinking* may well result"). But Vivian's own interest in the topic is unmistakable. This is not a setup; this is a topic of genuine fascination *for her*. *She* wants to play this exploring game as well as watch how the children play it and help them to probe as fully as possible. This is a classic instance of inquiry demonstration, as well as an opportunity for children's engagement.

Text No. 9: Languages

1. TEACHER: If you were in charge of the world, would you make only one language or many languages, the way it is now?
2. TANYA: One language. Oh yes! Then I could understand everyone in the whole world.
3. EDDIE: No, let it stay this way so different countries keeps on being not the same. Then you take trips to see what those countries are like and how they talk.
4. ELLEN: I like the world the way it is but I don't like fighting.
5. TEACHER: Is that because they have different languages?
6. ELLEN: Well, if they can't understand each other they might think good words sound like bad words.
7. WALLY: She means like if someone says, "Let's play," in French, then in Chinese they might think he said, "Let's fight."
8. WARREN: (Warren is Chinese) Keep it this way because if you're Chinese you would have to learn English.
9. TEACHER: Would English have to be the language everyone learns?
10. WARREN: I don't know what God likes to talk. Wait, I changed my mind. Let everyone say the same language. Then when my mommy and daddy speak quietly I could understand them.
11. TANYA: I changed my mind too. Better not have the same language. Here's why: Whenever this whole world had the same language everyone would say they want *their* language to be the

one everyone has to have. Then everyone would blame someone else for giving them the wrong language.
12. AKEMI: (Akemi is Japanese) If everyone speak Japan, everyone
have to live here. My country too small for the big America.
13. WARREN: Everyone can come to China. It's much bigger. Let Chinese be the language. No, I changed my mind. Let my
mommy and daddy talk English *all* the time. (Paley, 1981,
pp. 119–120)

The initiating inquiry invites the children into a discussion of an explicitly hypothetical issue (not a discussion that "is meant to lead to a
decision"). We hear the children "continually ponder[ing]" an issue and
the teacher repeating "in some form what the speaker has said or connect[ing] one contribution to others." We hear an enacting of the structures of expectation that Vivian noted: the "act of discussing . . . is, in and
of itself, helpful and rewarding"; "as many ideas as possible" are to be
brought forward; there is "no single answer which closes the topic."

Examination "of the human condition" is evident here as the children
consider the human desire to understand others, human tendencies toward conflict, possibilities of misunderstanding, inclination toward com-
petition and so on. The essence of this event is the articulation of "individual points of view and differences" and the gaining of "interesting ideas
from each other." The children do indeed play out the structures of expectation that Vivian articulates. There is a shared understanding that the
issue is worth considering. There is a seriousness here, too (focus; attention and response to each other), but also a "playfulness" (a playing with
ideas) that is the essence of wondering inquiry (as contrasted with information-seeking inquiry). Also typical of wondering inquiry, we hear the
participants avoiding closure—keeping the dialogue open so that more
ideas come onto the floor; we hear interaction that—while drawing on
real-life examples—revels in considering possible worlds; we hear discourse whose purpose is engagement in the process of considering possibilities. This interaction seems to have no larger pragmatic purpose or
goal: Engaging in reflection—together—is all, and the process "in and of
itself [is] helpful and rewarding."

This discussion—indeed, the genre discussion itself in this classroom—is clearly an inquiry event in that its purpose is that individuals
shall turn toward others to help them go beyond in their own thinking,
as well as contributing to the thinking of others. If this were not the intention, then the participants would not verbalize their ideas in conscious
awareness of the presence of others and in conscious awareness of the
frame that they are in. Giving voice—literally—to their ideas, these chil-

dren turn toward one another in a way that is both tentative and invitational. Because these children are engaged in inquiry, it is no surprise to find them drawing on their present knowledge base to go beyond it, for inquiry arises in one's knowledge and the use one makes of it. It is activated knowledge. The knowledge base that the children are drawing on is impressive:

- Misunderstandings between people can cause fighting.
- There are many specific languages in the world (French, Chinese, Japanese).
- English is a dominant language.
- Language is power and people disagree as to whose will be dominant.
- If one lives in a particular country, one speaks a particular language.
- Countries differ in size.
- Shared ways of speaking bring people together; different ways threaten relationships.

Nor is it surprising to find a high energy level, though the energizing nature of the inquiry utterances may be more difficult to hear in this event than in the bedtime storytelling interaction (Susan and Jack), in which the contrasting rhythms of the narrative episodes and the inquiry episodes alternated with one another. Here there is no such contrast and the energy level is sustained throughout. Notice how much more accurately this discussion is characterized by Bakhtin's notion of inquiry than by Berlyne's. There is no attempt to end the "aversive" off-balance state of uncertainty by asking questions that will lead to resolution—to a state of rest and balance (Berlyne). Rather, it is the purpose of this event to wallow in uncertainty and hypothetical possibilities, a most Bakhtinian thing to do!

In this example, the teacher and children step into the frame called discussion knowing that they have come together to reflect on an issue, not (in this instance) to resolve or answer it. In their probing, it is understood that all participants will go beyond present understanding, extending the boundaries of their individual worlds, and that they will do so with each other's help. It is the very presence of a variety of different views that enables the going-beyond for each individual. There is active inquiry here. And there is power. Yet, for me, the notion of power as fixed-amount entity (more for me means less for you) does not capture what is happening here. Wherever these participants are when they begin this discussion, they are at a different place—a beyond place—when they finish (not a finish in the sense of over-and-done). And no one arrived at her new place at the expense of someone else. No one gave up her agenda for someone else's. Quite the opposite: each one's expressed possibilities become available to all.[3]

Consideration of the individual utterances (conversational turns) within this discussion again reveals how uninformative it would be to consider only interrogatives. All the interrogatives are Vivian's (#1, 5, 9), yet the inquirers are the children and teacher both. Individual children commit to a position . . . and change their minds; agree with others . . . and disagree; state what they like . . . and what they don't like. Their utterances explain, elaborate, suggest, support, consider consequences. Yet all are inquiry acts because, occurring within this exploratory frame, their way of turning toward others is to ask, "How 'bout this?" in an attempt to go beyond, and help others go beyond, their present thinking.

"How Do You Know If Somebody Likes You?"

The next discussion example introduces acts in which the same children describe, share, and savor past experiences of friendship. Such language acts would seem to be unlikely candidates for inquiry acts. Yet they address the unspoken but understood invitation which underlies discussion in this classroom: "Can you match the idea under discussion with an example of your own?" The children's responses are further instances of "How 'bout this?" This particular discussion focuses on friendship, and again it is Vivian who introduces the topic with an initiating inquiry.

Text No. 10: Friendship

1. T: How do you know if somebody likes you? . . .
2. WALLY: Watch a person and see if they stay and play.
3. JILL: And lots of people get in fights and they act like they're not being nice but the next day they want to be friends again.
4. EDDIE: If he talks to you a lot he likes you.
5. DEANNA: I can tell if someone doesn't like me. I like someone who doesn't like me. I chase him and he doesn't run after me. He tries to hit me and I duck.
6. EDDIE: I know the boy next door is my enemy because we know we're enemies.
7. ELLEN: They say bad words to you if someone doesn't like you. . . .

8. DEANA: Jill, remember when you and me were in your father's car sucking our thumbs?

9. JILL: Oh, yeah. That was so much fun. My daddy kept singing, "Rockabye baby in the treetop." Remember?

10. FRED: Hey, Wally. Remember at Eddie's birthday party we put those metal kettles on our heads?

11. TANYA: Lisa, remember when I first came to your house and I didn't know where the bathroom was? And then we put the boats in the bathtub?

12. T: Are you children saying that you know someone likes you if you remember nice things you did together?

13. ELLEN: Remember when we were looking for the black kitty at your house, Kim? And we said, "Here, Kitty, here's kitty" and we were laughing so much?

14. KIM: And it was in the closet? I remember that.

15. WARREN: Kenny, remember in nursery school we brought snow inside in our hats and the teacher was laughing?

16. KENNY: Hey, let's do that again. Okay? (Paley, 1981, pp. 150–152)

How strong is the influence that the genre frame exerts here. The members of this classroom community share an expectation about relevance in discussion: Discussions "are issue-focused" events in which participants "continually ponder a question . . . in a fairly open-ended manner." "Seldom is a comment considered irrelevant," Vivian tells me. "It is understood that something reminded a classmate of his particular response. . . . We always expect thinking to jump around, back and forth" (personal letter, April 26, 1996). It is this shared structure of expectation that provides unity across this wide range of diverse utterances. Vivian's "Are you children saying that you know someone likes you if you remember nice things you did together?" is an explicit articulation of what is—at some level—already understood: To recall pleasant shared experience is to contribute relevantly to the issue being explored.

How strange it seems, given our history of focusing on children's classroom questions, to interpret these kindergartners' shared recollections as acts of inquiry. Yet an understanding of genre—an understanding of shared expectations of utterances living within purposeful exploratory text—requires just such a reinterpretation. These interaction events push us to extend our notions of inquiry in classroom dialogue. In the inquiry genres of classroom life, "remember when" becomes an act of inquiry, held as it is within a frame of "How 'bout this?" How different it is to consider individual utterances *within* their own genres, instead of considering lists of "questions" *extracted from* real dialogue, as earlier education research tended to do, busying itself with the tallying of interrogative sentences. Utterances are not separable from the texts in which they live. Remove an utterance from its text and you are left holding a lifeless thing—a sentence, but no longer an utterance.

It is *life* that resounds in the kindergartners' words. I am struck by how much feeling imbues the children's talk. Their talk gives life and breath to Bakhtin's (1986) distinction between words out of a dictionary and words out of people's mouths, as well as to Vygotsky's (1986) distinction between meaning and sense. *Kettle* in the dictionary is one thing; on one's head it is quite another. There's *snow* in the dictionary, or in one's hat. The dictionary's *boat* is a different boat from the one in the bathtub, and the dictionary's *Chinese* is different from what my mommy and daddy speak quietly.

"Is Voice Matter?"

Let's suppose that Jill, Justin, and Susan have spent a year in Vivian's kindergarten and now go to Karen Gallas's first-second grade. Here they will participate in a genre called science talk that is similar to Vivian's discussion in many ways. Karen introduces science talks to the children as times "when they can speak with each other about important questions" (1995, p. 20), times "when children [can] wonder out loud about the world" (p. 69). *Wonder* is certainly the operative word. As with Vivian's discussions, one immediately recognizes the strong presence of the characteristics of wondering inquiry in science talks: the openness, the orientation toward engagement in a process of playing with possibilities. Typically in science talks, "the children are satisfied simply to talk about the question. They will not ask to know the 'real' answer. . . . It is the asking and the talking that are the focus of those kinds of talks" (p. 70). Like Vivian's genre discussion, Karen's science talks are clearly framed as interactive events that are separate and distinct from others. Recall that Vivian's discussions are "differentiated from conversations, chats, or storytelling." Similarly, Karen's "Science Talks occur in a separate and formally prescribed time frame and within a whole class discussion format" (p. 1) and are "distinguished from both the more formal times when I 'teach' science through direct instruction, as well as those times when children work with science materials and activities" (p. 1). Also reminiscent of Vivian's discussion genre, Karen adds that "as Science Talks progress, almost every idea is taken seriously and worked with for a time" (p. 40) and that the children "naturally engage in theoretical speculation about a question" in a "mode [that] is unusually flexible and open ended, filled with metaphor, analogy, imagination, and wonder" (p. 43).

For all the striking similarities between discussions and science talks, there are two major differences: topic domain and teacher's role. Whereas appropriate topics for Vivian's discussion come from any area of thought, it is science topics that are explored in science talks, for Karen is apprenticing the children into scientific discourse. She "strive[s] to have each child be admitted to conversations about the world of science . . . hoping to help all children find a way to own, or appropriate, some understanding of the language, attitude, mind, and psyche of the scientist. I am . . . attending to the construction of a discourse in my classroom" (p. 99). It is a discourse whose essence is "collaborative theory building" (p. 99).

Besides the difference in topic domain, we find a difference in the teacher's role in discussions and in science talks. Whereas Vivian is both inquiring participant and coach (e.g., articulating children's implied connections or inviting a child to elaborate), Karen's role is entirely a scaffolding one: She coaches from the sidelines (e.g., "Could you say your question again, Tom?") but does not come onto the field as a player. Karen preserves science talk as a time for the children to discuss science topics with one another.

With these similarities and differences in mind, consider the following excerpts from a science talk (Gallas, 1995) in which the children discuss "Is voice matter?"—a question originally posed by a seven-year-old girl in this first-second grade classroom.[4] (In the following example, I have preserved only the transcript, deleting Karen's commentary on it. Also, I have numbered the utterances for easy reference in my subsequent discussion of this example. Ellipses are in the original and indicate a long pause.)

Text No. 11: A Science Talk

1. TOM: Air takes up, um, space, but does voice?
2. LESTER: I think it sort of does because like, it's like air, and voice is like air so it's
3. ELLEN: Sort of . . .
4. TOM: Like if you, like if she can blow up a balloon up with your, with your, um, with your, um, breath, it, um, must take up, it must be matter, sort of.
5. ELI: It must be matter sort of, 'cause . . .
6. TOM: Like if you blow up a balloon, like it takes matter.
7. ELLEN: I think it might be matter because, um, when you talk you breathe out and you breathe in, so . . .
8. TOM: Yeah, but if you breathe, um, talking, um, you can you still,

um, when some people talk, um, they're like talking a lot, they have to like, get their breath.

9. TOM: If voice is, um, matter, um, is, like, would we be getting squished right now, if it's like, taking up room?

10. LESTER: No, it wouldn't exactly be getting like squished.

11. ELLEN: Because air's taking up space, and it's not squeezing us.

12. ZACH: And it takes up more space than we do.

13. TEACHER: Could you say your question again, Tom?

14. ZACH: How could it not really like

15. TIM: If, if . . .

16. ZACH: squeeze us

17. TOM: if voice is matter . . .

18. ZACH: to death?

19. TOM: why isn't it, like, smushing us against the walls?

20. MICHAEL: Because air is matter, but when there's like, like take a big wind, for instance. When hurricanes or tornadoes come along, they take up a lot of air, and space, and they are air. But it's just a big quantity of air . . .

21. LESTER: Sometimes the voice waves are, are not as hard as winds can be. Voices waves aren't.

22. IAN: But how can you tell voice is matter if . . . It seems like air *doesn't* take up space, but it actually *does*. So, so you can't, you can't exactly tell with air where, like, where it is. There's not like, one piece of air going in a different place. That's not the same as with voice. So, it doesn't seem like it would take up room. It's not like every day you see a chunk of air floating around in the sky.

23. ELLEN: Not if it's really cold and you're breathing, and it gets really cold. (Sounds of many children breathing in and out.)

24. IAN: Yea, so. You don't see a chunk of voice flying around if someone says something. It's not like you see these words coming up in a chunk of voice flying up into the air. (Pointing into the air) "Ohhhh, there's your voice."

25. ELI: Air can sorta talk. Because when, if, if it's blowing really hard you can make a noise.

26. LESTER: Voice like, like your voice is the sound.

27. IAN: Um, I want to, um, add something to Ellen's but I'm kind of protesting it. But air, air and voice, I don't think they're the same thing. 'Cause if, if voice was air, why wouldn't you just be breathing it instead of talking with it, using it to talk.

28. MICHAEL: We didn't say they were the same, we just said they were kinda similar.

29. TEACHER: Ian can you ask that question again because some people have, who've said air is like voice 'cause you breathe out, might want to respond to that. So Ian, will you ask that again?

30. IAN: Yeah, yeah, I don't, I don't think voice and air would be the same thing . . . 'Cause it doesn't seem like they're the same thing. Voice, you talk with it, and air, you breathe. So, if they were the same thing, if they were just air, you might not talk 'cause you wouldn't have any voice.

(skipping a bit here)

31. ZACH: I think voice is matter because like, when you talk, you can feel something like hot on your hand. If you put your hand near your mouth and if you don't talk, you don't have something hot on your hand.

32. IAN: I just tried that experiment and what I found out, see, I said, "I can." And I found out that when I . . . That hot stuff that I felt on my hand is just breath. I was just breathing.

33. ELI: But Zach, if that is true, then why can't we really see it happening? Why can't we really see it happening?

34. MICHAEL: I don't know. It's like air, you can't see air happen.

35. ZACH: You can see it on frosty days.

36. MICHAEL: Yeah, you can. You see your breath. And your breath is air.

37. NATE: Well, if you didn't have those tubes in your body, you couldn't speak. . . . If you were trying to speak, you would try to speak, you'd say nothing. You were saying air. (Based on Gallas, 1995, pp. 63–66)

Shared structures of expectation clearly guide this collaborative inquiry event. It is easy to hear the children enacting their understanding that this genre is a wondering exploration. We hear the characteristics of wondering in

- the *openness*, the children's welcoming of various ideas (including conflicting ones);
- the *play* in the children's examples of balloons and squishing, squeezing air; in their dramatizing ("Oh, there's your voice") and experimenting; and especially in their analogy and metaphor (e.g., voice waves and winds, chunks of voice);
- the *possibility* orientation, the children's tentative expression—their use of words (if, sort of, I think, like, seem, might, kinda) that mark the talk as hypothetical;
- the engagement in *process*, evident in both what is present in the

children's talk (active involvement with ideas) and what is absent (attempts to reach consensus).

It's easy, too, to hear the children's shared understanding that this genre is a *collaborative* event, one in which participants create "beyond" possibilities together. Their utterances connect:

TOM: Air takes up . . . space, but does voice?
LESTER: I think it sort of does because . . .
ELLEN: . . . when you talk you breathe out and you breathe in, so
TOM: Yeah, but if you breathe . . .

TOM: . . . would we be getting squished right now . . .
LESTER: No . . .
ELLEN: Because . . .
ZACH: And . . .

IAN: . . . I want to . . . add something to Ellen's but I'm kind of pro-
     testing it.

IAN: . . . air and voice, I don't think they're the same thing . . .
MICHAEL: We didn't say they were the same, we just said they were
         kinda similar.

There is close contingency here, one turn connecting with and building on another. One might wonder whether Bakhtin had been listening in on this science talk:

> Utterances are not indifferent to one another, and are not self-sufficient; they are aware of and mutually reflect one another. . . . Each utterance is filled with echoes and reverberations of other utterances to which it is related by the communality of the sphere of speech communication. . . . The utterance is filled with *dialogic overtones*. . . . [O]ur thought itself . . . is born and shaped in the process of interaction and struggle with others' thought, and this cannot but be reflected in the forms that verbally express our thought as well. (Bakhtin, 1986, pp. 91, 92)

Discussion and science talks surely invite a reconsideration of the "common knowledge" that young children are too egocentric to listen to each other and to take another's point of view, or that young children can't stay on a topic because they have such short attention spans.

Notice that what we do not hear in this science talk speaks just as loudly to the presence of shared expectations for this frame as what we do hear. The children make observations and suggestions, but we do not hear pronouncements. They draw on facts by way of probing an idea further, but we do not hear them using facts by way of providing a conclusive answer. We also do not hear monologic text—extended conversational turns in which a child holds forth in lecture style. The text here is profoundly dialogic, the speaker in each turn turning to others for active understanding and response. Also absent is performance talk—perfectly crafted and executed conversational turns. The talk here is messy. It is rough draft talk, thought-becoming-word talk. Absent, too, is authoritative stance. In its place is a tentative, "perhaps" orientation. These absent features are *systematically* absent, not coincidentally so. And it is no accident that what is absent is the opposite of what is present.

TEACHER GUIDANCE

The children's shared structures of expectation for discussions and science talks did not magically happen, nor did the children come into these classrooms already proficient in carrying out these events. These children learned how to participate in discussions and science talks with the intentional help of their teachers. Sometimes their guidance is explicit. When Karen was concerned about several boys "taking over" the science talks—dominating the talk and speaking only to one another—she gave them very specific instructions for changing their speaking behavior: "I want you to say one thing and then sit back and let the next person in" (p. 84); "Ask him a question. That way he can say more" (p. 86); "I want to ask . . . for the boys who talk a lot to not act like it's just a conversation between themselves. . . . when you guys talk, the sentences go on and on and on. . . . It's important that when you say one thing, you stop, and sit back, and let people think about it" (p. 87). Sometimes the guidance these teachers provide is not explicit although it is intentional as, for example, when Karen asks a child to repeat her question or when Vivian asks a question that nudges the discussion or articulates a connection implied in the children's talk. At the end of *Wally's Stories*, Vivian describes her role in discussions: She uses "material that children want to discuss" (p. 213); she tries to "help the child see how one thing he knows relates to other things he knows" (p. 213); she tries "to keep the inquiry open long enough for the consequences of [the children's] ideas to become apparent to them" (p. 213); she acts "as the ancient Greek chorus, seeking connections and keeping track of events, but the decisions must come from the children" (p. 214). In these ways Vivian provides "guided participation" for her "apprentices" in the genre discussion (Rogoff, 1990).

Whether by repairing the children's talk when it does not enact genre expectations, or by helping the children talk in ways that carry out those expectations more fully, Vivian and Karen are guiding the children into a particular type of discourse. Both teachers are apparently well aware that the "apprenticeship" they guide the children in is an "apprenticeship in thinking" (Rogoff 1990) as well as in talk. These teachers tell us that discussions "result in better thinking" (Paley, personal letter, April 26, 1996) and that science talks foster "the language, attitude, mind, and psyche of the scientist" (Gallas, 1995, p. 99). In these events, the children's articulation of their thought renders that thought the social act that we call inquiry. And because individual thought becomes a social act, the sharing of new territory becomes possible.

SHARED TERRITORY

The listener speaks. The speaker listens. The speaker listens in the very act of speaking, orienting self toward other. And the listener speaks, not only in the literal sense of articulating the response that follows the listening/interpreting act, but also in the listening/interpreting act itself, for the interpretation completes the speaker's act: "The only way the speaker's act can mean [and thus be complete] is to be understood" (Clark & Holquist, 1984, p. 213). The speaker does not express meaning alone. She does so in partnership with the addressee. What Bakhtin (1986) calls "sharing territory" might more accurately be called *sharing the creating of territory.*

In the three preceding examples, we hear the participants' "attunement to the attunement of other" (Rommetveit, 1992, quoting Barwise & Perry, 1983). Besides being closely connected turn-by-turn, the talk is characterized by shared expressive features. The children's intuneness can be heard in the shared *tunes* of their speech:

- *Tentativeness* markers are abundant—the I don't knows, sort ofs, ifs, and maybes—and doubtless many more that we cannot pick up from the transcripts alone (e.g., intonation contours, pauses, speech rhythms, body language, pitch patterns);
- The talk is *imaginative, dramatic, visual.* Across participants, images are created (taking trips to other countries, people thinking good words sound like bad ones, God liking to talk one language or another, Mommy and Daddy speaking quietly, people in conflict

over which language should dominate, everyone coming to Japan
... or China to live, getting squeezed to death by air, hurricanes or
tornadoes coming along, a chunk of air floating around, air talking,
the look of air on frosty days) or re-created in memory (wearing
kettles on our heads, sailing boats in the bathtub, putting snow in
our hats). Talk is dramatized, not simply reported ("Let's play,"
"Let's fight," "Ohhhh, there's your voice"). These are all acts of
imagination.

- The children rely heavily on *reaching devices*—analogy, comparison,
  metaphor—devices that help them go beyond by stretching what
  they know into what they sense beyond it. These types of rhetorical
  devices allow one to stand with one foot in the known, while placing the other in the unknown. They carry creative thinking
  forward.
- *Specific words* are picked up and used by different participants (*sort
  of* [Gallas #2, #3, #4, #5], *squished* [Gallas #9, #10], *squeeze* [Gallas
  #11, #16], *remember* [Paley (Text No. 10) #8, #9, #10, #11, #12, #13,
  #14, #15], *everyone* [Paley (Text No. 9) #2, #9, #10, #11, #12, #13)].

These are the sounds of collaborative inquiry.

I am struck, too, by the children's sharing of discourse moves. The
first discussion (about language) offers a particularly good example. We
might expect a speaker to put forward an idea that other participants
would then agree or disagree with. This does happen, but it also happens
that speakers disagree with *their own* ideas (I changed my mind). Also,
we might expect a speaker to offer support or clarification for an idea she
has initiated. Indeed, we do find speakers doing this, but we also find
other participants supporting or clarifying the original speaker's idea (She
means . . .).

However closely attuned to one another these children and teachers
are in their discussions and science talks, they do not merge. They remain
distinctive consciousnesses, distinctive voices. The listening here does not
involve "passive understanding that, so to speak, only duplicates [the
speaker's] idea in someone else's mind" (Bakhtin, 1986, p. 69). Rather, the
listener *creates* meaning in the act we call interpretation. Understanding
is dialogic.

"If an answer does not give rise to a new question from itself, it
falls out of the dialogue," says Bakhtin (1986, p. 168). Clearly Bakhtin's
"question" here is our "inquiry," an act that expresses uncertainty and
turns toward another for response. Yet, as I listen to the children's talk in
the three examples, it seems to me that the "question" is not in the speaker's utterance, but rather in that utterance-as-understood-by-another. It

takes (at least) two to render an utterance inquiring in its thrust. In the children's discussions and science talk, inquiry acts live in the speaker's words *because listeners hear/interpret these utterances as inquiry acts and respond to them as inquiry.* And it is wondering inquiry, not information-seeking inquiry, that these listeners/responders hear: invitations to hold the discussion *open*, to *play* with *possibilities*, to engage actively in a *process*. Together these speakers and listeners/responders create new territory. Together they make inquiry acts.

Why do the children in our three examples hear inquiry's intent in speakers' words? If that intent is not in the words as *spoken*, but rather in the words as *understood*, then why do the children understand the utterances in this way rather than some other? The answer must be genre. The structures of expectation for discussion and science talk foster this inquiry interpretation, for collaborative inquiry is what this genre is; it is what the children understand themselves to be doing. And this genre is not simply a way of using words; it is a way of using the mind as well. This is a genre in which thought is rendered social act and thus the possibility of changed consciousness is available to all.

Notice how the teachers' utterances are heard in these events. The influence of genre is clear once again. Researchers have described in great detail the workings of that classroom staple "recitation" (often called whole-group discussion). Who is not familiar with its dominant IRE pattern in which teacher initiates (asks a question to ascertain whether children know the answer), a student responds, and the teacher evaluates the response (Mehan, 1979). The expectation for this genre is that the purpose is to demonstrate one's knowledge. It is performance talk that is appropriate within this frame. But the children in the discussions and science talk above do not interpret Vivian's and Karen's contributions as eliciting performance. They know they are in a different frame, a collaborative inquiry frame. Thus the teachers' questions ("If you were in charge of the world, would you make only one language?" "How do you know if somebody likes you?" "Could you say your question again, Tom?") are understood as invitations to thinking aloud in a creative, wondering way. Together.

INQUIRY AND POWER: TAKING A SECOND LOOK

When we think about the *energizing, shaping, pulling* aspects of inquiry acts in discourse, we are thinking in a self-*or*-other way: who has greater status and control within the discourse? When we think about the *shared territory* aspects of inquiry acts in discourse, we are thinking in a self-*and*-other way. Both aspects are real and ever present. They are the double bind that is part of all interaction. We are ever attempting to balance separateness (the hands) and togetherness (the clapping) when self and other come together in dialogue.

I marvel that children so young as Vivian's and Karen's manage this delicate balance so exquisitely in the above examples. Individual voices— separate and distinct—do indeed energize, shape, and pull—do move the talk forward in directions of the individual's own choosing. But just as surely, voices join—take one another into account. The individual hands and the coordination that is their clapping are both apparent. I believe that the genres discussion and science talk are enabling; they support the children's managing of the self-*or*-other/self-*and*-other balance. Vivian and Karen continually demonstrate and engage their children in discourse framed as valuing both distinctive voice and joined voices. These genres are events of individuality:

> "Discussions are try-not-to-interrupt activities in which one person at a time speaks."
> "The point is to get as many ideas as possible. . . "
> Discussions are expected "to bring out individual points of view and differences." (Paley, personal communication, April 26, 1996)
> "[E]very idea is taken seriously. " (Gallas, 1995, p. 43)

They are also events of connectedness:

> The inquiry act reaches out to others: "Does this puzzle you as it does me?"
> "The teacher connects one contribution to others . . . made."
> "The children continually ponder a [shared] question."
> The understanding is that "discussing some problem in the formal, full-class review is . . . helpful." (Paley, personal communication, April 26, 1996)
> Participants engage in "the construction of a discourse." (Gallas, 1995, p. 99)
> "It's important . . . [to] say one thing . . . and let people think about it." (Gallas, 1995, p. 87)

The child's "structures of expectation" in discussion and science talk include "I articulate my wondering" and also "I collaborate with others in exploring an issue."

It is the collaboration, the sharing of (the creation of) territory, that offers the possibility of changed consciousness for all participants. As we saw in the Jill, Justin, and Susan transcripts, "going beyond" was evident in the talk of both the children and their parents, whether in the role of addressor or addressee. As the territory belonged to all, so too did the possibility of changed consciousness. And so it is in the discussion and science-talk transcripts: one participant's utterance opens a new possibility for others. The power of these events is that they are dialogic, bringing multiple voices into collaboratively creating a text, a relationship, an understanding that none could have forged alone. This is the power of inquiry discourse; this is the power of the classroom.

I like to think of Jill, Justin, and Susan participating in discussions and science talks when they come to school. What wonderfully expanded consciousness-changing possibilities these would offer beyond the children's home genres. Participating in such interactive inquiry events, these emergent inquirers would come to know in a new way the generative power of inquiry: that inquiry *of* itself (in the talk of teachers and children) creates *beyond* itself (in the changed consciousness that is possible for all).

What are we to make of the teacher's sense that she is giving something up when she takes children's inquiry seriously, even to the extent of making it the fundamental shared expectation in collaborative inquiry genres such as discussion and science talks? What does she lose? I submit that what the teacher is giving up is *control* but not *power*. Indeed, in exploratory classroom genres, the measure of her loss of control may be precisely the measure of her gain in power, for if her goal in such events is to better understand the children's thinking, then the more that the thinking can reveal itself, the more fully she reaches her goal. This occurs when the child's intellectual act of thinking becomes the social, expressive act of utterance.

In collaborative inquiry events such as discussions and science talks, I hear empowered children. I also hear empowered teachers.

CHAPTER 9

Inquiry Style

Is there such a thing as individual inquiry style? The question is really two questions. The first is about individual distinctiveness, what some call *voice:* At any given moment, do we hear distinctive personal presence in inquiry acts and events? The second is about stability or continuity over time, what some call *style:* Do individuals have characteristic ways of inquiry across diverse situations? Do individuals sound and act like particular recognizable selves when they inquire in different contexts, at different times, allowing others to say of them, "Yeah, that's Lyn, all right" or "Doesn't sound like Joseph somehow"?

Our focus is children: Do children inquire in ways that are *distinctive* in the moment and *characteristic* over time? In the first half of this chapter we focus on the distinctive (voice), first in a general sense and then in relation to inquiry specifically; in the second half we focus on the characteristic (style) in children's acts of inquiry.

VOICE

One of the stories Jill often asked her mother to read to her at bedtime was *Curious George Goes to the Hospital* (Rey & Rey, 1966), the story of a mischievous monkey who eats a puzzle piece thinking it is candy, and has to go to the hospital to have it removed. As her mother reads this book aloud, Jill has many inquiries. And because the book is so familiar and Jill knows the story line so well already, her inquiries are as diverse as they are abundant (Roser & Martinez, 1985). Some of her inquiries are predictable.

> In the story, a package arrives for the man George lives with and, since the man is not home, George is tempted to open it. "George could not resist," Mother reads, and Jill asks, "What does resist mean?"
> George is taken to the hospital and Mother reads, "I'll call a nurse

175

and have her take you to the admitting office." Jill asks, "What's admitting office?"

These we might well have predicted. However, the majority of Jill's inquiries are quite unpredictable, moving beyond the specific words of the text.

"Do you really take a monkey to a real hospital?" asks Jill, an inquiry
that is not directly related to the words of the text.
Mother reads, "Betsy [a child in the hospital with George] was
scared," and Jill responds, "I'm not scared. Are you scared?"

Some of her unpredictable inquiries show her attentiveness to the book's illustrations:

"What does that feel like?" Jill asks, pointing to a picture of an iv.
The climax of the story is captured in a two-page spread that pictures
George speeding down a ramp in a runaway go-cart, about to
crash into men pushing lunch carts, and doctors and nurses
showing the mayor around. But Jill does not ask about this im-
minent disaster. She asks, instead, about a minute figure (with
his leg in a cast), watching the action from the top edge of the
page: "How can he stand up with a broken leg?"
And when, at the story's end, George and his friend are in the car,
ready to drive home, and a nurse is pictured running toward
them, arm outstretched, holding a small box (containing the rescued puzzle piece), Jill asks, "Mommy, do you like to ride in the
front or the back?"

What a wonderfully unique voice we hear in Jill's inquiry. Yet perhaps it should not surprise us that this is so. Even adults who are well
informed in the ways of children oftentimes cannot anticipate what will
gain a child's attention in a given situation, sparking the child's curiosity
to the point where it becomes the social act of inquiry. Surely if there is
one place in a child's language where we would expect to hear an absolutely distinctive voice, that place will be a child's inquiry, for it is there
that the child literally voices his purposes, his focus, his stance toward
topic and toward partner, his expressive ways, his valuing, his level of
engagement, his structuring of the interaction event. His "imprint of individuality" (Bakhtin, 1986, p. 75). His *voice*.

But what is voice? Current discussions about voice have to do with
writing rather than talk. Insofar as talk is considered at all, it is by way
of identifying aspects of audible voice that relate to metaphoric voice

(voice in writing), for example, that individuals have unique voices ("voiceprints"), that an individual uses the voice differently in different contexts and with different partners, that the voice conveys one's feelings and moods, that it "issues from inside us and is a sign of life" (Elbow, 1994, pp. 3–4). Elbow distinguishes five characterizations of voice in writing that enter the current debate (and are relevant to a consideration of inquiry voice):

1. *Audible voice.* Elbow suggests that "hearing a [written] text is the norm" (p. 7) and when we are unable to hear speech in/through an author's written words, it is often because the author has arranged his words so they are unlike speech, or else because—as a member of a particular "culture of literacy"—the writer has deliberately attempted "to maximize the difference between speech and writing" so as to keep self distant from the text (p. 8).
2. *Dramatic voice.* This is to hear a character in the text, though not necessarily the speaker/writer himself.
3. *Distinctive voice.* This interpretation focuses on voice as a recognizable style that we identify with a particular author, although again the voice is not necessarily the author's "own self." It is a way or ways of expression that we associate with a particular writer.
4. *Authoritative voice.* Speaking/writing with sureness, strength, confidence is the essence of this interpretation. The expression conveys a sense of one who "ha[s] the authority to speak or wield influence" (p. 15).
5. *Resonant voice.* This is the author's own presence in the text. "[R]esonant voice in writing . . . has the self's resources behind or underneath it" (p. 20).

Resonant voice is the interpretation that matches Bakhtin's notion: "All of us who make utterances . . . whether spoken or written, are . . . authors. We operate out of a point of view and shape values into forms. How we do so is the means by which we *articulate who we are*" (italics mine) (Clark & Holquist, 1984, p. 10).[1]

I believe that resonant voice best characterizes inquiry voice, for if there is one place where voice is "a picture of the mind" (Elbow, 1994, paraphrasing Cicero, p. 4)—the very sound of one's consciousness at work—surely that place is inquiry utterances. It is worth noting, too, that Holquist's gloss for voice, as Bakhtin uses this term, is "the speaking personality, the speaking consciousness" (quoted in Bakhtin, 1981, p. 434). I hear in this definition of voice the personal ("*person*-ality") and intellectual ("consciousness") and social (a personality that is "speaking") aspects whose perfect union is the essence of inquiry utterances.

Clearly Elbow's five characterizations of voice overlap, and the major point of overlap is individual distinctiveness:

1. *Audible voice* is the "voiceprint," the individual sounding in his speech, in a recognizable way. The "voiceprint" does not identify the speaker/author as conclusively as the thumbprint or signature does, but the sound is individually identifiable nonetheless.
2. *Dramatic voice* is the inevitable distinctiveness of *a* particular character, the sensed presence of a particular human standing in the text.
3. *Distinctive voice* is just that: distinctive, expressive ways we recognize as those of so-and-so.
4. *Authoritative voice* suggests a force, a strength that necessarily belongs to someone.
5. *Resonant voice* is surely the most distinctly individual of all, for this interpretation asserts that it is the real person of the author that enters the text, not a "person" created to achieve an intentional effect. In this view, voice is the author's person, not persona.

What does this focus on voice as individual distinctiveness have to do with inquiry? A great deal, I think. The dialogue about voice in writing invites deeper reflection on voice in children's inquiry acts and events (especially those in classrooms).

INQUIRY VOICE

When I think of Jill, Justin, and Susan, I "hear" distinctive voices in the transcripts we have considered. In each one, the child is very much engaged in inquiry, attempting to elicit the parent's help in furthering his or her understanding. Jill attempts to learn more about animals' ways and hospital experience; Justin explores bird language, crying, and heaven; and Susan, inserting inquiry episodes into a narrative event, tries to visualize story characters and actions. In the next section of this chapter we'll consider the question of the continuity of individual voices across specific events and contexts. But here the question is whether, in these particular transcribed conversations, we hear distinctive inquiry voices.

Voice can only sound against our genre expectations. These are the ground against which—and because of which—distinctive voice emerges as figure. "[S]peech genres [are] relatively stable and normative forms" (Bakhtin, 1986, p. 81). What are our genre expectations for these transcript events? What do we consider normative? We have different frequently occurring events here: two bedtime-story-reading conversations, a bedtime-storytelling interaction, and a conversation during the ride to nursery school. Inquiry figures prominently in each one. The children's expression of their topics reveals a stance of curiosity. Each child turns to the parent in uncertainty and in expectation that the parent is both willing and able to help. The children's inquiry acts initiate episodes in which they collaborate with their partners in constructing texts that satisfy their inquiry intent (e.g., by providing answers, by carrying exploration/wondering further, by confirming). Thus Jill, Justin, and Susan conform to our (and presumably their) expectations for inquiry expression within these interactive events. It is against these expectations that their distinctive voices sound.

Jill

How is Jill's inquiry voice distinctive in the bedtime-story conversations? How does it stand out against our expectations? She frequently counters and challenges in a way that commands attention (especially in the "Nest-es" transcript). My expectation is that the inquirer's utterance acknowledges the partner as a likely source of the information she seeks, and that she turns toward the partner ready to receive what the partner offers. I expect to hear this in the inquirer's expression. But Jill often surprises me. "Uhn-uhn!" says Jill when mother tells her that "fish lay eggs" and "Nuh unh!" is her response when mother says that "turtles lay eggs." Even in the more open conversation about hospital experience, Jill's response, though sometimes accepting, is at other times evaluative ("Yuk"). I hear this evaluating, countering, challenging as "fiesty inquirer." It is a way of turning toward the partner that I do not expect. I do not hear this expressive aspect as evidence of inadequate mastery of this genre—as Jill not yet knowing how to inquire appropriately within this event. Quite the opposite. I hear a self who has considerable competence in doing bedtime-story conversation and thus is able to use this event for her inquiry purposes. "The better our command of genres, the more freely we employ them, the more fully and clearly we reveal our own individuality in them" (Bakhtin, 1986, p. 80). We hear Jill's "own individuality" loud and clear in her inquiry.

I also hear "persistent" in Jill, and this may have to do with length.

What constitutes "resolution" of her initial inquiry is far more than I expect. In fact, her initial inquiry in each episode ("Where do rabbits really
sleep?" and "Mommy, when I went to the hospital, did I cry when they
first put that thing on me?") barely hint at what is to come, her real
agenda: to build a body of information about animals' ways (not just
rabbits and not just sleeping) and to build in her imagination a rich picture of hospital experience. There is more here than her initial inquiries
lead me to expect. I am listening for prototypic patterns of inquirer asks/
partner provides/inquirer accepts. But Jill pushes much further. Again
this is not a matter of limited competence in carrying out inquiry episodes in bedtime-story conversations. Rather, it is Jill's facility with this
genre—especially with ways of inquiry within it—that enables her to
manipulate the event so effectively for her inquiry purposes. *Her* purposes. The purposes that are *Jill*—this particular self at this particular
moment.

Justin

The distinctive voice that speaks to me in Justin's inquiry is very
different from Jill's. I hear a voice that is more pensive and reflective, a
voice that borders on wondering (rather than information seeking). I hear
"reflective" in the forms Justin chooses. His conversation is heavy with
noninterrogative forms, which are more indirect expressions of inquiry
acts than are interrogatives. His talk is also heavy in "maybes." And when
he counters his mother's information, it is with "Yeah, but . . ." rather than
with the directly confrontational voice that is Jill's. Justin and his mother
ride to and from nursery school many times each week. They talk with
one another as they go. And because Justin well knows the possibilities
for talk within this frequent event, he, like Jill, can use it for his purposes,
can speak within it in his own distinctive voice.

In Justin's (and his mother's) combinations of forms in the construction of the whole, I hear "exploratory probing." In Jill's (and her mother's)
text, I hear a voice that is amassing data. The data-gathering sound may
be due to the fact that question-answer pairings dominate their conversation. Justin gathers information from his mother too, but they talk in clusters that negotiate possible meanings, clusters that include question-
answer pairings but are not dominated by them. The resulting voice
sounds exploratory, probing.

As with Jill's conversation, so with Justin's: The length surprises me.
Both Jill and Justin pursue their topics beyond perfunctory resolution,
but what I hear as "persistence" in Jill, I hear as "probing" in Justin.

Susan

With Susan and her father, the event is storytelling. It does not surprise me that Susan inserts inquiry episodes into this narrative event, but the episodes themselves offer some surprises. What strikes me about Susan's inquiry is both how visually oriented it is and how she herself provides so much of the information she seeks, turning to the partner for confirmation of her ideas. The first of these, visual orientation, is doubtless influenced by the event itself, in which Susan is imagining the world her father creates in his story. Yet her imagination could equally work to construct other sorts of details—sounds, perhaps, or relationships or motivations or actions. But Susan is drawn to the visual: the height of the pixie queen, the color of her hair, the movement of the dancers, the "hot dog" look of Albert the Abalone, his way of sitting, the presence/absence of his appendages. Given that anything could possibly arouse curiosity and thus be the topic of Susan's inquiry, it is noteworthy that a visual orientation predominates.

Susan's pattern of providing the very information she seeks influences the structure of the text she and her father construct. Her pattern is to ask for information, and then, on receiving it, to ask for confirmation of one or more of her own conjectures. "And why do they [the pixies] disappear?" she asks Jack. "Well, they just disappear in the daytime," he replies. And it is Susan who supplies the reason by making a suggestion and inviting Jack's confirmation of it: "Because they have to go to sleep at daytime?" Discussion of Irmagold's (and her own) age, of Albert's squatting, and of his foot follow a similar pattern. Though her preferred inquiry form is interrogative, it more often seeks confirmation of her own idea than eliciting information from her partner. Susan does the bulk of the work toward answering as well as asking:

Not "How old was she?" but rather, "Was she four?"
Not "What does Albert the Abalone look like?" but rather, "Does Albert the Abalone have any toes? Did he look like a hot dog? Can you stick Albert the Abalone's foot out? Does Albert the Abalone have any arms?"

Susan seems to be contributing more specific information about Albert than Jack is, which runs counter to our expectation that inquirers seek information and their partners provide it. Susan enacts inquiry within this storytelling genre in her own way and for her own purposes. Again the impression is that of mastery of a genre enabling a distinctive inquiry voice to speak within and through it.[2] These distinctive voices stand out against the background of my expectations for how inquiry works in the interaction events the children are participating in. If I hear Jill's inquiry voice as fiesty, it is only because her voice is fiestier than I expect in a child's bedtime-story conversation. To say that Justin's inquiry voice is reflective or that Susan's is oriented toward confirmation of her ideas is only to say that the presence of these characteristics somehow differs from my expectations.

INQUIRY VOICE AND EXPECTATION

Now if it is the case that Jill's, Justin's, and Susan's individual inquiry voices emerge against the background of my expectations, then it must also be the case that the voices I hear are as much a product of *my* making as they are of the *speaker's* making. To what extent does Jill's fiestiness reside in Jill, and to what extent does it reside in my "fiestiness expectations" for bedtime-story conversation? Clearly, as listener/responder I actively participate in creating these distinctive inquiry voices, just as I do when I interpret the meaning and purpose of a speaker's utterance. Once again, speaker and listener/responder are inextricably joined in the creation of the language act, specifically in the creation of voice in the utterance.

Central to the current discussion about voice in writing is the question of whether voice is face or mask, person or persona. Do we hear the real author in the text, or do we hear a crafted voice constructed to create a particular impression? Do we hear who the author is, or only who the author wants us to think he is? Whatever the answer to this question turns out to be in the area of writing, I believe that the voice we hear in a child's inquiry act is more real than crafted. Bakhtin's (1981) notion of voice as "the speaking *person*ality, the speaking consciousness" (p. 434) is particularly relevant in inquiry, for the inquirer seeks to understand, not to impress; to probe, not to perform. Inquiry is perhaps the most continuous and compelling thing we do. If there is a person anywhere in discourse—a self and not just a mask—surely we will find it in acts of inquiry.

Of course, in any language act there is some shaping of a speaker's expression toward the partner, and one might reasonably argue that this shaping constitutes a certain crafting: As I inquire, I do so nicely so that you will want to respond helpfully to this nice person. This might seem to be mask after all. Yet insofar as it is mask at all, it is not the comedian's or tragedian's opaque mask that hides the real actor, substituting another in his place. Rather, it must be the whiteface of the mime through which the actor's own face reveals itself. In the fifth and sixth graders' literature discussions, the kindergartners' discussions, the first and second graders' science talks, I hear children taking one another into account as they talk, but I do not hear them crafting personalities in order to create some impression on the other participants. I hear them engaging with others in order to pursue their understanding.

This notion of the inquirer's voice as the "real person" has important consequences for teachers. If we hear an inquiry voice that—against the background of our expectations—sounds insistent or off the wall or rude, then we hear the *child himself* as insistent, off the wall, rude. We say, "That child is so insistent," not "That child expresses his inquiries in an insistent way" or "That child creates insistent-sounding text." We know the inquirer through his words. It is the person, not the text, that *sounds*. Vološinov (1973) insists that although it is often assumed that the person creates language, actually the opposite is true: Language creates the person. The child's *inquiry utterances* create (our perception of) the *inquirer*. Our only notion of the inquirer *behind* the act, is the inquirer we hear *in* the act.

Of course, we do not necessarily perceive the child inquirer in negative ways. We may "hear" him in positive ways as well. We might say of a child whose inquiries surprise us, "He's a bit flaky." On the other hand, we might say of him, "He's so lively, so innovative, so bright, such a creative thinker." But whether positive or negative, our perception of the child is likely to be influenced by the inquiry voice we hear, the strong presence of person we hear in the talk.

As a teacher, I find it disconcerting to realize that if I consider a student (through his inquiry voice) rude or pushy, impulsive or disrespectful, it is *I* as much as the student who have created this person whose voice I hear. I have created him in terms of my own expectations for inquiry expression. It is even more unsettling when the student comes from a culture different from my own. My creation of his person (through his inquiry voice) is especially problematic in this case, for he and I speak and listen against different discourse expectations. It is no wonder that an inquirer one teacher hears as insistent another hears as persevering and engaged, or that an inquirer one teacher hears as intellectually creative another hears as irrelevant and always off the subject.[3]

To say that inquiry voice is distinctive is not to say that it is always the same. If voice is the person, it must be many faceted, because the individual is many faceted. As fiesty as Jill is, she has her more reflective moments. Justin is reflective, but not always and only reflective. Seeking confirmation is not Susan's only way. We know from research (and personal experience) that speakers adapt their expression to each social situation, taking into account the participants (age, status, familiarity, etc.), the genre, the public or private nature of the event, the formality level, the topic, the time, the place, and so on. We can be sure that Jill's, Justin's, and Susan's inquiry voices will sound differently in various classroom events. These children are not Johnny-One-Notes. Their inquiry voices, like their inquiry selves, are richly textured.

There is another sense, too, in which these children's inquiry voices are not single. The inquiry voices of others reverberate in these children's "own" voices.

> The unique speech experience of each individual is shaped and developed in continuous and constant interaction with others' individual utterances. This experience can be characterized to some degree as the process of *assimilation*—more or less creative—of others' words. . . . Our speech . . . is filled with others' words, varying degrees of otherness or varying degrees of "our-own-ness." . . . These words of others carry with them their own expression, their own evaluative tone, which we assimilate, re-work, and re-accentuate. (Bakhtin, 1986, p. 89)

And so in their own inquiry voices, Jill, Justin, and Susan *own* others' inquiry voices too, which they have "assimilat[ed], re-work[ed], and re-accentuate[d]." From the limited examples we have considered from these children's interactions with their parents, we could not hope to identify the others' inquiry voices that live within each of these children. Yet I think we can hear in Jill's fiesty voice, echoes of her mother—a strong, assertive, countering presence. And so with Justin and his mother. Justin inclines toward accommodation, negotiation, compromise, working through. So does his mother. Surely this is no coincidence. In Susan's voice, the echoes of her father are quite specific: She often incorporates his very words (Albert the Abalone is as happy as a clam, looks like an upside-down bowl, was once a handsome prince), though these are appropriated to serve her own confirmation-seeking purposes. Yet however much others' voices resound in Jill's, Justin's, and Susan's, these children's voices are not simply repositories for the voices of others. Rather, these children select, combine, and shape other voices into the new creations we hear as *Jill, Justin, Susan*.

If indeed a child's inquiry voice is populated by the inquiry voices of others, then collaborative exploratory events in classrooms become terribly important. What is literature study, science talk, discussion, if not an array of inquiry voices that the emergent inquirer encounters and may "assimilate, re-work, re-accentuate"? These voices may enrich his own ever-emergent inquiry voice.

If it is also the case that inquiry voice is jointly constructed by speaker and listener, then there is a third sense in which the inquiry voice of the speaker is not single. The speaker's voice is partly shaped by the response of the addressee in any interaction. Voice belongs to and is created by the speaker and the partner(s) as they collaborate in constructing the text in which the inquirer's voice is heard.

Inquiry voice, then, (1) adapts to different situations, (2) appropriates the voices of others, and (3) is constructed in partnership with others. Does it make sense to talk of (singular) voice at all? Voices perhaps. Is there some stable self across this range of adapted, appropriated, collaboratively constructed voices? Clearly Jill's, Justin's, and Susan's voices sounded distinctively in the conversations we have studied. But at different moments and in different contexts, do these children inquire in somewhat predictable expressive ways that confirm our expectations ("Just like Jill!"), or that surprise us ("Now that's strange coming from Susan"; "Justin wasn't himself in discussion today")? If so, we must have some sense of a stable, continuing, characteristic inquiry self that resounds in the child's inquiry behavior across social contexts.

INQUIRY STYLE

Drawing on Teachers' Experience

The 12 to 14 graduate students in my "Children's Questioning" seminar every year are present or former teachers, each with between 2 and 12 years of teaching experience. They wear various labels: early childhood/kindergarten teacher, math specialist, special education teacher, bilingual specialist, elementary teacher, junior high science teacher, teacher of the deaf, and so on. Several weeks into the semester, I invite them to engage in a brainstorming activity to help us begin focusing on inquiry style: Is there such a thing? What does it look and sound like in children? I tell them, "We're going to try something here. You've all worked with lots of children. I want you to think about some different ways that children have of inquiring. We're going to do this in pairs of opposites (in their inquiry, some children tend to X but others tend to Y) not because we expect to find children at polar extremes, but only because we're trying to identify dimensions along which inquiry behavior can range. For example, some researchers have suggested impulsive-reflective as such a dimension. Don't worry about overlap. Just say anything that comes to mind."

Each time I have done this, I have been a bit nervous, expecting to be greeted with either stony silence or confusion. But this has not happened. The students jump in immediately, calling out their suggestions as I write them on the chalkboard. There is no "What do you mean?" No "Could you please clarify?" They *know* what I mean. Quickly the chalkboard fills with their suggestions. I write until there are no more. The following actual unedited list from one class is typical:

> impulsive —— reflective
> global/whole —— parts
> linear —— nonlinear
> theoretical/abstract —— concrete/practical
> sequential —— random
> methodical —— serendipitous
> verbal —— imagistic
> product oriented —— process oriented
> active (physical) —— still
> searcher —— observer
> synthesizer —— analyzer
> wonderer —— sense-maker
> toward closure —— toward opensure
> inductive —— deductive
> depth —— breadth
> *****<> —— <>***** (As far as I can remember, this represented doing things such as observing or trying out first and then inquiring, versus inquiring first and then doing things.)
> facts/factual —— ideas/conceptual
> logical —— intuitive
> serious/goal directed —— playful
> planful —— spontaneous
> accepting —— considering (critical)
> risk taker —— cautious
> outside/distant/removed —— inside/within
> formal —— informal
> competitive —— cooperative
> solitary —— social

A brainstorming exercise, nothing more. We can call the inquiry dimensions the students generate and the means of generating them unscientific, and so they are. But there is a great deal of experience in that classroom with me year after year—12 to 14 graduate students each with 2 to 12 years of teaching experience, each of those years teaching some 25 children—a lot of experience. And it is real experience with real children engaged in real acts of inquiry, not experience involving children carrying out the controlled tasks of psychologists' designs in "uncontaminated" situations. I trust these students as a valid source of information about children trying to understand their world with the help of others.

It is immediately obvious from my students' brainstormed list that these (practicing and former) teachers need no Bakhtinian lectures about the union of action and language in children's inquiry. Through memory, they see and hear their child inquirers saying and doing, and they characterize the children's inquiry ways in terms of both. Individual inquiry style is what they think of. Style includes voice, but is more than voice. Voice focuses on the author's presence in his words; it is "the *speaking personality*"—the rhythms and intonation, the word choices and phrasings, and so on. But inquiry style is more inclusive, embracing the inquirer's ways with action as well as with words.

As my students and I discuss their suggested inquiry style dimensions further, it becomes clear that these teachers recall their students as stable inquiry selves across specific moments and situations. This feature of stability, coupled with the language-and-action composite feature, defines style as I am using it here. My students' recall of individual children as stable inquiry selves squares with the experience that I frequently have when I observe in a classroom. A particular child will pique my interest, and after the children have gone, I'll ask the teacher about him. "Tell me about Octavio," I say. And the teacher does—by providing a portrait of Octavio when he "is himself" (in contrast to his ways of behaving when he is "not himself"). Her verbal portrait does what artists' portraits do: captures some continuing essence of the person. In describing Octavio, the teacher does not summarize a conscientious collection of the total body of data relating to Octavio's behavior. Rather, she selects telling details that capture and portray what she feels is the essence of the self she knows as Octavio. She does not tell me specifics of what he did yesterday during math or music unless these serve as examples of Octavio's characteristic (or uncharacteristic) behavior.

Drawing on Research

We are well aware that individuals modify their behavior in response to each new situation, yet it does not square with our experience to deny enduring, across-situation continuities of personality. "We are obliged to experience ourselves [and others] as invariant across circumstances and continuous across time," says Bruner (1996, p. 16). We believe in some sort of enduring entity. Indeed, to say that an individual modifies his behavior in different contexts is to imply that there is some basic reality of individual behavior that "gets modified." We sense a stable, continuing, single center that holds self together, and we even take it as a sign of mental illness when the center does not hold. We speak of "divided self," or "split personality," of someone "at war with himself." We wonder what is wrong when someone we know is "not himself." We do not expect self to be single voiced or single styled, but we do expect the moment-to-moment behavior to emanate from a stable source. I think of centripetal and centrifugal forces again—the balance between the pulling out from the center (the diversity) and the pulling in toward center (the stability). We expect an individual's behavior to adapt to each social situation, but we do not expect it to fly outside of the individual's own orbit. We seem to think of "self" as a single personality with many sides, rather than as multiple personalities somehow cobbled together. The very phrase "multiple personality" signals mental illness.

And so when my students tell me about their children's inquiry styles, they are describing typical tendencies of particular children—preferred ways of perceiving, of acting, of expressing. They are suggesting that these ways are individually distinctive and that they show some coherence and constancy across momentary acts. From one perspective, it may seem strange to perceive inquiry style this way; yet from another perspective, it seems inevitable. We seem, as Bruner (1996) says, "obliged" to do this.

The obligation to experience self "as invariant across circumstances and continuous across time" is fundamental in our attempts to understand human behavior. Case-study research offers the classic example. When Dyson (1989, 1992) studies children's writing development within the social community that is their classroom, she studies Jake and Mitzi, Jameel and Lamar. And it is their styles she describes, "their individual styles as symbolizers and socializers" (1989, p. 104). She assumes that these styles—each individual writer's "approaches" and "preferred ways of responding" (1989, p. 259)—will show some continuity from day to day. She knows that Jake's and Mitzi's socializing and symbolizing ways will change over time. Indeed, a major reason to study these developing writers is to observe these changes. But whatever the changes, Jake will still be Jake, Mitzi still Mitzi. Dyson expects change, but not total discontinuity and disconnection. She also assumes that an individual child's moment-to-moment behavior will form a pattern, not simply a collection. And so Dyson can characterize one child as "a collaborative player and a social critic" (1992, p. 85), another as "a joyful performer" (1992, p. 98), descriptors that only make sense if there is some relatively stable identity. For all the diversity in a child's interaction in each social situation, and for all the child's changes over time, Dyson can characterize each child's ways because they are characteristic across the diversity. The child's momentary behavior surprises us or doesn't, against the continuing characteristic ways we recognize as Jake or Mitzi, Jameel or Lamar.

Fillmore's (1983) research provides another good example, this one from second-language learning. She observed Chinese (Cantonese)-speaking and Spanish-speaking children who were learning English as their second language, from the beginning of kindergarten to the end of second grade. She identified "language-learning style characteristics" and "social-style characteristics" in these language learners (categories that may remind you of Dyson's "symbolizers" and "socializers"). Fillmore observed and described the differential use subjects made of available resources as they attempted to learn English. Individual learners relied to greater or lesser degrees on various "language-learning style characteristics" such as verbal memory, verbal fluency and flexibility, and sensitivity to linguistic context and patterning, and on "social-style characteristics" such as outgoingness, desire for contact with others, talkativeness, and activity preferences (more interactive or more solitary) (Fillmore, 1983, pp. 160–161). Together, language-learning style characteristics and social-style characteristics for any given child combined to give a unique and relatively stable "portrait."

The key word in reading miscue analysis is *strategy*, not *style* (Goodman, Watson, Burke, 1987), but again the assumption is of a continuing approach that is characteristic of a given child. The underlying question is, From the options available for making sense of print, which does this child draw on especially and how does he use them? We observe particular oral reading behaviors in a given child, identify the strategies that these reveal, and assume that he will rely on similar strategies when he interacts with other texts at other moments. Indeed, if we did not make this assumption, miscue analysis could not inform our understanding of the child reader.

These are only three examples from language education research (studies of young children's development of reading, writing, and English as a second language). Notice the absence of absolutes. Reading this case study literature, one swims in a sea of nonabsolute words such as *tendency, preference, orientation, approach, inclination, likely* (to). These words create profiles of individual children who select and use available linguistic and social resources in ways that leave their own recognizable marks. Basic to all three studies is the notion of self as coherent, and style as the continuing expression of coherent self.

Now what about children's inquiry? Does that area of children's behavior—like literacy and (second-) language development—reveal distinctive individual styles that show continuity across time and circumstance? This is not the first time this question has been raised, nor is it the first time the hunch has been that the answer is *yes*. Kenzie (1977) reports a little-known but rather intriguing research study in which he attempted to develop a set of tasks that would assess "individual manipulative curiosity and inquiry style" (p. 2) in children. This in itself is important, for Kenzie was not asking, "Is there such a thing as inquiry style?" He was assuming that there is, and his research was oriented toward trying to "capture" it (e.g., describe it, devise ways to assess it and to facilitate it). In an interview setting, Kenzie presented each of 10 primary-grade children with five puzzling phenomena (e.g., a roller that rolled uphill or a plasticine ball that bounced on some surfaces but not on others). For each task, the researcher followed a set of eight steps, attempting to "elicit surprise, puzzlement, manipulative curiosity and inquiry" (p. 3) from the child in relation to the puzzling item. Then the child was free to explore the item and the researcher conversed with the child informally, following the child's lead. Every session (child engaging with five tasks, one at a time) was tape-recorded and nonverbal behaviors were recorded by hand. Each child's behavior was described in terms of six central qualities for each task: (1) surprise, puzzlement and wonder, (2) intrinsically motivated manipulative curiosity, (3) ideation about causes or conditions of the phenomena, (4) experimentalism, (5) objectivity/bias, (6) reasoning. The descriptions resulting from the task situations turned out to be similar to descriptions of the same children when they were observed in several small-group inquiry situations in their classrooms. Also, the descriptions from the task situations matched the teachers' perceptions of the children's ways of exploring. This is not surprising, for I assume that these teachers knew their children.

I believe that an important part of what a teacher knows when she "knows her children" is inquiry selves, each with a unique profile, a stable-self-across-contexts style that is a set of expected tendencies, orientation, stance—preferred language-and-action ways of relating to phenomena of interest and of engaging others in his sense-making. Yes, every response to every social situation is unique, but more often than not, it is in character. No wonder that my students respond as they do when I ask them to suggest polar points on dimensions of inquiry styles. They are (present or former) teachers who know their children, including their inquiry ways. Also, they live in a society that expects self to be stable.

It makes sense to ask what each child's inquiry style is like. It is also helpful to do so, for this aspect of a teacher's knowledge of her children enables her to appreciate, foster, and extend the inquiry ways of each emergent inquirer.

The child's inquiry style distinguishes him *from* others, while connecting his unique inquiry self *with* others. His characteristically distinctive hands are ever engaged in the coordinated act of clapping.

CHAPTER 10

Inquiry Style in the Classroom

Ask a parent to tell you about embarrassing moments with her child, and it probably won't be long before she gets to "the time my child asked an embarrassing question." The "question" is invariably a curious child's act of inquiry. Consider the case of my 5-year-old nephew Kevin.[1]

Besides Kevin, the cast of characters includes his mother and father, his mother's elderly Aunt Ida and Uncle Walter, and several other adult relatives (including myself). We were all in the host's living room, talking informally as a group while the hostess (another of Kevin's great-aunts) was getting dinner to the table. Feeling somewhat chilly, Aunt Ida still had her mink stole around her shoulders. In a loud voice, Kevin launched into a conversation with Aunt Ida that went something like this:

> KEVIN: How much did that fur coat cost?
> AUNT IDA: (in a joking voice) Oh, it cost plenty!
> KEVIN: How much?
> AUNT IDA: More money than you've seen in a while. (laughs awkwardly)
> KEVIN: Yeah, but how much did it cost? How many dollars?
> AUNT IDA: Kevin, you sure are interested in money. I think you're gonna be a banker someday.
> KEVIN: Did it cost a hundred dollars? How much?

And so it continued. It wasn't an interminable conversation; it only felt like it. My recollection is that the hostess rescued Aunt Ida (and the rest of us) by announcing that dinner was served.

What went wrong here? Why was this incident so uncomfortable for all of us in that room? After all, we were a cluster of relatives in a pleasant social situation, and a curious child whom we were all fond of did what curious children do: He asked the relevant person to provide the information he was seeking. So what was wrong with that? *Everything*, and that everything reveals what a minefield an inquiring child is in.

Topic is the first mine for the unwary child. Money just happens to be a sensitive subject for many adults in our society, adults such as the ones in that living room. If Kevin had inquired about what kind of fur it was or whether Aunt Ida had gotten it as a birthday gift or why she was wearing just the top part of a fur coat instead of a whole one—any of these would have been fine, but the topic of cost was embarrassing. The second mine that Kevin stepped on was addressee. The issue of whom you ask can be tricky. If he had asked his mother or a peer about the cost of a prized possession, it might have worked. But not his great-aunt Ida, an elderly relative he saw only occasionally and did not know very well. It was especially problematic that he asked his question in a group situation. The presence of other people in front of whom the conversation was "performed" heightened the embarrassment, not just for Aunt Ida, but for all of us who were agonizing on her behalf. The fact that we all saw each other rarely and thus did not know each other well—were trying to exhibit "good behavior"—only made matters worse. The child's persistence was a further problem. He simply would not give up. And his behavior also felt rude somehow. He seemed not to be speaking respectfully to his 80-year-old great-aunt.

But although everything in this event went wrong, there is a sense in which Kevin did nothing wrong. What's wrong, after all, with inquiring when you're curious about something? And what's wrong with directing your inquiry to the person who has the information you seek, someone who is fond of you and presumably willing to try to help you understand your world? And what's wrong with persisting until you get an answer? As a society, we value perseverance, and we compliment people for not giving up easily. Well, Kevin was doing just that. And what's wrong with initiating a conversation with one individual who is part of a friendly social group, while others listen in? We do this all the time. And if, from Kevin's point of view, there is nothing wrong, then what is there to be polite about, to manage with special indications of respect? He wasn't being *im*polite—wasn't using rude words or interrupting others. Why should more than this be required by way of conveying respect in this particular instance? Kevin did nothing—and everything—wrong.

As you can see from this example, inquiry acts are acts of imposition. Thus the inquirer must learn to inquire politely, in ways that assure the willing and helpful participation of the partner. In this chapter we focus first on the nature of the imposition inherent in inquiry acts, and then on the politeness they require. Next we consider what can—and often does—go wrong when a student inquires in her classroom. How can the classroom be a safer place for children's inquiry? We address this question next and, finally, reflect on the delicate balancing of self and other that inquiry acts entail.

IMPOSITION IN INQUIRY ACTS

You might be in for some surprises were you to ask a university student to "describe [in writing] a school experience (any grade or in college) where you asked a question and felt bad or discouraged about the response you received." Indira Nath (1994) did this with 307 university freshmen. Stories such as the following were all too typical. (I have preserved the students' exact words, punctuation, and spelling from the original surveys.)

> In 7th grade science I remember asking why we don't have clouds in our houses. I really wanted to know why they could form outside, but not inside. The teacher laughed histerically, as did the class.

> I once asked a question in Chemistry class in High School and my teacher said it was an irrelevant question and I felt embarassed and ashamed. I swore, from that day on that I would never ask another question in class.

> In grade school I asked a question in class, and the student teacher became frustrated and asked me how I could not possibly know the answer by now. I felt stupid and was very hurt. It was a long time before I was able to ask a question without feeling frightened.

> In chemistry Sr. year of HS, I asked a ? and it came out sounding awkward. My teacher told me I asked ?s just to hear myself speak. ACK! [2]

What is puzzling is that teacher after teacher in study after study says that she values student inquiry (or "questioning") and wants to foster it in her classroom. Yet student after student tells personal stories of inquiring in the classroom with dire consequences. Why? The reasons that come to mind first may have to do with the teacher:

- The teacher is insensitive.
- The teacher is under pressure to cover the curriculum or to raise children's test scores. She doesn't have time for student inquiry.
- The teacher is afraid she may not be able to answer students' questions and may lose face.
- The teacher wants to maintain control—does not want to relinquish her power by "turning it over" to the students, as she feels she will have to do if she encourages them to inquire freely.

But although these may sometimes be relevant factors, it is too simplistic to focus only on the teacher. The problem is far more complex, and far more interesting, than this. We can only begin to understand it by considering the nature of inquiry acts themselves. What is it about acts of inquiry that render them so sensitive in our interactions with others, whether in a living room or in a classroom?

Stated simply, inquiry acts are acts of imposition. Think again of our definition of an act of inquiry: a language act that is the speaker's attempt to elicit another's help in going beyond her own present understanding.

- The inquiry act brings participants to the speaker's agenda. The topic, the level of engagement, what constitutes resolution, the orientation itself (wondering, information-seeking)—all these the inquirer establishes in the inquiry act. This is imposition.
- The inquiry act largely determines the shape of the partner's response—how it is slotted into the conversation, what constitutes appropriate content of the partner's turn, what kind of discourse move it will be. This is imposition.
- The inquiry act requires verbal response from the partner—*pulls* more strongly for verbal response than does any other communication act. This is imposition.

No wonder, then, that inquiry acts require care. No wonder that they can easily offend. And because we feel the strong presence of the person in the act, we are likely to consider the person, not simply the language act, imposing.[3] We may celebrate individual inquiry style. We may appreciate the strong sound of a characteristic inquiry self that speaks across specific interaction events. But however strong, unique, characteristic that inquiry self might be, it must also learn to be flexible and diverse, adapting to constraints of genre, topic, participants, context. Above all, the emergent inquirer must learn to inquire *politely.*

POLITENESS AND INQUIRY STYLE

"[P]oliteness . . . is . . . a precondition of human cooperation" (Brown & Levinson, 1987, p. xiii). If there is one area of language where human cooperation is essential, that area is inquiry, for it takes two or more people to complete an act of inquiry. When we think of politeness, we usually think first of particular words—saying "please," "thank you," "excuse me." But Brown and Levinson have something different and larger in mind. To speak politely is to convey that you are taking the partner into account. The emergent inquirer must develop a style both strong and sensitive, expressive ways that simultaneously attend to the desires of self and other in a given situation.

Drawing on data from three unrelated languages (English, Tzeltal, and Tamil), Brown and Levinson (1987) have probed the complexities of *politeness phenomena*. They assert that basic to our interactions with one another is the assumption that we and our partners have "two specific kinds of desires . . . : the desire to be unimpeded in one's actions . . . and the desire . . . to be approved of" (p. 13). [4] Languages provide expressive means (politeness phenomena) for taking care of both of these desires. Brown and Levinson find rank, distance, and power (i.e., status) to be three especially important factors that one must take into account when imposing on another, so as to address the partner's desire to be unimpeded and/or to be approved of.

1. *Power* has to do with the relative status of the addressee and the speaker. To what extent does one have power over the other?
2. *Distance* concerns the question of how close the partners are to one another socially.
3. *Rank* refers to the heftiness of the imposition itself.

The greater the *power* of the addressee over the speaker and the greater the social *distance* between the two and the greater the imposition, the riskier the act is and the more attention the speaker must give to the politeness of her expression, that is, the more her expression must convey her attention to the partner's desire not to be impeded, or to be approved of, or both.

It is easy to see that Kevin's inquiry act was very imposing in terms of Brown and Levinson's factors of power, distance, and rank: Aunt Ida was substantially more powerful than Kevin; she and Kevin, though relatives, were distant in age and in having very limited contact with each other; and the inquiry was a heavy imposition in the sensitivity of the topic, the presence of others, and the persistence in Kevin's manner. It is also easy to see that Kevin's expression in no way suggested attention to Aunt Ida's desire not to be impeded (imposed on, in this case). He simply plunged in, again and again, with no expression of regard for her. His expression did not convey awareness of Aunt Ida's higher status, nor did it acknowledge in any way the heftiness of his imposition (the taboo nature of the topic, the presence of others).

What ways of taking care of Aunt Ida's desires are available in language? This is different from asking what ways were available to Kevin for modifying his style politely, for—being a young child—he was as yet unaware of many of the politeness resources that his language affords. Thus they were not really available to him. What sorts of politeness devices do languages offer?

Brown and Levinson differentiate between "negative politeness"—expression that addresses the desire to be unimpeded (the pull toward respecting separateness), and "positive politeness"—expression that addresses the desire to be approved of (the pull toward connection). For example, drawing on language resources that respect the partner's desire to be unimpeded (negative politeness), a speaker might do such things as "cushion" her expression ("I wonder if you could possibly find the time to X" rather than the direct "Do X"), or make it easy for the partner to refuse ("I don't suppose there's any chance you could X, is there?"), or apologize ("I'm really sorry to bother you, but . . . "). On the other hand, drawing on language resources that foster affiliation (positive politeness) a speaker might compliment the partner or use shared, "in-group" or affectionate terms of address, or seek the partner's agreement (e.g., by using tag questions), or use inclusive words like "we," "us," "let's." In his interaction with Aunt Ida, Kevin did none of these things. His talk expressed neither positive nor negative politeness and thus seemed rude and embarrassing. He was taking care of his desires, but not attending to Aunt Ida's.

Surely it would be unreasonable to expect that these complex and subtle aspects of politeness in imposing acts—inquiry acts specifically—will be well developed in young children. Indeed, even as adults we sometimes find ourselves offending others unintentionally and needing to do "repair work" by upping the politeness component of our talk when we engage in imposing acts. If we do not yet fully control these aspects of polite imposition, surely the young child will not. But over time the child's inquiry style will include an ever wider range of expressive options for conveying that she is taking the (imposed-upon) partner into account. The good news is that the classroom is the best of all possible places for politeness aspects of emergent inquiry style to develop. The essence of events such as discussion, science talks, literature study is taking self *and* other into account. That is the demonstration; that is the engagement.

The point here is not for teachers to become experts in the specifics of positive and negative politeness, or of power, rank, and distance factors. Neither is the point to be able to produce definitions for these. And the point is certainly not for teachers to provide children with a 25-ways-to-inquire-politely curriculum. Rather, the point is to appreciate the remarkable complexity and subtlety of this aspect of emergent inquiry. We can take comfort in the fact that, as adults, we know how to inquire politely and do so ... at least most of the time. Not perfectly, of course. And not always. Our inquiry, too, is ever emergent. Yet it is part of our own communicative competence that we know how to—and (mostly) we *do*—take others into account in our inquiry expression. We cannot explain the intricacies of what we do, but we don't need to. Our own intuitions as mature, expert language users (and inquirers) guide us well. Thus it is inevitable that an attentive teacher will, in her own characteristic ways, draw on the resources her language affords for polite expression of inquiry. Whether she wishes to or not, she demonstrates and engages her children as apprentices in inquiry expression that takes others into account by conveying respect for their separateness, by building solidarity, or both. When Vivian Paley (1981, p. 152) asks, "Are you children saying that you know someone likes you if you remember nice things you did together?" she is not thinking, "Now would be a good time for some positive politeness. I think I'll say something that will let the children know that I am listening intently to what they are saying and that I value their ideas." When Karen Smith (1990) says, "Seems like [Grandma] made it harder on Dicey by not telling her," she is not thinking to herself, "I'll express myself tentatively here ('seems like') so the kids will know they don't have to accept this view and that I'm respecting their right to have a different opinion." And though it is surely an implied compliment when Karen Gallas (1995) invites individual children to repeat their questions for the group to consider, she does not do this in order to demonstrate positive politeness. These teachers are simply attending to others in respectful and connecting ways, and their language inevitably expresses this. This is what it means to be communicatively competent, and these teachers surely are.

It is possible that an increased awareness of ways that politeness works in inquiry expression may help us figure out why it is that the inquiry ways of particular students sometimes annoy or irritate us. Just what IS it that is "going wrong"? If we can figure this out, we may be able to help particular student inquirers, and we may also be better able to separate the *child* from her *expression*. As Kevin and the university stu-

dents at the beginning of this chapter demonstrate, there is much that
can go wrong with acts of inquiry. Which is to say that there is much the
emergent inquirer needs to learn to attend to in her inquiry expression.

THE MINEFIELD

What, exactly, can—and often does—give emergent inquirers trouble
in a classroom?

The Student Inquires About the "Wrong" Thing

The student may inquire about a topic that is taboo or embarrassing,
inappropriate or irrelevant, off the subject or inconvenient and so on. The
list is long. Listen to these university students tell of negative inquiry
experiences in which topic was (part of) the problem.

> It was in high school and in health class I asked a question about
> AIDS and everybody started laughing at me. And till this day I re-
> member them laughing at me and I don't ask many questions be-
> cause of this.

> I asked an instructor of a large class one time and they responded
> with "Well, that really doesn't have anything to do with what I'm
> teaching, but if you want to come to my office during hours we can
> talk about it." NO! Obviously it had *something* to do with the teach-
> ing or I wouldn't have asked.

> There was an incident in my math class when I asked a question
> and my teacher said that my question was pointless and we should
> go on to something that needs further looking at. I felt so unimpor-
> tant and didn't want to ask questions anymore.

These examples suggest instances in which the topic of the student's inquiry was seen as taboo (making the teacher and classmates feel uncomfortable) or off the subject or trivial ("pointless," as the teacher called it).[5]

The Student Inquires at the "Wrong" Time

Timing may have been an issue in the second example above. In telling the student that her question "doesn't have anything to do with what
I'm teaching," the teacher may be saying that the student's inquiry is ill

timed, it doesn't fit into the discussion at that moment. Here is another example.

> I asked my English teacher in high school a question about *Macbeth*
> during the lecture because I was confused. She looked at me
> rudely and said, "If you didn't rudely interrupt, I could get to that."

The words "rudely interrupt" are telling. What is being "interrupted" here? The student's question is not an interruption in the sense of speaking at the same time as the teacher or cutting the teacher off. What is being ("rudely") interrupted is the flow of the teacher's talk, the implementation of her "speech plan." Besides disrupting the teacher's neat lecture design, the student has perhaps stolen her thunder a bit by getting to the point before she does. In any case, the student's insertion of her question at that particular moment is perceived as interruptive. The question is ill timed in the discourse (from the teacher's point of view).

With obvious frustration, a friend of mine who teaches 10th-grade English described a particular student of his this way: "This kid asks really interesting questions. The problem is, we'll be having a class discussion about something, and he sort of drops out and is thinking to himself about what we've been talking about. Then five minutes later he asks this terrific question, but by that time, we've moved on and are talking about something else. I never quite know what to do. I don't want to lose his really interesting question, but I'm afraid if I deal with it at that point, we'll lose the momentum of the discussion."

There is another way a student's inquiry act can be ill timed. This is the situation in which inquiry itself is unwelcome. "We're not doing that right now," that is, the event we're engaging in is not an inquiry event and so inquiring right now is the wrong kind of thing to be doing. Again, the time is wrong.[6]

The Student Asks the "Wrong" Person

A student can be in for some surprises. Sometimes the person a student assumes is the right person turns out not to be. My son's 12th-grade math teacher turned out to be the wrong person. When Erik got a test back and realized he was confused about the use of square brackets and curly braces, he asked his teacher what the difference was between them. Her answer came in a sarcastic voice: "Why don't you students ever read the textbook?" He did not learn the difference between square brackets and curly braces on that occasion, but he did learn that this teacher was the wrong person to ask. In his words, "I said to myself, 'I'll never ask you another question.'" (He never did.)

The status difference between teacher and student (Brown & Levinson's [1987] "power" factor) may need to be managed carefully by the student. Teacher-student relationships live within the larger society's expectations for adult-child relationships, especially how children shall express respect for adults. How often we hear adults express frustration when a child talks to the adult in ways that do not acknowledge the adult's higher status or the child's lower status. "Who do you think you are, talking to me like that!" the adult says angrily (i.e., your way of talking elevates your own status). Or, "Just who do you think you're talking to anyway!" (i.e., your way of talking reduces my status). Given that the child's inquiries are often directed to her teacher, the child will do well to express her inquiry in ways that indicate she knows that "who she is" is a child, and "who she is talking to" is an adult teacher.

The Student Asks "Too Persistently"

A persistent inquirer can be seen as pushy. Listen to Elaine, a 6th grader in an elite private school (Walther, 1978).

> E: Oh, yeah. Okay, if the sun, okay, the sun doesn't have doesn't have to explode; it could just not get oxygen and it could just go out like a candle.
> T: Elaine, we're not going to worry about the sun right now. No, it doesn't because when it is in there, it's billions of years from now and it's not going to . . .
> E: Yeah, I know, but . . . I know, I know, I know.
> T: And it's not going to . . . it's not going to disappear.
> E: I know, I know, I know, but, if it goes out like a candle, then, ahhh, how fast, how long does it take light to get here from the . . .
> (several turns involving the teacher and two other children)
> C: It's, umm, how do you figure out how long it takes, then?
> T: Ahhh, your science book has it figured out for you. The other science book, when we had that astronomy chapter, we figured it out then at . . .
> E: Somewhere I heard that it took a real long time so that if it did go out, we have about . . .
> T: Four and a half light years to the nearest star is what it was.
> E: So, what I was thinking (teacher makes a face)
> T: Elaine, *what!?*

E: Well, what I was going to say was that if it didn't take real long
to get here, like if it did take real long to get here, like if it was
four and a half light years, then we wouldn't have anything to
worry about, if the sun did go out.

T: Okay, we won't worry about that. (pp. 91–92)

One wonders whether persistence was an issue in the following recollection by a university student.

Once I went up to a teacher to make sure I understood . . . and I
was told that I asked too many questions.

The Student Inquires in a Public Setting

The partner is thereby put on the spot with the possibility of losing
face. This can be especially tricky if the one to whom the inquiry act is
directed is the teacher.

I have felt stupid when asking questions before. For example, I
asked a question that everyone else wanted to know the answer
also, but the teacher realized that his point wasn't getting through.
He blew up at me because I pointed that out.

The situation here would have been less problematic (and the teacher
might not have "blown up" at the student) if "everyone else" hadn't been
present. The public nature of this instance contributed to the teacher's
loss of face.

It isn't only the teacher who may lose face in an inquiry situation in
which many people are present. The student's face may be threatened
as well.

I asked a question once in my math class in which the teacher kept
asking me what I was talking about. This discouraged me because
it made me think, "If this lady is going to make an ass out of me in
front of all these people, why should I ask the question?"

Clearly there is teacher insensitivity here, but there is also the presence
of "all these people" that the inquiry is expressed "in front of."

Now add the fact that these various mines interact in complex ways.
The right person at one time and place is the wrong person at another.
An acceptable topic in a private conversation with people one is close
to may be an embarrassing topic in a more public setting with folks one

knows less well. The very persistence that works well when inquiring of peers may be problematic when the partner is an adult. It is no small task to learn to manage these imposing acts graciously. The child may mean to be respectful, but lack the expressive competence for conveying this.[7]

INCREASING THE SAFETY OF INQUIRY IN THE CLASSROOM

Given so much that can misfire, perhaps what should surprise us is not that students' inquiry acts often do *not* work in classrooms, but that they often *do* work, as in the Paley, Smith, and Gallas examples. The children and teachers in science talks, discussions, and literature study inquire vigorously, yet they do not offend. It is worth asking *why*. We can come at this question from two vantage points: Brown and Levinson's (1987) positive and negative politeness, and Goffman's (1974) notion of discourse frame.

Positive and Negative Politeness in Inquiry Events

In the classroom inquiry events we have focused on, Brown and Levinson's (1987) power, distance, and rank factors are all reduced, and this reduction correspondingly reduces the imposition in the inquiry acts. The participating children are peers and thus their power is relatively equal. Paley and Smith are participants in these events, but both contribute ideas, comments, suggestions, wonderings much as the children do. This kind of participation minimizes the asymmetrical power relationship between teacher and children. The status difference is surely not erased, nor should it be. As the children well know, these teachers possess relevant experience and expertise considerably beyond their own. But because their moves in the discussions are similar to those of the students, the "great divide" between teacher and student status is significantly reduced.

Unlike Paley and Smith, Gallas does not participate as a discussant, but leaves the content of the science talks to the children. She helps from the sidelines with the procedural workings of the discussion, but since the discussion itself belongs to the children, the teacher-child status issue is not much of a factor. The inquiry acts belong almost exclusively to the children, who are basically equal in status.[8]

Distance among participants is minimized also because, at the point in the year at which these collaborative inquiry events occur, the classroom members know each other well and have participated in many such events. Each of these classrooms is a strong, close community. As expected, reduced power differences and reduced social distance combine to reduce the rank (the heftiness) of the imposition in these children's inquiry acts.

Brown and Levinson (1987) observe that in situations of greater imposition, we tend to rely more on negative politeness (addressing the partner's desire to be unimpeded), whereas in situations of lesser imposition we are likely to rely more on positive politeness (addressing the partner's desire for solidarity and approval) (p. 60). Indeed, in the discussions, science talks, and literature study examples we have considered, the sound of connection (positive politeness) is stronger than the sound of respect for others' separateness (negative politeness). The kindergartners' shared recollections in the friendship conversation provide a particularly striking example of participants' exploiting affiliative language resources.

Notice that negative politeness is not altogether absent, however. We hear it a bit in the literature study excerpts when, instead of asking a direct question, the student uses a more indirect, "cushioning" phrasing: "There's a part I wanted to ask . . ." We also hear it in students' acceptance of personal responsibility for their understanding. When a student says, "I'm trying to figure out . . ." or ". . . I don't get when . . ." she indicates that although she is turning to the partner for help, she is not saddling the partner with the entire responsibility for her understanding. This is to respect the other's right not to be imposed on. Also, the students sometimes use open, nondirective phrasing ("I wonder why . . .") and typically address their inquiries to the group at large, rather than naming a particular individual to respond, both of which reduce the pressure on individuals in the group. These expressive ways suggest recognition of the imposing nature of inquiry acts and an attempt to lessen it so as not to intrude on (the rights of) others. Contrast this with the kindergartners' and first and second graders' more direct expression: "If voice is matter why isn't it like smushing us against the walls?" "Why can't we really see it happening?" These children just rip in. They don't seem to tiptoe around each other or handle each other with care as the fifth and sixth graders do. (Notice, however, the striking counterexample in Ian's "I want to add something to Ellen's [idea] but I'm *kind of* protesting it.")

However, although the older students sometimes inquire in an accent that respects others' desire to be unimpeded (negative politeness), still the overwhelming impression is one of strong connection—strong reliance on positive politeness: for example, the use of "you know" (". . . because you know how they bury people . . ." "You know it's weird if . . ."), agreements with and echoings of one another ("Yeah," "I know," "It sure is sad"), Karen's articulation of the student's implied inquiry ("And that surprised you?"), her checking of student understanding, and her own inquiries that convey her valuing of students' opinions ("What do you think?"). In all these ways, participants come close, express affiliation and approval, enhance solidarity. However, in all three groups' collaborative inquiry events, it is the linking of each turn to the next (discussed in Chapter 8) that most strongly reveals the forces of connection at work. These interactions foster closeness more than they maintain respectful distance. Affiliation is their dominant way of taking others into account in this inherently imposing kind of discourse.

Frames in Inquiry Events

Goffman's (1974) notion of frame offers a second perspective on why these collaborative inquiry events in our examples work so well. There is little need for negative politeness, because the frame itself reduces imposition. Recall that Goffman defines frame as participants' "answer" to the question "'What is it that's going on here?' . . . the answer . . . is presumed by the way the individuals then proceed to get on with the affairs at hand" (p. 8). "Discussion," "science talk," "literature study"—each names a "frame." It is an answer to the question "What is it that's going on here?" Each of these labeled events is demarked—set off—from other classroom events (particular time, place, group of participants, structure, stance, purpose), and the shared activities within it both reflect and further define it. Literature study, discussions, science talks create safe spaces for inquiry acts. The participants share the understanding that each is an exploratory frame in which inquiry is the essence. The participants are not likely to stumble on the mines discussed earlier. Each of these frames gives wide latitude to what qualifies as "appropriate *topic*." Though these three teachers would doubtless disallow topics which would be hurtful to any member of the group, it is understood as part of the frame, that the range of acceptable topics is very wide. And *time* will not be a problem, for these three frames say to the students, "This *is* the time for inquiry." What about *person*—whom you ask? Again the frame speaks: "*We*—all the members of this group—we are the persons; there is no 'wrong' person here. Our presence in this event identifies us as 'right' persons." The frame supports *persistence* too, even sees it as shared: The expectation is that the inquirer pursues her wondering until she is satisfied and that it is the responsibility of group members to come to the inquirer's agenda and contribute at that point. The *public* nature of inquiry acts that often jeopardizes them and threatens loss of face is taken care of by these frames also. In literature study the group is small, just teacher and six students who are friends and have chosen to explore a book together. That is as public as it is going to get. Discussions and science talks include more participants, but no one is pressured to speak. Thinking one's own thoughts (a distinctly private activity) is participation enough. If one chooses to speak, the understanding is that it is exploratory talk, not performance talk, that is called for, rough-draft talk, not polished prose. Also, it is understood—is part of these frames—that mutual respect and trust "hold" the participants and define each event. This shared understanding reduces the risk of children (or teacher) losing face in front of others.

Two Paradoxes

There are two paradoxes inherent in inquiry acts that make them especially promising places for children to develop both positive and negative politeness. The first paradox has to do with inquiry acts being both imposing acts and complimentary acts. The fact that inquiry acts are acts of imposition encourages the use and development of negative politeness—those language resources of considerateness that respect the partner's right to remain autonomous and unimpeded. But a compliment is built into inquiry acts too, and thus there is implied approval of the partner (an instance of positive politeness). The inquirer says, in essence, "I turn to you in my uncertainty because I believe you to be a person both willing and able to help me." This inherent compliment offers fertile ground for positive politeness, opportunities for fostering approval, connection, affiliation.

The second paradox is that inquiry acts are equally and simultaneously acts that separate the partners and acts that join them. These acts place the partners across from each other: One initiates ("asks"), the other responds ("answers"). There is a canonical opposition here. But just as surely, the two join in that an inquiry act is necessarily jointly constructed. It is not carried out except in partnership. The act is dialogic or it is nothing. And so the inquirer can build on the separateness, the connectedness, or both, inherent in these acts as suits her purposes at a particular moment in a particular situation. Being simultaneously imposing acts *and* complimentary acts, separating acts *and* connecting acts, inquiry offers opportunities par excellence for children to learn ways of balancing self and other, a balance that is the essence of all communication, not just inquiry interaction.

TOWARD SELF-OTHER BALANCE IN CLASSROOM INQUIRY

If it is the case that the emergent inquirer must learn to express her inquiries politely, taking her partners' desires into account, does this mean that her individual inquiry style is compromised, her voice muted?

Does the inquirer who attends to others lose individuality and distinctive presence in the act? I think not. When my voice inclines toward others, it is still *my* voice that does so. I attend to partners' desires in ways that bear my own mark, my own sound. If one's inquiry is concerned only with her own agenda, then the speaking personality risks being strident rather than strong. The point is to develop an inquiry self that is flexible, able to adapt readily to the constraints and possibilities of the context and the moment.

Again I turn to the expressive inquiry selves in the classroom examples. When I listen to the children's inquiry events, I do not hear voices that are muted, nor do I hear voices that are strident and self-centered.

> . . . this [book] shows how to deal with [problems] in a much better way than just start crying, crying, 'cause crying doesn't do much . . .
>
> I like the world the way it is but I don't like fighting.
>
> I don't know what [language] God likes to talk.
>
> . . . remember when you and me were in your father's car sucking our thumbs?
>
> . . . You don't see a chunk of voice flying around if someone says something. It's not like you see these words coming up in a chunk of voice flying up into the air. . . . "Oh, there's your voice."

I hear strong personal *and* other-attending presence here.

Another question arises. Is there something disingenuous here? If we foster politeness in our children's inquiry, are we replacing *style* with *stylistics*? That is, instead of encouraging children to follow their own characteristic inquiry ways, are we encouraging them to substitute expressive trappings used to court the partner so as to keep her good will and thus secure her help? If so, aren't we fostering behavior that is rather phony and manipulative? But again I listen to the children and the teachers in our examples, and the styles I find there do not strike me as disingenuous or self-serving.

> Well maybe she, maybe the grandma couldn't handle it that her last daughter died.
>
> Wait, I changed my mind.
>
> Hey, Wally. Remember at Eddie's birthday party we put those metal kettles on our heads?

> Like if you, like if she can blow up a balloon up with your, with your
> um, with your, um, breath, it, um, must take up, it must be mat-
> ter, sort of.
> I don't know.

I hear sincere, spontaneous utterances, not crafted ones. I hear inquirers
who are considerate and caring; I do not hear inquirers who are *trying to
sound as if* they are considerate and caring.

Emergent inquirers travel a long road as they learn to inquire with
strength and sensitivity, in ways that both respect others' rights and pro-
mote solidarity. As effective as the focal classroom inquiry events are,
they are not perfect. Like all communication events, they require constant
work. A good thing this is, too, for in addition to being safe places for
inquiry development, they are nudging places, that is, they gently push
the student to go beyond her present level of competence. This safe-yet-
nudging place sounds very like Vygotsky's (1978) *zone of proximal development*—that territory that is neither way beyond the child's reach nor already completely within the child's grasp, but is, rather, the cutting-edge
area where the child can function successfully with the help of a more
expert partner.[9] This zone combines support and nudge: going *beyond*
(the nudge) with *help* (the support). We have focused on the safety and
support that the focal inquiry events afford. Now what about the nudge
in these events? Although both the teachers and the children contribute
to the nudging, it is the teachers I want to focus on here.

Each teacher has been instrumental in putting in place a frame (discussion, literature study, science talk) that includes the structure of expectation that the focal issues will be challenging. The children come to these
events expecting nudging issues, not wimpy ones. In each example, the
teacher assures nudging issues either by initiating them herself or by
supporting a student's topic. In addition, in the course of each discussion,
these teachers nudge their students further in the ways of inquiry discourse. They

- push students to clarify their meanings and confusions;
- respond to some inquiry acts in ways that do not answer, but encourage the student to reflect further;
- articulate connections between one person's idea and another's;
- encourage the student to connect her idea explicitly to the issue on
  the floor;
- question children's suggestions in order to prompt further consideration;
- remind students to listen to points made by others;

• allow—protect—space for others' response.

There is demonstration here: This is how collaborative inquiry is carried out. There is also engagement: You do it. The demonstrations and engagements include at least the following:

• speakers articulate their inquiries and participants stay with them, actively trying to understand;
• paraphrases remain "true" to the speaker's original idea and expression;
• exploring, not answering, is central;
• staying connected to the focal issue is important;
• keeping on going is the thing—probing, probing;
• listening to others and building on their response is necessary.

Nudges, all.

Notice once again the absence of "positive reinforcement." These teachers do not say to a child, "You have asked a good question" or "That's an interesting inquiry" (the kind of teacher response that the university students in the Nath study remembered from their "positive questioning experiences"). Yet their valuing of the children's ideas is unmistakable. These teachers demonstrate, and nudge their students toward, profound respect for others' inquiry.

Every challenge in classroom inquiry discourse offers a nudge opportunity. I know of none greater than that in which children from culturally diverse backgrounds come together to inquire, probe, explore in classroom communities. It is tricky enough for one to impose without offending when both partners share the same cultural expectations for inquiry. But when the cultural inquiry expectations of participants differ, the situation is far more difficult and holds greater possibilities for offense or misinterpretation of intention and attitude.

One's own inquiry style is, at one and the same time, personal and cultural. It is the result of an active, curious individual mind within a social group. The "speaking personality" speaks within a cultural community. Each group offers its own ways, possibilities, approaches, orientation, constraints; each inquirer chooses from among these and uses them in her own ways. Seamlessly the personal and cultural join.

And so these distinct cultural-and-personal inquiry styles come together to create a new culture we call "classroom." There is much—so much—we do not know about the inquiry ways of different communities. I feel certain that it is classroom teachers who, more than anyone else, will illuminate for all of us the inquiry ways of children from different backgrounds. The importance of this cannot be overestimated, for such insights bear on the crucial question of what it is to be human in the world. It's a question about the universal and the particular. What is it that is universal in inquiry? What is the nature of this compelling urge we share as members of the human species (to make sense of our world with the help of others)? But just as important, what are its different ways of expression? This is a question simultaneously about culture and about individuals: What are the distinctive cultural and personal sounds that inquiry makes—its distinctive voices, its distinctive styles?

The cultural variation in a classroom seems to nudge inquirers in two directions at once. On the one hand, the nudge is toward *individual distinctiveness:* How can my own voice be heard except in contrast to the voices of others? What does it mean to have one's own distinctive inquiry style, after all, if not to have characteristic inquiry ways which are distinct from others'? My graduate students recall inquiry styles of individual children they have taught precisely because each voice sounds against the others. And the greater the range of voices and styles, the more forcefully each one emerges. Cultural diversity in a classoom increases that range and so has the potential to strengthen each child's awareness of distinctive inquiry styles, including her own.

Cultural diversity in a classroom also nudges emergent inquirers toward greater *other-awareness* and more finely tuned response. As with all aspects of language acquisition, so with emergent inquiry: It must ultimately take into account the entirety of one's language exposure and engagement. The greater the cultural diversity in the voices that speak to/with a child, the greater the range of responsive ways she must develop. Thus cultural diversity nudges toward the development of an inquiry style that is respectful and caring, as well as one that is individually distinctive. It is important for a child to learn to manage this self-other balance, for that balance is the essence of all communication, not only inquiry interaction.

This self-other balance is also the essence of a just and caring society, and this may matter most of all.

PART IV

Context

The familiar phrase *language in context* points to the fact that we tend to think of two entities: language and context. Yet perhaps it is more accurate to speak of *context in language,* for we express and interpret utterances in one way rather than another depending on context. One has the sense of context infusing utterances and interaction events. When thought of in this way, the notion of context and language as two distinct entities begins to blur. This wonderful alchemy hints at the fascination and complexity that is *context.*

We explore context in Chapter 11, drawing on two different and complementary notions of context: context as the surround, and context as weaving (Cole, 1996).

Chapter 12 brings us back to the beginning (Chapter 1) and also takes us beyond it. We'll reconsider the original reasons for studying children's inquiry (the joining of social, intellectual, and personal factors; the managing of imposition; the relation of inquiry to learning; the new insights currently available). These turn out not only to be reasons to *understand* inquiry and its emergence more fully, but also to be reasons to intentionally *foster* children's inquiry in classrooms.

We end by reflecting on a most important notion that some new voices contribute to an understanding and appreciation of children's inquiry: the notion of inner dialogue. It is perhaps strange that this final going-beyond in our own thinking—instead of taking us farther away from where we now stand—should instead take us deeper into our own selves. The act of inquiry that is the essence of social dialogue just may be the essence of inner dialogue as well.

CHAPTER 11

Inquiry Context

The goal of this chapter is to explore context in relation to classroom inquiry acts and events. We begin by drawing informally on our day-to-day experience of language-in-context. Then we consider two different notions of context: the *surround* view and the *weaving* view (Cole, 1996). Both are relevant to children's classroom inquiry, and both are interrelated.

STARTING WITH WHAT WE KNOW

One morning as I was walking down the hall toward my office in the education building, I passed two female students and overheard one say to the other, "Next week we're going to try to do aggression." I know what each word in this sentence means, yet taken together the words meant nothing to me, although they were perfectly comprehensible to the two students. They had a context for these words; I did not. I tried to create one so that the utterance would be meaningful for me. My assumption that the two young women were students was my first context-creating move: They looked to be the age of undergraduates, they were draped with book bags and carried student paraphernalia (books, notebooks, papers, pens), it was the time for changing classes, with many students in the hall, and they were in an area of the building where classes are held. I reasoned that they were students coming from an Educational Psychology class. Other departments hold classes in this building (Special Education, Educational Administration, Curriculum and Instruction), but the word "aggression" suggested Ed Psych to me. I guessed that in the class they had just left, they had been focusing on emotions, and perhaps next week the focus was going to be on the topic of aggression. Perhaps. Having no context for the remark except the one that I created, I will never know. What is of interest here is what I was drawing on as I created a (possible) context: my knowledge of that particular place (a university building where education courses are held), of the purposes and activities of the people typically found there, of what students look like, of how they behave, of how they talk when they are in their student roles ("next week" suggested a routine in which they attend classes once a week, "aggression" seemed more an academic word than an everyday one, "*do* aggression" suggested dealing with it as a topic rather than as a personal experience).

Context is crucial to the understanding of written utterances no less than spoken ones. How often a teacher encourages a child to "use the context" to figure out a particular word in a written text. We think first of the most immediate context—the other words in the sentence the child is trying to read. But clearly there is more context that the child might draw on: knowledge of previous events in the text, familiarity with the structure and language of other similar texts, knowledge of human behavior and motivation, and so on. Like spoken utterances, written ones are embedded within rich and complex personal and social worlds. However, it was the experience of a professor friend of mine at another university that brought this fact home to me with particular force.

My friend was teaching an undergraduate language arts methods course. A graduate teaching assistant (TA) had been assigned to help with the course. The TA sometimes came to class. He would sit at the back of the room, some distance from the students. Occasionally he spoke up in class but did so by way of uttering pronouncements rather than commenting as a participant in the ongoing discussion. When my friend engaged the students in small group activities (as he frequently did), he would encourage his TA to join the groups in order to get to know the students. The TA did not do this, choosing instead to stay seated at the back of the classroom. By the end of the course, the TA did not know the students' names.

The students in this class kept reading-response journals in which they wrote their reactions to each reading assignment. It was the TA's job to write his own dialogic comments in the margins of each student's journal. The purpose was to engage the students in an ongoing written dialogue about the ideas from the readings.

Several weeks into the course, the students began coming to my friend to complain about the TA's comments in the journals. As the course continued, the complaints became a chorus. My friend confronted his TA with the students' growing discontent. He told the TA that the students found his comments critical and felt that he was "putting them down." The TA protested adamantly. "You show me one single comment I have written that is a 'put down'—one single sentence where I have criticized the student!" My friend flipped through a few journals, looking for an example—*and could not find one!* The words themselves—but wait! That's exactly the point. In communication, there is no such thing as "words themselves." There are only words spoken, written, signed, heard, felt, responded to . . . words enmeshed in an intricate web of knowledge and feeling, of "meaning" and "sense" (to use Vygotsky's terms again), of expectations, associations, connections, relationships—all these reverberate in the words when they become utterances. The students perceived the TA as haughty, judgmental, critical, cold. When they read his comments in their journals, they heard disdainful words that emanated from some lofty height and were intended to make them feel small and inadequate. Had my friend written the very same words, the students would have heard them differently. The TA's "And do you agree with this position?" or "Can you explain what you mean?" were responses the students would have heard as invitations to carry their thinking further had they been written by my friend, for the students knew him to be warm and supportive and respectful of their ideas. They knew this professor to value their wondering, their probing; they knew his stance to be exploratory. This was their context for this professor and it would have infused his words. But coming from the TA, these same words were critical, cold. The meaning here was not in the "words themselves" but in the associations the students had for those words in this particular situation. Like all words in spoken and written utterances, these were contextualized experientially, personally, emotionally, socially.

Sensitivity to context is evident early in a child's life. Even before a child is saying his first words, he demonstrates "an appreciation of context" (Bruner, 1990, p. 71). He is figuring out the sense of others' words by figuring out the context in which the words are spoken. "[T]he acquisition of a first language is very context sensitive . . . the child already grasps in some *prelinguistic* way the significance of what is being talked about or of the situation in which the talk is occurring" (p. 71). Margaret Donaldson (1979) gives this example:

> An English woman is in the company of an Arab woman and her two children, a boy of seven and a little girl of thirteen months who is just beginning to walk. . . . The English woman speaks no Arabic, the Arab woman and her son speak no English.
>
> The little girl walks to the English woman and back to her mother. Then she turns as if to start off in the direction of the English woman once again. But the latter now smiles, points to the boy and says: "Walk to your brother this time." . . . the boy . . . holds out his arms. The baby smiles, changes direction and walks to her brother. . . . she appears to have understood the situation perfectly. (pp. 31–32)

We continue throughout life to interpret others' utterances in terms of the contexts in which they occur.

The above examples, taken together, hint at the complexity of context. Some scholars have gone so far as to suggest that the notion of context is too complex and variable and ever shifting to be defined: "it does not seem possible at the present time to give a single, precise, technical definition of *context,* and eventually we may have to accept that such a definition may not be possible" (Goodwin & Duranti, 1992, p. 2). So if we cannot even define "context" with any confidence, how can we hope to achieve the goal of this chapter: to relate context to inquiry acts and events in classroom communities? The answer to this quandary is that we turn toward the matter of context by way of probing it, not defining it. If our orientation inclines toward exploration, then the closure of a definition is not what we seek. The complexity and indeterminateness of "context" now become invitational rather than daunting. Perhaps this exploratory stance is what Goodwin and Duranti had in mind when they concluded that "lack of a single formal definition, or even general agreement about what is meant by context, is not a situation that necessarily requires a remedy." It is enough that we "recognize the importance and are actively involved in trying to unravel how it works" (p. 2).

Our recognition of the importance of context and our attempt to unravel its workings in classroom inquiry acts and events begins with what we already know. The preceding examples suggest that our informal, everyday knowledge of context is considerable.

- We understand why politicians rail at journalists for taking/reporting their remarks "out of context."
- We know how violated we sometimes feel when our own remarks are taken out of context and passed along to someone else.
- A friend tells us of a hurtful remark another friend has made, and we say, "Oh I'm sure he didn't mean it that way. Perhaps he . . . " and we go on to create a new context for the offending remark that allows it to be interpreted in a less hurtful way.

To contextualize words differently is to make them mean differently. And we will—must—always contextualize them *somehow.* We tend to think of context as surrounding people's words, but these familiar kinds of experiences suggest that context infuses people's words—is part of their meaning and sense. "The only way the speaker's act can mean is to be understood" (Clark & Holquist, 1984, p. 213); and we understand by bringing context to bear on spoken and written words.

Notice how it is often a *mis*interpretation or *mis*understanding that calls our attention to the importance and the workings of context. Though context is always present, woven in and around and through speakers' utterances, we notice it most when the interaction is problematic in some way: The politician is upset, a friend is hurt, a child is unable to read a sentence, a TA is offending students, I am unable to understand a remark I overhear. In these instances context becomes opaque. Normally it is transparent. We are told that the fish is the last to discover water. Notice, however, that water is essential to the life of the fish. So, too, with context in our daily experience: It is something we are usually unaware of, but it is essential to the life of our utterances.

The examples so far suggest that although we may most often remain unaware of the workings of context in our daily interactions, we can bring this knowledge to a conscious level if we wish to. The examples suggest, too, that our informal, everyday understanding of context is considerable. However, teachers' knowledge of context goes well beyond this informal everyday sort, for teachers actively and intentionally work *with* and *on* context in the classroom all the time. A teacher may speak of "setting a tone," of "creating an atmosphere," of "fostering a climate," of "establishing an environment" for her classroom. Whatever the expression she chooses, she is speaking of classroom *context.* She names this context-creating in her own professional idiom—tone, climate, atmosphere, environment. She recognizes that she is working to establish a particular kind of place that her classroom will be—accepted ways of carrying out activities, of relating to one another, of considering topics of interest, and so on. She is dealing here with what Cole (1996) calls "the surround view" of context (in contrast to "the weaving view" that I mentioned briefly in Chapter 1 and will return to shortly). Both notions of context (surround, weave) are important in classrooms. They are part and parcel of the language that happens there—how it is carried out and how it is understood. And both have everything to do with inquiry acts and events: Some classroom surround contexts foster children's and teachers' inquiry, and others do not; some offer a rich array of resources—threads—from which inquiry acts and events can be woven, and others do not.

THE SURROUND VIEW

Location is the dominant metaphor in this view of context. We say an interaction is "located in," "situated in," "embedded in," "occurring in," "surrounded by" a given context. Recall the politician complaining that his remarks were "taken out of" context, another instance of the location metaphor.

The word *in* in English names different types of containment, for example, when coffee is in a cup, there is an opening at the top; whereas a tree in the woods is in an open area. But the containment in the context metaphor is typically conceptualized as being complete. The usual graphic image is a set of concentric circles, bounded by solid black lines, and representing a set of *within-a* relationships: A child's inquiry utterance occurs within a particular science talk within a particular classroom within a particular school within a particular neighborhood and so on. The suggestion is that the outer circles impinge on the focal utterance that occupies the center circle. Thus, it seems incongruous that, more often than not, the concentric circles are drawn with solid dark lines that look quite impenetrable, not open to any sort of impinging.[1]

This location metaphor fails in several important ways. Clearly, language acts are located in time as well as space. Susan's inquiries about Albert the Abalone occur within a history of shared Irmagold stories; and the student's inquiry about cremation occurs within a history of literature-study events in Karen Smith's classroom. These are particular moments situated in particular histories. Further, the physical locating that the verbal and visual metaphors suggest does not adequately recognize that the space is also psychological, drenched in emotion and sense. Recall Paley's kindergartners pursuing their understanding of friendship within a rich web of associations, memories, feelings.

The surround context we focus on in this chapter is classroom. The assumption is that it is a context that holds the members' inquiry acts and events within it. We must recognize, however, that its boundaries are not impenetrable (the bold lines of the concentric circles of the familiar diagrams). Quite the opposite. Each child's and teacher's "outside" comes in, each one's knowledge, beliefs, values, expectations, experiences, expressive ways .... These interact with what is already there in a classroom (as well as with what the members of that classroom community build together over time), to contextualize utterances and interaction events. Expectations from outside and inside constitute a pool of resources for each individual—a set of possibilities and constraints—for creating and interpreting utterances. Each child draws on these contextual features differently in each unrepeatable instance.

It is surely impossible to specify all the contextual resources a child is drawing on in a given situation of speaking or interpreting, but we often hear traces of the child's outside experience in her classroom talk: Mommy and Daddy speaking Chinese, toy boats in bathtubs, metal kettles on heads—children in class making sense of world languages and of friendship in terms of their home experience of these. Also, a particular aspect of a child's larger surround context will be relevant in one classroom inquiry event and not in another. For example, being an older sister to a younger brother may be experience that a child draws on in interpreting events from *Dicey's Song* in a literature-study event, but not in a discussion of whether voice is matter. Notice, too, that although I speak of *the* surround context of the classroom, as if it were a single entity, it is not. Though much of that surround context is shared and pulls toward unity, much is also individual and pulls toward multiplicity. And of course, the surround context changes day by day, as the teacher and children live their classroom lives together. And so it seems that the idea of a surround context in terms of which we understand utterances is a close, familiar, and easy concept at one level, but a rather complex and elusive one at another level: impossible to specify completely, different for each individual, drawn on differently in each instance of speaking and interpreting, and ever in a process of change.

When we apply Cole's (1996) notion of surround context to the classroom, we readily slip into using the term *community*. What is the classroom community, after all, if not the shared expectations and experiences participants build over time, within which utterances are expressed and understood? Community is the surround context which provides the resources for and also the constraints on interaction.

Now as every teacher knows, the members of a classroom community all bring their outside experience *in*. A teacher cannot possibly know all of a child's "outside" resources, nor can she know fully how the child utilizes these resources in making sense of classroom interactions. But the more the teacher does know of the children's lives beyond the classroom, the better position she is in to draw on these resources inside the classroom as she and the children create (and continually re-create) their classroom community. This, of course, is why teachers try so hard to build strong connections between home and classroom. I think immediately of first-grade teacher Carol Avery:

> The night before school begins, I phone all the children to introduce myself to them, chat briefly, and ask them to bring a favorite book to school the next day. . . .
> The phone conversations with the children are fun and fascinating. I ask how I might recognize them tomorrow and they eagerly tell me of their new clothes and physical descriptions:
> "I'll tell you one thing. I have dark brown hair and light shoes."
> "I have freckles and blond hair and blue jeans."
> "I don't know what I look like. I'll have to ask my Mom."
> When I ask about books, the children respond quite candidly:
> "I already got one in my bookbag."

"I'm learning to read, but I can't read yet."
"I do a little books. I'd rather play Nintendo."
"I don't have no books, not really. I watch TV." (Avery, 1993, pp. 77–78)

With her phone calls, Carol tells these children about the surround context of the classroom they will enter: "The boundaries of this surround will be permeable, and what you bring to this community will contribute to its creation."

Carol is not casual about the first day of school. I know no teacher who is. Why? What makes the beginning of each new school year so important? Why does the teacher plan that first day so carefully: how she arranges the furniture, selects and schedules activities, organizes materials, chooses the story she will read aloud, introduces procedures for various activities ... Why such careful attention to these matters? It is because she is acutely aware that she and the children are beginning the work of creating their community. Together they are constructing the surround context that will hold everything participants do in this place. Every unrepeatable utterance, event, interaction will be construed with reference to this surround—the structures, values, expressive ways, constraints, possibilities it offers.

- The selection and placement of furniture says something about the kind of social relationships the teacher expects, and also gives some hints about what activities she values. (For example, is there a library area? Is it large? Is it inviting? Where is it located?)
- The arrangement, accessibility, and management of materials indicates how she views student initiative and sharing.
- The activities of the first days—what they are and how they are carried out—give messages about the teacher's stance toward learning (what she believes it to be, how she thinks it happens).
- The early days of Writing Workshop will play out more than writing procedures. They will also demonstrate the teacher's respect for student choice, initiative, response, and interaction, and her expectation that membership in this community entails responsibility toward others.
- The teacher's introduction of various oral genres (science talks, perhaps, or discussions or literature studies?) will convey particular speaking norms, but will also convey messages about ways of relating to what we find interesting, and ways of connecting with one another in regard to these matters of interest.
- Even the teacher's read-aloud on that first day—the book she

chooses and the way she guides the talk in response to it—contributes to the building of community. Listen to Karen Smith:

> I often read *Crow Boy* (Yashima, 1955) on the first day of school. After the students share their thoughts and feelings, I share my thoughts about the responsibility of a community to its citizens. I ponder with the class how Chibi's classmates might have seen him differently if they had focused on what he could do rather than on what he didn't do. Usually this leads to some sharings of personal experiences when we have felt like outsiders. (K. Smith, 1990a, p. 23)

Karen knows this sharing of *Crow Boy* is about much more than a literary work. It is also demonstration of and engagement in ways that members of this community are to turn toward topics of interest and toward one another in their talk. Karen is saying to her students, "This story is not just about Chibi. It is also about us, about the kind of community we can be."[2]

Community, the Random House dictionary tells me, is "a social group sharing common characteristics or interests and perceived or perceiving itself as distinct in some respect from the larger society within which it exists," or "a social group whose members . . . share government, and have a common cultural and historical heritage." But consider the classroom on the first day of school. Here come 25 students and one teacher— 26 yet-to-be members of a yet-to-be community. And the community is one that will create itself over time and then, suddenly on the last day of the school year, will destruct. Think how different it is for a newborn coming into a community. The community is already there—has its own norms and values, history and customs, traditions and stories, procedures, genres and social activities. And it is full of experts who will help the newcomer come into full membership, nurturing the novice into the community's ways of thinking, valuing, behaving, expressing, and so on. Dollard (1935) put it this way: "Accept two units for our consideration: first, the group which exists before the individual; and second, a new organism envisioned as approaching this functioning collectivity" (quoted in Cole, 1996, p. 180). But on the first day of the school year, there is no "functioning collectivity" that will hand on its traditions, procedures, values to the newcomer. Everyone is a newcomer. Unless it is a multiage classroom, there are no experts in this not-yet community's norms, values, history, traditions. Children and teacher do not enter a community; they become one.

I do not mean to suggest that the 26 arrive as blank slates regarding the classroom. The entering child may have overheard snatches of parent conversation relating to school, may know some school legends perpetuated by older siblings, may have played school with neighborhood children, may have attended preschool, Hebrew school or Sunday school, or earlier grades. The teacher arrives with plans and arrangements, with her own expectations and wonderings, and probably with the experience of creating classroom communities with other groups of children . . . but not this one.[3] The school itself is there, with its own schedules and structures, its own character and philosophy. And so the teacher and children do not create their community entirely from scratch, but considerably more so than other communities do. From that first day, teacher and children are creating the surround context within which they will make sense of all classroom interaction, including inquiry acts and events.

No wonder teachers take the beginning of a new school year very seriously. No wonder every teacher remembers the special character of each class of children she has taught: She speaks of the unique "chemistry" of one, the unusual "dynamics" of another. The fact that this community-creating happens anew with each class may blind us to how extraordinary it is for each new group to enter a community that isn't there. Yet.

Many of the demonstrations and engagements of the very first day will be about inquiry: whether or not it is important, how it is to be pursued, how expressed, in what situations and activities, in what genres, and so on. Having built some understanding of inquiry over the past chapters—its purposes, its expressive ways, its dialogues, its individual styles—we are now in a position to ask, What kind of surround context in a classroom will be most supportive of the ongoing inquiry of its members?

THE SURROUND CONTEXT THAT FOSTERS INQUIRY

The Social

Inquiry utterances are acts of connection. A speaker reaches out to others with the intention of drawing them in to his probing. The child inquirer, therefore, must know that his classroom is a social place, and this means a place where interaction is valued, not simply tolerated. We have all known teachers who say, "Well, might as well let the kids talk 'cuz they're gonna do it anyway." Throw up the hands, shrug the shoulders, say, "I give up," sigh. The surround context such teachers shape does not forbid interaction, but neither does that context encourage it. The classroom context that is good for inquiry is one that values interaction.

Now, certainly no teacher or child could endure unrelieved chatter from 8:00 to 3:00 every day. Every child must have opportunities to be silent, to be alone. But so must he have opportunities to connect with others in his community. The interaction expectations of the inquiry-fostering classroom are not that talk will be endless. Rather, participants share the expectation that this is a place where we talk with one another because it enhances both learning and friendship to do so.

How does the child come to know that his classroom community is this kind of place? Again I think about the messages of the first days and weeks, that especially important time for this emergent community. The room the child enters makes a visual statement in its physical arrangement, for example, the clustering of desks so that informal talk can occur, and the presence of areas for whole-group meetings, and also areas for small-group projects and informal conversations. The teacher would not create areas conducive to children's large group and small group talk if she did not intend for interaction to occur there.

Within the first several weeks of the new school year, the child will have a sense of how time is organized in his classroom and of the kinds of activities in which he will participate there. He will doubtless engage in activities labeled math, science, social studies. In a classroom context supportive of children's inquiry, these activities will provide for social connection.

- Can we expect a child to inquire in math if math is always and only a solitary event—with no problem-solving and problem-creating group times, no times for sharing discoveries and challenges?
- Can we expect a child to inquire in science if science is always and only "final form," devoid of collaborative exploration? Whatever we mean by "scientific community," the term surely designates a group of people who interact with one another in the excitement of exploration and discovery, in wonder, in doubt, in skepticism, in challenge—all tentative, nonfinal orientations.
- And shall we expect a child to inquire as historian, anthropologist, geographer if we take the "social" out of "social studies," depriving children of the very interactions that are the essence of social science: learners coming together to probe, reflect, imagine; to consider the whys and hows of social life?

The message in a classroom that values interaction across the curriculum is this: We are all learning resources for one another. If this shared understanding is not part of the surround context, why would one child inquire of another? Why would a teacher inquire of a child?

The demonstrations and engagements of the first few weeks do not simply tell the members of this emergent community that social interaction is valued here; they also tell the child what kinds of interaction are valued. The strongest message for emergent inquirers may have to do with trust. Remember that an inquiry act is an act of courage—going beyond to . . . where? To what? It is also an imposing act that can misfire in a whole host of ways (as we saw in Chapter 10). It is imperative, then, that a safe surround hold each child inquirer. Each must know that trust anchors all interactions in this place. Adults' hurtful memories of inquiring in unsafe learning communities are powerful reminders of just how crucial trust is to the creation of an inquiry-fostering surround context. "When I asked a question in class

> . . . the teacher laughed hysterically as did the class
> . . . my teacher said it was an irrelevant question
> . . . everybody started laughing at me
> . . . my teacher said that my question was pointless."

These responses told these student inquirers that they were in an unsafe, untrusting community. Not surprisingly, they shut down:

> . . . I swore from that day on that I would never ask another question in class.
> . . . It was a long time before I was able to ask a question without feeling frightened.

One of the most important demonstrations of all relating to the building of a trusting community where inquiry can flourish, may be the teacher's responses to her students' acts of inquiry.[4] Contrast Karen Smith's responses to those preceding:

> "Do you understand they cremated [Dicey's mother]? . . . Maybe that's what was confusing you."
> "Yeah, I wonder why . . ."
> "So you think maybe it was . . . ? Hmmm."

Unlike the earlier hurtful examples, these responses of Karen's tell the student, "This is a safe place for you to inquire in."

Another important demonstration in Karen's responses is about listening. It goes without saying that if we are learning resources for one another, we surely must listen to each other. But the demands of inquiry go beyond a courteous kind of listening to an active, co-constructing kind.

Inquiry acts and events are jointly constructed. In the focal transcripts, we have seen a variety of teacher moves in response to a student's inquiry (e.g., seeking clarification, agreeing, countering), but in each response, the teacher was joining the inquirer in his inquiry place. The response was tightly contingent on what the child said. Only active listening can generate such responses. Classroom inquiry requires children to understand that inquiry is deeply and continually dialogic, belonging not just to the speaker, but to listener/responders as well. The kind of listening and responding a teacher demonstrates makes a vital contribution to building this shared understanding into the surround context.

Trust and active listening are not the only characteristics of the social surround context that support inquiry. Inquiry acts are acts in progress, happening *now,* in the moment of speaking. Thus the surround context that fosters inquiry will be one that appreciates rough draft talk, messy talk, idea-becoming-word talk. (We heard this appreciation operating in the science-talk and literature-study excerpts we considered.) Further, the child inquirer must know that the context that holds his inquiry honors variety as well as messiness—a variety of moves, structures, voices.

To consider the social aspects of the surround context that supports inquiry in a classroom is to engage in an if-then exercise:

> If inquiry acts are acts of connection, then in the classroom surround context, connection must be valued.
>
> If inquiry acts are acts of creativity and courage and imposition, then the classroom surround context must be safe and trusting.
>
> If inquiry acts are collaboratively constructed by speaker and listener/responder, then in the classroom surround context, active listening must be expected.
>
> If inquiry acts are acts in progress, then in the classroom surround context, rough-draft talk that reflects thought in the process of becoming must be appreciated.
>
> If inquiry acts occur in a variety of expressive forms and discourse moves, then in the classroom surround context, diverse expression must be welcomed.

Above all, the classroom context that supports children's inquiry will tell them that inquiry is important. Students in Gallas's, Paley's, and Smith's classrooms can have no doubt of this, for it is evident in these teachers' posing of their own inquiries, in their appreciative response to student inquiries, and in their provision for collaborative inquiry events in their curriculum. In all these ways they tell their students: "Inquiry is a major way of our connection in this place where we learn *together.*"

As suggested earlier, we sometimes speak of an individual's behavior as being "in character," meaning that it is in keeping with our expectations for that individual. We know him to be such-and-such a kind of person and we expect him to behave in such-and-such ways. Classroom context is like this. Each classroom has its own character—is such-and-such a kind of place. We expect members of that community to behave in ways that are in character within that surrounding context—the shared values, resources, and expectations that characterize this community. There is little hope that a child will reach out to connect with another in his act of inquiry, if such reaching out and connecting are "out of character" in his classroom context.

The Intellectual

To value certain kinds of talk in a particular classroom is to value certain kinds of communication work that the talk is doing. In a classroom, much of this work has to do with use of the mind, for the classroom is, after all, a learning place. I have suggested that social aspects of an inquiry-fostering context will include the valuing of rough draft talk and talk which is diverse.

- If students' (and teachers') talk is rough-draft talk, that is because it is expressing rough-draft thought—in-process thought, ideas emerging. To value rough-draft talk is also to value in-process thought.
- If students' (and teachers') talk is diverse, that is because their thinking is diverse. To value diverse talk is to value diverse thinking as well.

Thus the social messages of the surround context are not only about ways of interacting; they are also messages about using one's mind in the place of learning that we call classroom. When Karen Smith demonstrates and engages her students in talk that is diverse, she is validating using the mind diversely—reflecting, wondering, challenging, empathizing, seeking information, clarifying, disagreeing, and so on. When Karen Gallas legitimizes the rough-draft expression of science talks, she legitimizes in-process thinking.

I do not mean to suggest that there is a simple one-to-one match between thought and expression, with each thought tumbling forth, out of one's mouth, as words. Questions about the relation of thought and language have fascinated scholars for centuries. They will not be resolved anytime soon. However, we do know that language and thought are different entities, and that the images of thought must be translated into language—literally re-formed as words in order to become language acts. Vygotsky (1986) gives this example:

> Thought, unlike speech, does not consist of separate units. When I wish to communicate the thought that today I saw a barefoot boy in a blue shirt running down the street, I do not see every item separately: the boy, the shirt, its blue color, his running, the absence of shoes. I conceive of all this in one thought, but I put it into separate words. A speaker often takes several minutes to disclose one thought. In his mind the whole thought is present at once, but in speech it has to be developed successively. (p. 251)

However, although the relationship between thought and expression is not a simple, direct think-the-thought ⟶ say-the-word connection, there *is* a relationship and it is one we can hear in the talk of children. Final-form talk reflects a different kind of mental activity than rough-draft talk does. A single way of considering a topic will result in a single-ness in language use (e.g., the performance talk so prevalent in IRE recitation events), whereas multifaceted consideration of a topic results in talk which is various in perspective and in function. And so those *social* characteristics of the surround context that support inquiry talk, simultaneously and inevitably support inquiry's *intellectual* orientation as well—an orientation that is tentative, nonfinal, and multifaceted in its ways of considering issues of interest.

Further, each surround context that supports children's inquiry will, in its own unique ways, demonstrate and engage children in a view of knowledge that includes the understandings: (1) that knowledge is creatively constructed by the knower, (2) that present knowledge is the starting place for going beyond it, and (3) that knowledge involves feeling as well as thought, sense as well as meaning.

Knowledge is creative construction. The view that knowledge is creatively constructed by the knower stands in stark contrast to the view that knowledge is received from an authority (teacher, text). A receiving notion is antithetical to inquiry. An inquirer is a doer, not a receptacle—not even a receptacle that speaks and writes, allowing another (teacher, test) to know that he has received. The classroom community's construal of the nature of knowledge will influence the intellectual acts that happen there. It is unrealistic to expect that children will actively probe if the shared assumption surrounding them is that their appropriate role is to receive.

Present knowledge is a starting place. We often encounter the notion of knowledge as an ending place. Gallas, Smith, and Paley don't see it this way. For them, the children's knowledge is the starting place for going-beyond conversations: science talks and discussions and literature studies. These three teachers encourage their children to connect what they know to what they are constructing beyond it. For Paley, this often means articulating for the children the connections she senses in their talk. "Are you children saying you know someone likes you if you remember nice things you did together?" she asks after they have provided many specific instances of good times with friends. "I think I know what reminded you of that," she tells Deana when, during a discussion about choosing "cubby" partners, Deana unexpectedly asks about choosing actors to dramatize the stories the children create. "Choosing your own actors *is* a bit like picking a cubby partner," Vivian tells the children, again making a connection (Paley, 1981, p. 216). When, in a science talk, Gallas requests that a child repeat what he has said, it is because she hears in the child's observation the promise for going beyond in interesting ways. And Karen Smith, when her students are confused about cremation, tells them, "You know, there's two ways" (i.e., there is the way you know already, and another way as well). There is respect here for what these children know, not because the children's knowledge is in and of itself impressive, but because of the enabling possibilities it holds for going beyond. What a restless business inquiry is!

It is unlikely that these children would carry out their discussions, science talks, and literature studies as they do, if they did not know that they are in a place that values their present knowledge as a starting place for going beyond it.

Knowledge includes feeling. There is a myth afoot that research and scholarship are objective, neutral, dispassionate enterprises. Now, I have known many researchers and scholars from many disciplines. Some I have known personally, others through their writing. I have yet to encounter one who is dispassionate in his work. Whether historian, biologist, mathematician, literary critic, geologist, ethnomusicologist—it doesn't matter. A driving curiosity and fascination propel the work. How could it be otherwise? Researchers and scholars are inquirers, and there is nothing dispassionate about probing and wondering in areas of compelling personal interest. We say that we want our students to engage in social science, math, art, literature, science in the real ways of these disciplines, actively taking on the stance of each and the ways of thinking and exploring and expressing as an insider in each discipline. This is not simply to build particular domains of knowledge. It is also to care about the compelling issues of each discipline, to bring our own experiences to bear, to share the excitement of the historian, mathematician, biologist.

It would be strange, then, if the classroom surround context was one that did not welcome children's feeling selves, did not recognize the sense as well as the meaning in what and how they know. We have heard both meaning and sense in the classroom transcripts we've considered. Suppose we took those science talks, discussions, and literature-study events, and we stripped them of all feeling—no evocation of experiences of friendship, of seeing your breath on a cold day, of Mommy and Daddy talking quietly; no excitement in response to another's idea about voice, no imagining, no dramatizing; no empathy with a story character whose mother is dying, no weighing the moral dilemma facing an author who writes fiction for children—all of this suddenly *gone*. What would we be left with? We would be left with human organisms exchanging words-as-dictionary-entries. No utterances here; just linguistic structures, for utterances, as Bakhtin reminds us, are never neutral. Of course, this stripping away of feeling in the children's talk would negatively influence their active, engaged participation; but so would it negatively influence their intellectual understanding. To explore science, history, art, math, literature is to do so with feeling, for the child apprentice no less than for the adult expert. The classroom context that welcomes children's inquiry necessarily welcomes their feeling selves as well.

The Self

With that phone call the night before the first day, Carol Avery tells each new student that he is important. Why else would Carol call each one, ask how she can recognize him, and invite him to bring a book from home? And when each of these children comes to his new classroom in the morning, he will find more indications that this place is one that values him as an individual.

Again and again, in the classrooms I visit, I am struck by how powerfully the physical environment itself conveys the message that each individual contributes distinctively and significantly to the whole. In one kindergarten, after the teacher has shared with the children different versions of *I Know an Old Woman Who Swallowed a Fly*, the children make their own "Big Book" for this favorite, each child contributing a page for one line of the song. In another kindergarten the book the children make is *The Halloween Monster Book*, each child's monster picture and dictated verbal description constituting one page of the book. Small groups of children linger over these books during Free Choice time each day, but they always return them to their privileged place on the chalk tray, front and

center of the room. Bar graphs occupy a special space in yet another kindergarten—a graph for the kinds of shoes the children are wearing, another for the kinds of pets they either have or wish they had at home.
The children's individual squares, side by side, extend the bars of each
graph. Near the graphs is a portable display board that is a collection of
Polaroid pictures of individual children working at centers during Centers Time. And near the graphs is a cubbies wall, each cubby clearly labeled with one child's name. Personal presence is clear: my page in the
book, my pet and my sneakers represented on the graph, my cubby on
the wall, a picture of me painting at the easel. Yet in each case, the distinct
individual contribution stands within a larger whole. The pages and the
squares are individual; together they make a book or a graph. The Polaroid pictures and cubbies are individual; together they comprise collec-
tions that fill a bounded space. The visual message seems equally about
the individual and the collective, about self and other(s). Self-presence is
strong, but self is not alone. The self-other message I find in these visual
arrays is consistent with the self-other awareness that inquiry acts require.
I think of inquiry's essentially dialogic nature: the necessary distinctiveness of each participant, but also their coming together to create the
larger whole that is dialogue.

From the child's point of view, the activities he engages in may be
more important than the physical setting that surrounds him. Freedom
of choice will figure prominently in the activities of an inquiry-fostering
classroom. The child in Becky King's K/one/two classroom who comes
to her and says, "Ms. King, I wanna do an investigation," is a child who
knows that he has choices in this classroom and that "doing an investigation" is a way of acting on them. He probably also knows what Becky
will say in response: "O.K. What is it you want to investigate?" With this
question, Becky is seeking information from the child, but she is also
promising to help. Patti Seifert's kindergartners have choices too. From
the beginning of the year, Patti and the children have many informal discussions "about what we would like to learn about, what we are curious
about, what we are interested in." In February, Explorers Club begins with
Patti interviewing the children individually about what each one might
be interested in exploring, why these topics are of particular interest, and
what the child already knows and what he wants to know about these
possible topics. Here is what some of the children tell her.

> "I'm curious about potions. How do they mix stuff?"
> "The stars and the moon. I know some stars shine brightly, because I've seen
>   them. How do they make stars? How does the moon change shape?"
> "I want to know about deer and elk because I see them a lot when I'm

coming home. I know they know how to run fast. I know they can jump over the fences fast. I want to know what they eat and where do they have babies?"

"Ocean and beaches. I know how the water got there. Somebody spends all their life getting buckets of water and pouring it there. But I don't know how the sand got there."

(Seifert, forthcoming)

In Explorers Club, these children pursue their selected topics. Lynne Strieb, in her first/second-grade classroom, provides daily Centers Time, that favorite of kindergarten teachers, because Lynne knows that children need the continuing freedom to choose, to initiate, and to shape their daily experiences, long after their kindergarten days are over (Strieb, forthcoming). The valuing of individual choice permeates these classrooms. To value the individual's choice is also to value the individual who chooses.

Many aspects of the surround context of a classroom will convey to the child what his place is in that community. He needs to know that his own distinctive presence matters. It's an understanding we would hope surrounds members of classroom communities for many reasons, but fostering inquiry is a particularly important one. Inquiry acts bring self into the act in a major way: It is *my* topic, *my* purpose, *my* voice that is central and urges the attention of others. In order to inquire in a classroom, a child must know that he matters. How can his act of inquiry matter if he does not?

It's possible to feel a bit of a letdown at this point. We work hard to build a deeper understanding of children's inquiry, then turn to the classroom to consider implications: If this is what children's inquiry is like, what will the classroom be like that best supports it? We hope for an answer that is new and groundbreaking. We'd like trumpets and drumrolls. There are none. The classroom community we are looking for turns out to be one that we, at some level, have believed in all along as the most supportive of children's learning. And yet it is possible that, although we end up at a place in our thinking that is already familiar, we may know that place in a new way—may know it with greater conviction.

Now imagine a classroom community in which teacher and children share this surround context which I have suggested supports participants' inquiry. How do the members of this community draw on these shared norms, values, understandings, and expectations as they engage in collaborative inquiry events? It's a question about weaving.

THE WEAVING VIEW

"Each moment is a place you've never been," Strand reminds us (Kehl, 1983, p. 30). And so it is; but it is also the case that each moment remembers places you *have* been, experiences you *have* had. In a classroom community, some of these are experiences that community members have shared; others are experiences individuals bring from outside. Now the metaphor changes from context as something that *surrounds* participants, to context as something participants *weave*. It's a shift from noun to verb, a shift from what participants know, to what participants do. Surely the surround context is ever changing, but if we zoom in on a particular moment, we find a particular surround context in place, providing a set of resources—possibilities and constraints—that participants draw on in creating and interpreting the interaction event of this particular moment. Bakhtin's notion of the repeatable and the unrepeatable is relevant once again. The weaving metaphor would see the surround context as the total set of available threads—repeatable in the sense of being there for use in various interactions; and would see the interaction of the moment as a unique selecting and weaving of those threads into a one-of-a-kind cloth. The weaving metaphor highlights participants' activation of their knowledge of the norms and values that surround them. And so the surround and weave notions of context come together in specific interaction events: Participants draw on the surround *context* to *contextualize* (weave) each interaction.

The classroom interaction events of special interest are collaborative explorations. It is instructive to consider an excerpt of a familiar transcript one last time. Ultimately what we want to understand is *how* participants weave, but for now we must be content with increasing our awareness of *what* the threads are in the weaving. Specifically, in constructing a collaborative exploration event, do participants draw *on* and draw *into* their weaving the social, intellectual, and self threads that I have identified as supportive of emergent inquiry? Listen again to the beginning of the science talk in which the children focus on the question, Is voice matter? The numbering of conversational turns below is slightly different from the numbering that appears on pp. 165–167): Zach's "How could it not really like squeeze us to death?" (#14, #16, #18 in the original) and Tom's "If, if, if voice is matter, why isn't it, like, smushing us against the walls?" (#15, #17, #19 in the original). I am numbering as single, overlapping conversational turns, rather than as three turns for each speaker. (I use underlining to indicate overlap.) Our focal unit is utterance, and I believe that Zach's question and Tom's question were both single utterances for these speakers.

1. Tom: Air takes up, um, space, but does voice?
2. Lester: I think it sort of does because like, it's like air, and voice is like air so it's
3. Ellen: sort of . . .
4. Tom: Like if you, like if she can blow up a balloon up with your, with your um, with your, um, breath, it, um, must take up, it must be matter, sort of.
5. Eli: It must be matter sort of, 'cause . . .
6. Tom: Like if you blow up a balloon, like it takes matter.
7. Ellen: I think it might be matter because, um, when you talk you breathe out and you breathe in, so . . .
8. Tom: Yeah, but if you breathe, um, talking, um, you can you still um, when some people talk, um, they're like talking a lot, they have to like, get their breath.
9. Tom: If voice is, um, matter, um, is, like, would we be getting squished right now, if it's like, taking up room?
10. Lester: No, it wouldn't exactly be getting like squished.
11. Ellen: Because air's taking up space, and it's not squeezing us.
12. Zach: And it takes up more space than we do.
13. T: Could you say your question again, Tom?
14. Zach: *How could it not really like squeeze us to death?*
15. Tom: *If, if, if voice is matter . . . why isn't it, like, smushing us against the walls?*
16. Michael: Because air is matter, but when there's like, like take a big wind, for instance. When hurricanes or tornadoes come along, they take up a lot of air, and space, and they are air. But it's just a big quantity of air . . .

Tom's opening utterance (relating the property of occupying space to both air and voice) enacts his understanding that what you know already is the starting point for going beyond it. His is not the only contribution that uses present knowledge to move beyond it. Indeed, the entire excerpt occurs at the intersection of know/don't know: what these children know of properties of matter and of air, of blowing up balloons, of breathing in and out, of using breath in speech, of hurricanes and tornadoes—these threads are their starting places for considering possibilities beyond. The active nature of knowledge here is unmistakable: new possibilities being creatively constructed. Totally absent is talk that reflects a perception of knowledge as something given and the knower as receiver. Entertaining new possibilities together requires talk that is messy—messy in a wonderful way, the way of exploratory talk: "because um," "if, if, if," "with your um, with your, um." How different is the messiness of this talk, from that of the talk in the reciprocal teaching sessions. Recall Charles's original question: "What is found in the southeastern snakes, also the copperhead, rattlesnakes, vipers—they have" (Palincsar & Brown, 1984, p. 138). Talk can be messy in all sorts of ways. Some relate to inquiry; others do not.

The children's talk in the excerpt above is striking in its diversity. In these 16 utterances—just a few moments of conversation—we hear children offer possibilities, give reasons, connect one thing with another, provide hypothetical examples, reason logically (if . . . then), challenge, formulate specific inquiries, agree and disagree, modify one anothers' ideas, elaborate and extend, offer counterexamples, clarify, imagine, and so on. This diversity is possible because the participants share an understanding that many expressive ways and discourse moves can serve collaborative inquiry. It is out of this shared understanding that they weave this rich expressive tapestry.

The diverse ways of the children's talk in these few utterances are ways of turning toward others and toward the topic of consideration. They are ways of connection with other participants. The contingency of utterances to one another leaves no doubt of the active nature of the listening here. But I also hear the sounds of close interpersonal connection in the phrasings that sing their way across participants' utterances: "sort of" (#2, #3, #4, #5), "it must be matter sort of" (#4, #5), "you breathe (in)" (#7, #8), "getting squished/squeezed" (#9, #10), "squeezing us/smushing us" (#11, #14, #15). Such connection! Participants building together, yet remaining individual and distinct. Six distinct children's voices across these 16 utterances, each child a speaking personality who leaves his "imprint of individuality" (Bakhtin, 1986, p. 75). Again we find distinct "hands" coordinated in their "clapping," the essence of inquiry dialogue.

One might ask whether the presence of these social, intellectual, and personal features woven together in the children's science talk may be a matter of coincidence and not a matter of these children drawing on contextualizing resources that they share—the social, intellectual, and self norms and values of their classroom community. But I think it could not possibly be coincidence that this many children could proceed with the weaving, turn by turn, that is happening here. The participants do not focus their (conscious) attention on the *workings* of the conversation; they focus on the *ideas* they are considering. If the workings of collaborative exploration were not in place, shared by the participants, then these would need to be negotiated, clarified, repaired. But for the most part they are not; they are assumed. In the main, the children negotiate their ideas, not the mechanisms for connecting, reflecting, expressing. Norms for these are understood and shared. It must be so for this conversation to move along as it does in smoothly coordinated fashion.

One might also ask whether it is possible that the shared social, intellectual, and personal understandings that are reflected in the children's talk are—not threads from the larger surround context of this community—but only features of this particular genre: science talks. Do the children perhaps understand these to be the threads of "doing science talks," but not aspects of their relationships to one another and to "content" more generally?

It is impossible to answer this question on the basis of 16 utterances in a single conversation. I have no doubt that these children select and weave these threads in the making of a science talk, in ways that are different from their selecting and weaving in other oral genres in their classroom. They share structures of expectation specific to this particular genre, and these guide how they construct these events and how they interpret them.

However, doing science talks *at all* lives within the larger classroom surround context. If that context were one that did not value connection, active listening, exploratory talk; did not foster respect and safety for risk taking; did not view knowledge as creative construction, as starting points, as infused with feeling; did not value the individual voice within the group—in such a classroom context, science talks would not occur *at all*.

Science talks provide a safe and special place for intense social connection, for vigorous and diverse probing, for strong personal presence. They occur in this classroom precisely because their character is *in* character with the surround context of this community.

CHAPTER 12

Going Beyond

So far we have been exploring children's inquiry in their social lives. It is perhaps ironic that we now go *beyond* this by going *within*. The domain we consider in this chapter is inner speech, for inquiry lives there, in the child's inner life, no less than it does in her social life. We begin the chapter with a reconsideration of the rationale for this book (originally presented in Chapter 1), and this leads us to our final focus on dialogue and inquiry in inner speech.

RECONSIDERING THE RATIONALE

What does it matter if children's classrooms foster their emergent inquiry? What does it matter if schoolchildren use their minds, their talk, and each other in inquiry's ways? In Chapter 1, I offered reasons for children's inquiry warranting study at this time. I return to these now. They are not only reasons to *study* children's inquiry; they are also reasons to actively *foster* it in the classroom.

Inquiry Weds the Social, the Intellectual, the Personal/Self

These three join seamlessly in inquiry acts and events. I do not mean to suggest that these three aspects are not present in other language acts; but I do mean to suggest that the *intensity* of each one and also the *balance* among them are especially noteworthy in inquiry acts. This strong presence and perfect balance may make inquiry a particularly fruitful kind of discourse, in which the child can hone these aspects that figure in all interaction, not just in inquiry. That is, the child's engagement in inquiry acts and events may make an important contribution to language development even beyond the development of inquiry.

But I can't help wondering whether the benefits may reach even beyond this. If it is the case that inquiry acts carry out those three compelling urges that make us human in the world—to connect with others, to understand the world, to reveal ourselves within it—then might it not also be the case that a child's engagement in inquiry acts and events may deepen her understanding of her own (and others') humanness? I can only wonder.

Inquiry Requires the Managing of Imposition

In her act of inquiry, the inquirer pursues her own wants but must simultaneously take her partner's wants into account. If she does not, her act may offend the very one whose help she seeks. There is good reason to be concerned that schoolchildren learn how to inquire without offending others. We want children to be able to turn to knowledgeable others for help as they try to further their own understanding. Yet when they manage the imposition that inquiry acts entail, they may be doing something more, something beyond the particular inquiry acts themselves. The necessity of simultaneously tending to the wants of self and of other is the double bind that lives at the heart of all social interaction, not just inquiry. Inquiry acts, but also social relationships, must be about self, but cannot be *only* about self; they must be about other, but cannot be *only* about other. Whatever else we might mean by "social relationship," we surely mean self and other in some sort of balanced togetherness.

Inquiry events such as discussions, literature studies, and science talks play out this self-other balancing game on the playing field that is the classroom. Where could the players possibly get a more vigorous and demanding workout? Their community supports the intensity and diversity of their engagement and provides safety for their risk taking. But the self-other balancing game they play as they manage the imposition of inquiry acts has relevance far beyond these acts and events, for it is the essence of all social interaction.

Again I wonder whether there is something even beyond this. Isn't this managing of the desires of self and other basic to life in a democratic society? When we focus on self's wants and needs, we speak of *justice*, and *rights*: "We seek a just society," we say, that "protects the individual's rights." And when we focus on the wants and needs of others, we speak of "a caring society," words that have an empathetic ring. The double bind again: autonomy on the one hand, affiliation on the other. My needs and wants. And yours, too.[1]

Inquiry Enhances Learning

This is not a new idea. The earlier educational literature that was concerned about teachers asking too many questions and children asking too few was rooted in the assumption that asking one's own questions was central to one's learning. It is true that this earlier research, focusing as it did on interrogative forms, missed much of what it was trying to understand and foster, namely, children's inquiry—their turning to others for help with their own sense-making. But despite the limitations of this work, it was prompted by a belief that children's own initiative and active engagement were important to their learning and that both would increase if children had more opportunities to pursue their own inquiries in the classroom. It was correctly recognized that children's learning would be enhanced if the learners themselves played a greater role in determining its focus and direction—if the child could ask about what it was that she wanted to know. With the clarity of hindsight, we can see the limitations of that early work that considered only interrogative forms. However, we can also see the appropriateness of its intention: to give children greater control of their own learning.

Currently in education, we see many attempts to entice, coax, even coerce children into "learning." The endless competitions of one sort or another, the ever-present rewards, the lure of high grades and test scores—these are but a few of the ways some would try to "make" children learn. But these enticements don't bring about learning; they only bring about the appearance of learning; they only bring about certain types of performance. The possibility of learning resides in the learner. How easy it is to lose sight of this! But the English language does not lose sight of it. English is quite clear about agency in learning: The learner learns. We can say, "The *child learned* that the earth goes around the sun," but we cannot say, "The *teacher learned the child* that the earth goes around the sun." We can say that the teacher told the child this, or showed her this, or demonstrated it, but not "learned her" this. That wonderfully mysterious act that we call "learning" is the child's. She will—she must—do it in her own way. Our best hope and best help is to support her inquiry, for in these acts she tells us where she is and where (and how) she is trying to go as a learner. If we provide opportunities for her to tell us, then we also provide opportunities for ourselves to help her.

To honor the child's inquiry is to acknowledge this child as an active, initiating, constructing learner. It is to support the child's use of what may be the most important tool of all for helping her do what she has in mind.

Yes, *in mind*. Once again, the inquiry act or event in a classroom reaches beyond itself to something more. Yes, there is importance in each inquiry act or event in and of itself: It is important that fifth and sixth graders probe deeper potential meanings in *Dicey's Song*, that kindergartners reflect on world languages and friendship, that first and second graders wonder together about whether voice is matter. But of still greater importance may be what these particular interactions tell the participants about use of the mind. The particular inquiry event—what children actually do and say on a particular occasion—is but one enactment of the *kind of thing* they do with their minds, with their talk, with each other:

- how they use language to render their thoughts shareable;
- how they carry out their roles as learners;
- how they connect with one another in exploration, speaking with distinctive, yet coordinated, voices;
- how they orient themselves in an open and tentative way toward topics of interest.

These are "lessons" about *inquiry*. And about *learning*. And about the *use of the mind*.

New Voices Enrich the Inquiry Dialogue

As I suggested in Chapter 1, the time is right for a study of children's inquiry: Voices of scholars and researchers and educators from the past meet voices (especially those of Vygotsky and Bakhtin) new to a discussion of children's inquiry. Thus we have considerable knowledge and also the possibility of going beyond it. Inquiry requires both. Indeed, our exploration of children's inquiry has itself been an act of inquiry. Like all inquiry acts,

- it has arisen in what we know already—of children's language development, of their ways of expressing curiosity and turning to others for help, of teaching and learning in classrooms.
- it has been an attempt to go beyond this present knowledge—to probe further from that place where known and not-known meet, a reaching place, the place where probing begins.
- it has prompted us to turn to many others for help with our understanding—to young children and their parents, to students and their teachers, to scholars, to researchers.

And to Vygotsky and Bakhtin. The voices of these two have been heard before now in other domains, but they are new to a discussion of children's inquiry. Their ideas have helped us go beyond—have enriched our conceptualization of children's inquiry purposes, expression, collaborations, styles, contexts. Now we turn to them one last time, attempting to understand how social (inquiry) dialogue becomes the (inquiry) dialogue of mind.

INNER SPEECH

Dialogue

Vygotsky believed that initially a child's speech is social in nature: it is speech for and with other people. Social speech continues throughout life, but according to Vygotsky, from about age three to about age seven, the child develops a second kind of speech as well: "inner speech" or speech for and with oneself. The word speech here is more metaphoric than literal, for inner speech is not a matter of the child now saying things to herself that she used to say to others, nor is it speech with the sound turned off. It is, rather, the formation of a new kind of consciousness in the child. It's an important development, for it is in this new consciousness that higher mental functions reside—mental activities such as reflection, problem solving, reasoning. It is also a development that has important classroom implications, for the child's continuing development of inner speech can be influenced significantly by the dialogic events of the classroom. But before we can consider those classroom implications, we need some background about (1) the dialogic character of inner speech, (2) the course of its development, and (3) the relationship of inner speech to the child's language and thought.

The dialogic character of inner speech. The word *speech* (in the label "inner speech") is problematic. Since "inner speech is inherently dialogic" (Wertsch, 1985, p. 112), the translation "inner *dialogue*" is preferable to the more familiar "inner *speech.*" In choosing between these two translations, we are not engaging in a petty semantic quibble. The choice has theoretical import, for "inner dialogue" conveys a central tenet of Vygotsky's theory, namely, that social dialogue is the origin of inner dialogue. Vygotsky maintained that social dialogue is internalized and that *"inter*-mental/psychological" processes eventually become *"intra*-mental/psychological" processes within the child: "Structural properties of interpsychological functioning, such as its dialogical question-answer organization, are part of the resulting internal intrapsychological plane of functioning" (Wertsch, 1985, p. 65). Vygotsky was not claiming that the social dialogues of the child's experience are somehow copied or stamped into the child's mind; rather, he was suggesting that inner dialogue retains the multivoiced and interactive character of social dialogue. Vygotsky's characterization of inner dialogue as "quasi-social" or a "form of internal collaboration with oneself" (quoted in Wertsch & Stone, 1985, p. 173) suggests the continuing dialogic essence of "inner speech." (How quickly the words *inter-mental, multivoiced, collaboration, interactive* bring to mind our focal classroom transcripts!)

The course of development of inner speech. Vygotsky's claims about the child's development of inner dialogue were based on his research in which he documented children's move from social dialogue to egocentric speech to inner dialogue. His study of the transitional stage (i.e., egocentric speech) is especially helpful because the child's egocentric, audible speech "provides a 'window' into the inner world of silent speech-for-oneself" (Kozulin, 1990, p. 177). "Egocentric speech is a transitory phenomenon; its roots are to be found in the primitive communicative speech-for-others, but its 'fate' is to become internalized as inner speech-for-oneself" (p. 174). And so to describe egocentric speech is to capture a development in process, speech on its way to becoming "inner." The child's egocentric speech indicates that a new and different kind of language-and-consciousness is branching off from the child's social speech. Also, it gives hints—in the child's actual talk—of the kind of process that is taking place. With the onset of egocentric speech, the child engages in a new kind of talk that serves a new kind of purpose—one that is intellectually oriented. Over time, while the child's social speech continues to be fully expressive, her egocentric speech, in contrast, becomes increasingly abbreviated, "leaving out" (i.e., not verbalizing) the subject of the sentence. These subject-less sentences Vygotsky calls "predicative," because they have only predicates. Knowing already what the spoken sentence is about (its subject), the child does not need to speak it. The claim is that the features that increasingly get left out of the child's egocentric speech are not lost; they become internalized. They move from outer (spoken) to inner (silent).

> The predicative character of inner speech seems to be a direct result of the shrinkage of the distance between addresser and addressee . . . inner speech is . . . the ultimate point . . . of "intimacy" between addresser and addressee. (Kozulin, 1990, p. 178)

In inner dialogue, addresser and addresse have become one: self. Egocentric speech is the journey toward this point. It is the transition from the expressed (for and with others) to the understood (for and with self).

The child's egocentric (and ultimately, inner) speech carries out a different function for the child than does her social speech, and it is this different function that accounts for its different (increasingly nonsocial) character. Vygotsky believed that the child's egocentric speech served to direct or guide her problem solving. In a well-known series of experiments, he engaged child subjects in various activities (e.g., drawing) and along the way introduced some obstacle. Predictably, the amount of egocentric speech increased dramatically with the introduction of the obstacle, "when the child face[d] difficulties that demand[ed] consciousness and reflection" (Vygotsky, 1986, p. 228).

> Our experimental results indicate that ... egocentric speech ... does not merely accompany the child's activity; it serves mental orientation, conscious understanding; it helps in overcoming difficulties; it is speech for oneself, intimately and usefully connected with the child's thinking. (Vygotsky, 1986, p. 228)

Indeed, one scholar describes egocentric speech as "thinking aloud": "difficulties confronting children stimulate them to 'think aloud' ... in response to a problematic situation" (Kozulin, 1990, p. 175). (Not unlike ourselves, perhaps?)

We must assume, I think, that children, throughout the school years, continue to develop both their social speech (their interaction for and with others) and also their inner speech, the internal, dialogic consciousness that guides their reflection and problem solving. We must assume, too, that throughout these years, social dialogue will continue to be the source and sustenance of the child's inner dialogue. It is impossible not to immediately think of the contribution that classroom discourse may make to the child's continuing development of inner dialogue.

The relationship of inner speech to the child's language and thought. Now, what exactly is this inner dialogue? We can get some sense of how it develops and the purposes it serves for a child, but what IS it? This one is difficult. It may be easier to begin with what inner dialogue is *not:*

- Inner dialogue is *not* talk without the volume, as if someone had pointed the remote control toward the child and pressed the mute button. Inner dialogue is not words moving through the child's mind one by one in a temporal sequence.
- Inner dialogue is *not* thought, for thought includes more than language (e.g., images) and, unlike language, it is a-temporal, an all-at-onceness rather than a one-by-one procession of words in time. (Recall Vygotsky's barefoot boy in a blue shirt running down the street.)
- Inner dialogue is *not* the stored accumulation of the social dialogues of one's experience.

But although inner dialogue is none of these, it is close to all of them. Though it is not talk without the volume, we are told repeatedly that inner dialogue is "mediated" by language.[2] And though inner dialogue is not thought, it is very close to thought; it is that part of "thought [that is] connected with words." In inner dialogue, "words die as they bring forth thought" (Vygotsky, 1986, p. 249). And although inner dialogue is not a set of social dialogues imprinted in the mind, the development of this new intellectual function has its origin in social dialogue and retains a dialogic structure.

Now, what are we to make of this language-enabled development of mind that originates in and is sustained by social interaction? Three messages emerge that I believe have profound implications for the classroom. First, the social dialogues of daily life are the source and sustenance of inner dialogue. The move from inter- to intra- does not play itself out once and for all, with the child relentlessly marching forward from social to internalized dialogue. Rather, it repeats over and over again, each new social dialogue offering new possibilities for the child's inner dialogue. Thus it is crucial that there be abundant opportunities for the child to participate actively in social dialogue in the classroom community.

Second, the nature of the social dialogues of the child's experience influences the nature of the "new plane of consciousness" she forms. Vygotsky "argued that the form of interpsychological functioning has a powerful impact on the resulting form of intrapsychological functioning" (Wertsch, 1985, p. 61). This means that it is not only the *presence* of social dialogues in a classroom that is important to the child's continuing development of inner dialogue; it is also—and especially—the *nature* of these social dialogues: What they are like will influence what the child's inner dialogue is like. What sort of consciousness does the child form out of her participation in classroom dialogues that are transmission-and-performance scripts placing the child always on the receiving end of someone else's telling? We must expect that the child's experience of these will foster the making of a mind that takes in, but does not construct or create. In contrast, what sort of consciousness does the child form out of her experience of science talks, discussions, and literature studies such as those we have considered, dialogues that are truly *dialogic*, interactions that are exploratory, tentative, and invitational? We must expect these to engender a quite different and actively constructing kind of consciousness. After all, "a 'form of discourse' is not just a vocabulary and style to be imitated: it is a way of understanding the world" (Barnes, Britton, & Torbe, 1986, p. 57).

Third, the boundaries between "outer" and "inner" are not impenetrable. One moves back and forth between them: "There remains a con-

stant interaction between outer and inner operations, one form effortlessly and frequently changing into the other and back again" (Vygotsky,
1986, pp. 87–88). This fluidity is familiar in our everyday experience. Are
we "outer" or "inner" when we talk to ourselves? Here's another example.
I am reading along and come to a passage that is particularly difficult to
understand. I stop, return to the beginning of the passage, and read it
aloud—slowly, deliberately. Or what of the situation in which a friend
comes to me with a problem, tells me about her problem and—along the
way—begins to see (and tell me) possible solutions, and finally thanks
me for being so helpful, though I said not a word! She talked her own
way through the problem. And what is personal journal writing in which
we give (written) voice to our reflections? Are we in the land of "inner"
or "outer" in these examples? The act of wondering may be the ultimate
example of this inner/outer, back-and-forth movement, acts that Townsend (1991) defines as "the questions [social] we ask ourselves [inner]."
In all these everyday examples, our act seems to draw on—and move
back and forth between—both inner and outer dialogue. Each seems to
support the other.

It could be said that in the above examples one is trying to marshal
attention and block out potential distractions. If so, this seems very like
the egocentric speech of the child, which guides her through her present
task. And, like the child's egocentric speech, our own increases with the
increasing difficulty of the task at hand. But I wonder if there isn't also
another kind of help we find when we move from "inner" to a more social
kind of speech. Is it just a matter of controlling attention, or do we also
get help by returning to the kind of dialogue that initially gave support?
In the absence of a copresent other, do I "otherize" myself and in so doing
create supportive social dialogue? This is not simply a matter of going
from not-vocalizing to vocalizing. It isn't that I turn up my voice; rather,
that I "turn up" the social component. I look at my copious handwritten
dialogue in the margins of those written texts that have especially engaged and challenged me, and I wonder to whom my inquiries were
addressed. To the author? To my otherized self? To both of us? In any
case, I seem to be recasting an inner event in a social form, in support of
my intellectual challenge.

Again I turn to the classroom. What implications does this back-and-
forth movement between inner and outer dialogue have for teachers and
children? It seems that the social dialogues of the classroom are a constant
source—wellspring—to which each member can return. Over the past
several decades, we have come to a deeper appreciation of the social nature of children's literacy development. This awareness has informed the
ways of teaching and learning in many classrooms. Nowadays we expect

to find reading workshops in which social and independent options are present and mutually supportive. Yes, we continue to value and provide for the child's individual, silent (though dialogic) engagement with a text. But so, too, do we value and provide for social dialogue involving written text—read alouds, partner reading, literature studies, book talks and so on. Writing workshops are not quiet places and we do not expect them to be. Not anymore. The child's writing experience in the classroom is infused with continuing connection with others in the community.[3] And if an individual's movement between inner and outer is so fluid, then this movement must reside mainly within the child's control, for she more than anyone else will know when to seek the resources that social interaction affords.

Finally, what is the place of inquiry in the child's inner dialogue?

Inquiry

If we care about nurturing children's inner dialogue—that consciousness where higher mental activity occurs—then we must also care about providing abundant opportunities for children to participate in inquiry discourse in their classrooms. Just as inquiry acts are fundamental in social dialogue, so are they fundamental in inner dialogue.

Ask-and-answer is the prototypic structural relationship one finds over and over again in descriptions of social dialogue. Dialogue is sometimes characterized as conversation that composes itself according to a question-answer design, for example, the prototypic "adjacency pair" that is the basic exchange unit of larger stretches of interaction. Bakhtin (1986) stresses the central role of inquiry act (or "question") in dialogue when he characterizes dialogue as "inquiry and conversation" (p. 114). He asserts that dialogue ends when inquiry ends: "If an answer does not give rise to a new question from itself, it falls out of the dialogue" (p. 168). A favorite metaphor of Bakhtin's is that of dialogue as a chain: Each inquiry utterance is a link that connects with a response that gives rise to another inquiry utterance that connects with a response . . . and so on. Inquiry act is the move that carries the discourse forward.

In inner dialogue, too, the inquiry act is fundamental. Inner dialogue retains the question-answer structure of its social origin. Recall Wertsch's (1985) words: "Structural properties of interpsychological functioning, such as its dialogical, question-answer organization, are part of the resulting internal, intrapsychological plane of functioning" (p. 65). Thus inquiry acts are essential to both social and inner dialogue. Somehow it is unsurprising that the sounds that inquiry makes in social dialogues should re-sound—*sound again*—in the dialogues of mind. It is unsurpris-

ing that in inner dialogue as in social dialogue, inquiry acts should energize and shape the dialogue, and pull into it "voices of others [that] are
indispensable in the 'theater' of our inner speech" (Kozulin, 1990, p. 179).

The claim that inquiry acts live in inner dialogue is not only theoretical; it is also research-based. I mentioned already Vygotsky's (1986) finding that in egocentric speech, subjects of sentences disappear from the
child's talk, although they are retained—understood—in the child's inner
dialogue. There is evidence in Vygotsky's research that "questions" follow a similar course. Vygotsky (and his followers) observed instances in
which children's egocentric speech had the distinct character of answers,
though the inquiry acts being "answered" were unspoken.

> Vygotsky's writings suggest that the questions to which the "answers" corre-
> spond [come to] occur in inner speech. This does not mean that a full-blown
> version of each question is somehow represented (perhaps subvocally) in
> internal mental functioning. . . . Instead, the question is *presupposed*. . . . [T]he
> answer, as it occurs in the flow of problem-solving activity, changes to reflect
> the question that had formerly been part of an overt, social interaction.
> (Wertsch, 1991, p. 90)

Bakhtin goes further than anyone I know in claiming importance for
inquiry acts in inner dialogue ("hidden dialogicality," as he sometimes
called it). For him, "question" is necessary to any act of understanding.
Spoken or not, the inquiry must be "there" for understanding to be possible. "With meaning," says Bakhtin (1986), "I give *answers* to questions.
Anything that does not answer a question is devoid of sense for us" (p.
145). He is asserting here that we can only understand that which we
construe within an inquiry-response relationship. "Meaning always responds to particular questions" (p. 145). We can be sure that Bakhtin is
not speaking of "questions" here in the sense of syntactic forms—types
of sentences. His insistence throughout his work that it is utterance (a
unit of communication), not sentence (a unit of grammar), that is relevant
to an understanding of interaction suggests that "inquiry-response" may
capture his meaning better than "question-answer" does. For him, inquiry acts, within an inquiry-response structure, enable understanding.

It is interesting that these quotes from Bakhtin (1986) come from
notebooks in which he carried out a "lifelong dialogue with himself" (p.
xvii). Reading his notebook entries, one has the strong impression of
reading responses to deep and personally compelling inquiries, though
the inquiry utterances themselves often do not occur in the writing. His
inquiries are clearly present, even when unexpressed. In his notebook
writing, Bakhtin unintentionally becomes a superb example of the very

thing he writes about: making meaning through an inquiry-response dialogue for and with oneself. He demonstrates, too, that one moves back and forth between inner and outer dialogue in a very fluid way. Indeed, in Bakhtin's notebook entries, he seems to engage in both inner and outer dialogue simultaneously.

Inquiry acts, I believe, play a crucial role in this easy movement between outer and inner dialogue. It is not only that inquiry lives within both inner and outer dialogue; inquiry also links the two. Inquiry is a kind of boundary phenomenon. Impelled outward, inquiry acts enter dialogue with others; impelled inward, they enter dialogue with self. I wonder whether, instead of conceptualizing of inner and outer dialogue as distinct domains—circles that do not touch (and seeing the individual as stepping in and out of one circle and then the other)—it may make better sense to think of the two as intersecting circles, with inquiry as their shared segment. Facing in one direction, the inquiry act participates in outer dialogue; facing the other direction, it enters inner dialogue.

The focus of this book has been inquiry as social behavior—language acts of communication purpose and expression, necessarily involving participants and social context. But inquiry is not only an act of discourse; it is also an act of mind. In inner dialogue, too, inquiry is purposeful and reverberates with the sense, expression, voices, collaborations and contexts we originally—and continually—come to know through social interaction.

I know of no more important goal in education than that the child shall discover the power of his or her own mind. And I know of no more important source of that discovery for every child, than the inquiry that lives in the continuing exploratory dialogues of classroom life.

Notes

CHAPTER 1

1. I am grateful to Carol Peterson for this example.

2. I alternate generic "he" and generic "she" by chapters, using "he" in odd-numbered chapters and "she" in even-numbered chapters.

3. I do not mean to suggest that this way of viewing language is inherently better than other ways. Language can be explored from various perspectives and each illuminates some aspects of this amazing phenomenon while ignoring others. I choose this language act perspective because it illuminates what I am trying to understand: children's inquiry development and its relation to learning in a classroom.

4. Many other units have been proposed, for example, the discourse move (Bellack, Kliebard, Hyman, & Smith, 1966), the speech act (Searle, 1970), the T-unit (O'Donnell, Griffin, & Norris, 1967).

5. Fillmore (1976) uses the terms *informational* and *interactional* to designate the message-oriented and relationship-oriented aspects of interaction. Tannen (1984) makes a similar distinction between *message* and *meta-message*.

CHAPTER 2

1. My focus for the present is social. I am not including in this discussion the inner dialogue we may carry on with ourselves in speech and writing. (We will consider this in Chapter 12.)

2. I thank Carol Peterson for this example.

3. I thank Jane Townsend (1991) for this example.

4. Tentativeness markers do other kinds of communication work also, for example, leaving the speaker an "out" if she is not very confident, or reducing one's own status in relation to the partner's. It is interesting that this teacher sometimes used tentativeness markers even when she was quite certain, apparently in order to invite the students to offer their ideas. See Townsend (1991) for further discussion of this point.

5. I call these inquiries "seemingly" mundane because we cannot know

what they are for the speaker; we cannot know what kind of building work the speaker is doing. "Mundane" may be just the look and sound that an inquiry act has to an outsider.

6. I am using the term *dialogue* here in a more everyday sense than Bakhtin did. Dialogism for him was a way of thinking about existence itself, not simply interaction between two or more persons. See Holquist (1990).

7. Ascribing specific intentionality is apparently not limited to mainstream communities, though it gets played out differently in different social groups. Heath (1983) has noted that adults in Trackton (a Black working-class community she studied), unlike mainstream adults, do not interpret the infant's vocalizations as attempts to say actual words. However, they do treat the infant's nonverbal behaviors as communicative, and "they praise the baby's nonverbal responses which seem to them appropriate to the circumstances: a coo and smile for Darett's new hat, and a grasp of Miss Lula's hand when she pokes at the baby" or the baby's excited movements on hearing a familiar voice over the telephone ("'Dis baby know you on de phone, Berta, you better ought to see dis baby'") (pp. 75–76). Thus the adults in both communities apparently see many of the infant's behaviors as communicative. The difference seems to be the status granted the various behaviors, for example, the relative importance of verbal and nonverbal behaviors and, especially, the interpretation of vocalizations (whether or not they are heard as words).

8. I thank Cyndy Hoffman for this material.

9. In natural contexts of daily life, adults often do give children explicit instruction as to what they should say in particular situations (e.g., "Say please"). See Heath (1983), Miller (1982) and Schieffelin & Ochs (1986) for examples from a variety of cultures. However, these explicit directives are simply the ways that adults and older children in these communities feel are appropriate in socializing the young. Thus, they are explicit, yet remain natural; they are not contrived or artificial in the way that school instruction often is (e.g., memorization tasks aimed at getting a high test score). They are ways of being a member of the particular community and behaving appropriately within it.

10. I am using Smith's term *engagement,* but not with his meaning. Smith (1983) defines *engagement* as "the productive interaction of a brain with a demonstration" (p. 103). I am using this term in the more everyday sense of actually participating in some activity.

CHAPTER 3

1. "Eskimos" was the term used at the time; the proper term used today is "Inuit."

2. Notice, too, that inquiries are rooted in one's knowledge and so can't all occur at the beginning of a study, before students have built a knowledge base. I shall have more to say on this point in coming chapters.

CHAPTER 4

1. I use *purpose* and *function* interchangeably.

2. The study that I find especially fascinating is Ross and Balzar (1975), that contrasted "answer" and "no-answer" conditions. First, third, and fifth grade children were shown slides and told a bit of descriptive information about each one in a detective game. The children were then to ask the experimenter questions. Half the children received answers to their questions, but for the other half (the children in the no-answer condition), when the child asked a question, the experimenter would establish eye contact with the child, then smile at the child—*and not answer the child's question*! Not surprisingly, the no-answer children asked fewer questions than those in the answer condition. The interpretation of these results was that children ask more questions when they get answers than when they don't. But this is a good example of how a research question can determine what the researcher can see. Once the research question was cast as answer/no-answer, the results were interpreted solely within that framework, and what seems to be a more likely interpretation—totally bizarre vs. normal responding behavior on the part of the experimenter—was not a possibility. It is hard to imagine a more outrageous conversational situation than one in which you ask your partner a question and the partner looks directly at you and smiles (Ah! She heard me and understands) and then remains silent and looks away. She has simply dropped out of the interaction with you (smiling all the while) and gone on with her interaction with others present. Interaction does not get more bizarre than this.

3. I thank Ann Barbour for this example from her data, and Justin and Sherry Tschoepe, who are the source.

4. For the moment, I am staying with the basic message of the utterance here, ignoring the loss of particular tone or interpersonal factors that such a paraphrase might entail.

5. There is some disagreement about whether Vološinov or Bakhtin is the author of the work from which this quotation comes. For political reasons, Bakhtin may have written under the name of Vološinov, who was a member of the "Bakhtin Circle," an intellectual discussion group led by Bakhtin. There is general agreement among scholars that even if Vološinov is the actual author of this work, his ideas were strongly influenced by Bakhtin.

CHAPTER 5

1. I am reminded of the remarkable complexity of time concepts and also of the remarkable imaginative powers of the child's mind, whenever I recall the following incident. A father had been using a spatial metaphor to help his young son understand the meanings of *yesterday* and *tomorrow*. He had characterized yesterday as "the day behind this day," and tomorrow as "the day in front of this day." He was not prepared for his son's next question: "Well, if 'yesterday' is the day *behind* this day, and 'tomorrow' is the day *in front of* this day, what do we call the day *beside* this day?" Surely this is one more example of the fact that inquiries

arise out of knowledge (however partial) and the use one makes of it. (I am indebted to Shirley Thomas for this incident.)

2. Cognitive development is not the only influence on the course of development of interrogative semantics. See especially Bloom, Merkin, and Wootten (1982) for a consideration of discourse factors and the child's use of particular verbs.

3. This phrase echoes Frank Smith's (1988) notion of the emergent reader/writer as a "member of the literacy club." See Bruner and Haste (1987) for a discussion of three ways that adult-child interaction appears to contribute to children's language development: scaffolding, negotiation of meaning, and transfer of cultural representations.

CHAPTER 6

1. A number of scholars have suggested that the teacher use moves other than questions to foster discussion (Dillon, 1983, 1988b, 1994; Wood & Wood, 1983). See Townsend (1991) for a rich description of teacher moves in discussion that were and were not in question form.

2. This advice is somewhat problematic because existing category schemes that identify "higher" and "lower" level questions do so on the basis of the words in a particular question. For example, Hunkins (1995) bases his work on Bloom's (1956) taxonomy, which includes (from lower to higher) these categories: knowledge, comprehension, application, analysis, synthesis, evaluation. Hunkins (1995) tells us, "Teachers can classify questions as to cognitive level by looking at the wording of the questions," and he goes on to list the words "that can be used at the various cognitive levels," for example, *knowledge*—what, when, who . . . *comprehension*—compare, conclude, contrast . . . *application*—solve, test, indicate . . . and so on (p. 68). But "level," it seems to me, has to do with the intellectual processes at work, not with the speaker's words per se. Jill's question "Do [rabbits] lay eggs?" would seem to kick in at the lowest level of Bloom's taxonomy: knowledge. Judging from the words themselves, this question seeks a specific fact. But Jill's "question" is an *utterance,* and the conversation in which it occurs indicates that she is doing the quite rigorous intellectual work of furthering her understanding of the "home life" of different animals—the similarities and differences among them. But even when we treat a speaker's expression as an utterance (carrying out communicative intention) rather than a sentence (a sequence of particular words), we still have a problem, for we may not know what sort of intellectual work the speaker's utterance is carrying out *for her.* We attribute to the speaker's utterance the purpose it would have if it were ours. And if the "question" is the teacher's (i.e., her probe in a discussion), although she may know her own intention in uttering it, she is not likely to know how a student takes it, that is, what level that utterance has in the student's listening response. It is quite possible that the teacher's (intended) level and the student's (processing/constructing) level are different. Thus the identification of utterances as cognitively "higher" or "lower"—while intuitively satisfying—is replete with problems.

3. We are all acutely aware of the many teachers who do not themselves hold this view of teaching and learning, but are expected to carry it out. These teachers are often pressured by principal, parents, administration, fellow teachers to "cover the curriculum" and to give evidence, in the form of students' high standardized test scores, that they have done so. Many teachers are constantly, often painfully, pulled between what they believe, on the one hand, and what the system expects them to do, on the other.

4. Knowledge as thing/object is not the only pervasive metaphor in education. The industry image is frequent, using terms such as *input* and *output, efficiency, accountability, outcomes*. And what about the pathology metaphor that sees the teacher's job as *diagnosing* and *treating*? Passive images of students are all too familiar—the blank slates to be written on, empty vessels to be filled, clay lumps to be shaped. And so the teacher's questioning—the centerpiece of classroom talk—serves largely to fill, to write on, to shape.

5. Notice that this does not mean that the teacher does not direct. Consider the structure of writing workshop—different in each classroom, but in each one, including some predictable set of procedures for managing materials, space, time, interaction, and so on. Though negotiable, the structure is largely teacher designed. Consider minilessons, an invaluable component of writing workshop in many classrooms (Calkins, 1994). Instruction is rarely more explicitly and intentionally teacher directed than it is in many minilessons. Karen's literature discussion is another classroom structure that results largely from teacher decision and direction: Literature discussions occur in this classroom because Karen decided they are a good idea, and they follow certain procedures because Karen believes these to be helpful. Teacher direction—deliberate and focused guidance—does not conflict with teacher-inquirer role in classrooms where this direction does not replace inquiry, but exists beside it to help children do their learning work.

6. It took me a while to realize that this student's hero was Clint Eastwood.

CHAPTER 7

1. I thank Carol Sharp for this material from an original research study, carried out in fulfillment of the requirements for the course Children's Questioning, a graduate seminar at The University of Texas. I also thank Jack and Susan, Carol's research subjects.

2. Again a caution is in order. The subjects in mother-infant synchronization studies have been mainly Anglo and middle class. But although the specifics of burst-pause synchrony might play out differently in different social groups, I would expect that it would play itself out in some way across cultures.

3. Notice that even oral or written text whose purpose is to inform often seems to respond to an implied act of inquiry that is the impetus for the text in the first place:

- Goffman's (1981) essay "Replies and Responses" responds to the implied inquiries "What is the nature of replies and responses? How do they work?"

- My telling you about the movie I have seen is a response to (my assumption of) your unspoken inquiry "What was the movie about?"
- My husband begins what promises to be a lengthy oration of projects and pressures of the coming week, and I hear myself say, "Did I ask?" I am telling him that there was no implicit inquiry on my part, as he has assumed.

Uttered or implied, inquiry acts propel discourse.

4. Pappas (1991) carries this suggestion further. Kindergartners' retellings of the expository and narrative texts that adults read to them preserve the distinctive structural features of each of these genres. This suggests an early sensitivity to different kinds of text structure, as well as early ability to (re)construct distinct text types.

5. Note that I am talking here of Western, mainstream imaginative story narrative only, not everyday narratives or narratives in other cultural contexts in which stories may be jointly constructed, etc. (Au, 1980; Heath, 1982b).

6. We will focus on the classroom in the next chapter, but already you can see why a student's act of inquiry may not always be welcome in a classroom. There are surely times when a teacher (often with good reason) does not wish to have the discourse event destabilized, its text structure altered, its topic focus shifted. And she may not care to be repositioned—given a new role in the communication event. It is less challenging for Jack to support Susan's inquiry during an Irmagold story event involving just the two of them than it is for a teacher to support students' inquiry in a classroom of 25. It is easy to love children's inquiry acts in the abstract, but it is sometimes difficult to love these highly imposing acts in the moment-to-moment busyness of classroom life.

7. It is not literally true that he cannot go on, but to do so would be to behave in a way that he would feel was inappropriate or rude. He could choose to end the event, of course ("I think I hear the phone"), but if he chooses to stay in the event, with its well-established traditions of Irmagold stories, then he either responds to Susan's inquiry acts in expected ways, or else gives her a reason for not doing so ("That's coming in a minute"), or pretends he doesn't hear her.

8. Not all cultures privilege speaking over listening. See Philips, 1972, 1983; John, 1972.

9. I use the term *active listening*, recognizing that it is redundant. Listening, by definition, is active.

10. Rosenblatt (1978) makes an analogous point about reading: "A text, once it leaves its author's hands, is simply paper and ink until a reader evokes from it a literary work" (p. ix).

11. It is usual to think of question-answer as an initiate-respond pair. But clearly Susan's questions are often responses to Jack's answers, and thus they both initiate and respond. The notion of initiate-respond as a closed pair is unsatisfactory, as is the notion that an utterance is either an initiation *or* a response. As classroom teachers well know, many acts of inquiry in real dialogues both initiate and respond. Susan's responses to Jack's answers demonstrate this two-sidedness of inquiry acts.

12. This is as true of writing as it is of conversation. The author writes with

his audience very much in mind, shaping his text in anticipation of audience interpretation and response.

CHAPTER 8

1. Notice, too, how quickly the word *power* partners with *authority* and *privilege* in the phrases *power and authority* and *power and privilege.*

2. I am grateful to Phyllis Whitin for calling my attention to Karen Gallas's work.

3. This squares with the personal experience many of us had as students. Another student would ask a question and I would wonder, "Why didn't I think of that?" But because someone else did, and her inquiry became available to me, so too did new ways of thinking. Another's inquiry act opened a door for me.

4. You will notice differences in Vivian's and Karen's transcripts. Each teacher transcribes in ways that are most appropriate to her own purpose and will best illuminate what it is that she is trying to understand in the children's talk. Vivian wants to probe the line of the children's thinking, and so she retains the children's own words, but edits out their performance imperfections (repetitions, hesitations, interruptions)—"clutter" and messiness that intrude on her focus. She wants to hold a steady, unencumbered gaze on the line of thinking the children pursue. For Karen, the messiness itself is of interest, so she preserves it in her transcripts. Karen traces the children's ideas as they weave in and out of the discussion, seem to get lost, and then, oftentimes, reappear in some form. Finding these patterns and connections through talk that seems to meander is Karen's interest, so preserving the totality of the talk, with all its apparent meanderings, is crucial.

CHAPTER 9

1. I am struck by how important the sounds of speech are to Bakhtin. Metaphors drawing on the actual sounds of the voice abound: "The utterance is filled with *dialogic overtones*" (Bakhtin, 1986, p. 102); "Intonation is the *sound* that value makes (Clark & Holquist, 1984, p. 10).

2. I find it interesting that each of these three children engages in imagining in the focal transcripts: Jill imagines what hospital experience is like; Justin imagines heaven; Susan imagines how Albert the Abalone looks. I hear different voices in these acts of imagination. I hear a businesslike quality in Jill ("Three [times you have been in the hospital]? O.K. What was the first one?"); I hear an almost playful quality in Justin ("And we'll be standing up just like we are now."); I hear a working tone in Susan, but work with an exploratory accent (in contrast to Jill's businesslike tone).

3. It was my colleague Tere Escobedo who pointed out to me many years ago that the vigorous, initiating kind of inquiry I so valued in schoolchildren was considered disrespectful in child-adult interactions in the community in which she grew up.

CHAPTER 10

1. I have changed all names in this incident.

2. Students in the Nath study also described positive questioning experiences. The overwhelming majority recounted asking a question and being complimented by the teacher for having asked "a good question." Only a few found the experience positive because of having derived personal intellectual satisfaction. These responses suggested that the students valued teacher approval above all else.

3. Notice that a number of the words that cluster around *inquiry* suggest strong imposition, even control. *Inquisitor* and *inquisition* are quite ominous. *Interrogative* and *question* are neutral enough as words that name inquiry's canonical syntactic form. But consider the word *interrogate*. And what about *question(ing)* in "He was brought in for questioning" or "She questioned the authority of the church." These uses of *question* suggest confrontation, challenge, an adversarial relationship. One wonders whether some of these connotations of challenge cling to our sense of the word *inquiry* as well.

4. These desires may remind you of the "double bind" Tannen (1984) writes of—the simultaneous pulls toward autonomy/separateness and affiliation/connection; the "desire to be unimpeded" stresses respect for and protection of autonomy and separateness, whereas the "desire to be approved of" stresses affiliation and connection.

5. There seems to be increasing social pressure to avoid sensitive topics in the classroom. Yet the classroom is the very place where children can learn to discuss sensitive and controversial issues in ways that do not hurt others. Such discussion would seem to be a major contribution that public education can make to children's development, as well as to the strengthening of a caring society. See Noddings (1993) for a compelling argument against keeping controversial topics outside of classroom exploration and debate.

6. Wrong place can be problematic also, often overlapping with time. That is, time and place often go together.

7. Another major consideration (one that would require a book all its own) is cultural differences in the ways in which respect for adults is to be expressed by children. Differences from one culture to another can be considerable: who one asks about what and how one does it. When teacher and child are members of different social groups, it is likely that each will have to extend her repertoire of inquiry politeness, both that which she uses and that which she interprets appropriately.

8. Notice that it is when the children's equal status is threatened by a few boys claiming more power for themselves and excluding other children from the talk that Gallas takes strong and explicit action to alter the situation toward equality for all participants.

9. I think that Vygotsky's *zone of proximal development* is similar to what teachers sometimes call "teachable moments." The metaphors are different: Vygotsky's is *place* (a "zone"), and the teacher's is *time* (a "moment"). However, basic to both is a sense of a particular situation offering the opportunity for an adult to help a child go beyond—a sense that with a bit of a boost, the child will be able to then move forward on her own.

CHAPTER 11

1. For a particularly noteworthy exception, see Dyson, 1992 (p. 3) for a graphic representation of the child's membership in three overlapping and intersecting "worlds."

2. I am struck by how deeply moral these matters are (see Coles, 1997). See also Harwayne (1992, pp. 10–11) for further examples of read-alouds selected to help with early community-building.

3. At the beginning and throughout the year, the teacher's influence is enormous, of course. However, the uniqueness of each class of children she teaches over the years reminds us that her influence—enormous as it undoubtedly is— is but one among many.

4. A study by Dillon (1981) indicates that such negative teacher responses are very much a part of the college/university scene. Dillon administered a questionnaire to 166 student teachers in university education courses. Ninety-five percent of the respondents indicated that they "have questions but do not ask them" in classes (p. 136). The reason given by 72% of these students was fear. Although some respondents indicated fear of negative responses from classmates, "the greatest fear cited [was] . . . of the teacher's negative reaction" (p. 137). The respondents stated that "the teacher will get angry and furious, upset and defensive, rude and sarcastic, discourteous and condemnatory. The teacher will say: 'I am amazed at the amount of ignorance you have just displayed,' or 'That's so obvious it's not even worth asking'" (p. 137). This study indicated that negative teacher responses to the questions of classmates, as well as to respondents' own questions, had caused these student inquirers to shut down. Inquiry needs a safe and trusting surround context in a classroom.

CHAPTER 12

1. Robert Coles (1997) would, I think, call this self-and-other awareness moral, as well as democratic. He describes the "moral intelligence" of a much admired mentor from his youth, citing "his respect for other people as well as himself, [and] the deep awareness he acknowledged of our human connectedness" (p. 5).

2. I don't quite understand this. The term "mediate" is typically offered as an *explanation* for the process of internalization; but to me it is quite the opposite: It seems to be a placeholder for the *inexplicable*. I am reminded of a math cartoon in which the adult stands at a chalkboard in front of a class. The writing on the board begins with a complex formula and ends with an answer, and in between are the words "A miracle happens here." So it seems with inner dialogue: the child starts with social dialogue, ends up with inner dialogue, and in between, a miracle. It is a miracle that involves language. Language is the enabler without which the miracle could not occur.

3. My examples involve reading and writing, but similar principles apply to other curricular areas as well.

References

Albritton, T. (1992). Honest questions and the teaching of English. *English Education, 24*(2), 91–100.

Allender, J. S. (1969). A study of inquiry activity in elementary school children. *American Educational Research Journal, 6*, 543–558.

Allender, J. S. (1970). Some determinants of inquiry activity in elementary school children. *Journal of Educational Psychology, 61*(3), 220–225.

Andre, T. (1987). Questions and learning from reading. *Questioning Exchange, 1*(1), 47–86.

Au, K. (1980). Participation structures in a reading lesson with Hawaiian children: Analysis of a culturally appropriate instruction event. *Anthropology and Education Quarterly, 11*(2), 91–115.

Austin, J. L. (1962). *How to do things with words.* Oxford: Clarendon Press.

Avery, C. (1993). *. . . And with a light touch: Learning about reading, writing, and teaching with first graders.* Portsmouth, NH: Heinemann.

Bakhtin, M. M. (1981). *The dialogic imagination.* Austin: The University of Texas Press.

Bakhtin, M. M. (1986). *Speech genres & other late essays.* Austin: The University of Texas Press.

Barnes, D. (1986). Language in the secondary classroom. In D. Barnes, J. Britton, & M. Torbe, *Language, the learner and the school* (3rd ed.; pp. 9–97). New York: Penguin Books.

Barnes, D., Britton, J., & Torbe, M. (1986). *Language, the learner and the school* (3rd ed.). New York: Penguin Books.

Bates, E. (1976). *Language and context: The acquisition of pragmatics.* New York: Academic Press.

Bateson, G. (1972). A theory of play and fantasy. Reprinted in G. Bateson, *Steps to an ecology of mind.* New York: Ballantine Books.

Baugh, J. (1983). *Black street speech: Its history, structure and survival.* Austin: The University of Texas Press.

Bellack, A. A., Kliebard, H. M., Hyman, R. T., & Smith, F. L. (1966). *The language of the classroom.* New York: Teachers College Press.

Berlyne, D. E. (1965). Curiosity and education. In J. D. Krumboltz (Ed.), *Learning and the educational process* (pp. 67–89). Chicago: Rand McNally & Co.

Berninger, G., & Garvey, C. (1981). Questions and the allocation, construction, and timing of turns in child discourse. *Journal of Psycholinguistic Research, 10*(4).

Berninger, G., & Garvey, C. (1981). Relevant replies to questions: Answers versus evasions. *Journal of Psycholinguistic Research, 10*(4), 375–402.

Blank, S. S., & Covington, M. (1965). Inducing children to ask questions in solving problems. *Journal of Educational Research, 59*, 21–27.

Bloom, B. S. (1956). *Taxonomy of educational objectives. Book I: Cognitive Domain.* New York: Longman.

Bloom, L., Merkin, S., & Wootten, J. (1982). *Wh*-questions: Linguistic factors that contribute to the sequence of acquisition. *Child Development, 53*, 1084–1092.

Brenneis, D., & Lein, L. (1977). "You fruithead": A sociolinguistic approach to children's dispute settlement. In S. Ervin-Tripp & C. Mitchell-Kernan (Eds.), *Child discourse* (pp. 49–65). New York: Academic Press.

Britton, J. (1973). *Language and learning.* Hammondsworth, England: Pelican.

Brown, P., & Levinson, S. (1987). *Some universals in language usage.* New York: Cambridge University Press.

Brown, R. (1968). The development of wh questions in child speech. *Journal of Verbal Learning and Behavior, 7*, 279–290.

Bruner, J. S. (1978). From communication to language: A psychological perspective. In I. Markova (Ed.), *The social context of language* (pp. 17–48). New York: John Wiley & Sons.

Bruner, J. S. (1981). The pragmatics of acquisition. In W. Deutsch (Ed.), *The child's construction of language* (pp. 39–55). New York: Academic Press.

Bruner, J. S. (1986). *Actual minds, possible worlds.* Cambridge, MA: Harvard University Press.

Bruner, J. S. (1990). *Acts of meaning.* Cambridge, MA: Harvard University Press.

Bruner, J. S. (1996). *The culture of education.* Cambridge, MA: Harvard University Press.

Bruner, J. S., & Haste, H. (1987). Introduction. In J. S. Bruner & H. Haste (Eds.), *Making sense: The child's construction of the world* (pp. 1–25). New York: Methuen.

Bruner, J. S., Roy, C., & Ratner, N. (1982). The beginnings of request. In K. Nelson (Ed.), *Children's language* (Vol. 3, pp. 91–138). Hillsdale, NJ: Erlbaum.

Cairns, H. S., & Hsu, J. R. (1978). *Who, why, when,* and *how:* A development study. *Journal of Child Language, 5*, 477–488.

Calkins, L. M. (1994). *The art of teaching writing* (new edition). Portsmouth, NH: Heinemann.

Cazden, C. B. (1988). *Classroom discourse: The language of teaching and learning.* Portsmouth, NH: Heinemann.

Christenbury, L., & Kelly, P. P. (1993). *Questioning: A path to critical thinking.* Urbana, IL: National Council of Teachers of English.

Chukovksy, K. (1968). *From two to five.* Berkeley and Los Angeles: University of California Press.

Clark, K., & Holquist, M. (1984). *Mikhail Bakhtin.* Cambridge, MA: Harvard University Press, Belknap Press.

Clay, M. M. (1966). Emergent reading behavior. Unpublished doctoral dissertation. University of Auckland.

Cole, M. (1996). *Cultural psychology: A once and future discipline.* Cambridge, MA: Harvard University Press, Belknap Press.

Coles, R. (1997). *The moral intelligence of children.* New York: Random House.

Cook-Gumperz, J. (1977). Situated instructions: Language socialization of school age children. In S. Ervin-Tripp & C. Mitchell-Kernan (Eds.), *Child discourse* (pp. 103–121). New York: Academic Press.

Copenhaver, J. (1993). Instances of inquiry. *Primary Voices K–6* (Premier Issue), 6–14.

Davis, R. M. S. (1971). A study of the relationship between pupil questions and selected variables. *Dissertation Abstracts, 31A,* 5027–5028.

Denney, N. W., & Connors, G. J. (1974). Altering the questioning strategies of preschool children. *Child Development, 45,* 1108–1112.

Dillon, J. T. (1981). A norm against student questions. *The Clearing House, 55,* 136–139.

Dillon, J. T. (1983). *Teaching and the art of questioning.* Bloomington, IN: Phi Delta Kappa Educational Foundation.

Dillon, J. T. (1984). Research on questioning and discussion. *Educational Leadership, 42*(3), 50–56.

Dillon, J. T. (1987). Question-answer models in a dozen fields. *Questioning Exchange: A Multidisciplinary Review, 1*(2), 151–169.

Dillon, J. T. (Ed.). (1988a). *Questioning and discussion: A multidisciplinary study.* Norwood, NJ: Ablex.

Dillon, J. T. (1988b). *Questioning and teaching: A manual of practice.* New York: Teachers College Press.

Dillon, J. T. (1994). *Using discussion in classrooms.* Philadelphia: Open University Press.

Donaldson, M. (1979). *Children's minds.* New York: W. W. Norton.

Dore, J. (1975). Holophrases, speech acts, and language universals. *Journal of Child Language, 2*(1), 21–40.

Dyson, A. H. (1989). *Multiple worlds of child writers: Friends learning to write.* New York: Teachers College Press.

Dyson, A. H. (1992). *Social worlds of children learning to write in an urban primary school.* New York: Teachers College Press.

Edelsky, C. (1991). *With literacy and justice for all: Rethinking the social in language and education.* New York: Falmer Press.

Eeds, M., & Wells, D. (1989). Grand conversations: An exploration of meaning construction in literature study groups. *Research in the Teaching of English, 23*(1), 4–29.

Eimas, P. D., Sigueland, E. R., Jusczyk, P., & Vigorito, J. (1971). Speech perception in infants. *Science, 171,* 303–306.

Eisenberg, A., & Garvey, C. (1981). Children's use of verbal strategies in resolving conflicts. *Discourse Processes, 4,* 149–170.

Elbow, P. (1994). What do we mean when we talk about voice in texts? In K. B.

Yancey (Ed.), *Voices on voice: Perspectives, definitions, inquiry* (pp. 1–35). Urbana, IL: National Council of Teachers of English.

Emerson, C., & Holquist, M. (1986). Introduction. In M. M. Bakhtin, *Speech genres & other late essays* (pp. ix–xxiii). Austin: The University of Texas Press.

Erickson, F. (1982). Classroom discourse as improvisation: Relationships between academic task structure and social participation structure in lessons. In L. C. Wilkinson (Ed.), *Communicating in the classroom* (pp. 153–181). New York: Academic Press.

Erickson, F., & Mohatt, G. (1982). Cultural organization of participation structures in two classrooms of Indian students. In G. Spindler (Ed.), *Doing the ethnography of schooling: Educational anthropology in action.* New York: Holt, Rinehart, and Winston.

Ervin-Tripp, S. (1970). Discourse agreement: How children answer questions. In J. R. Hayes (Ed.), *Cognition and the development of language* (pp. 79–107). New York: Wiley.

Feldman, C., & Wertsch, J. (1976). Context dependent properties of teachers' speech. *Youth and Society, 8,* 227–258.

Fillmore, L. W. (1976). *The second time around: Cognitive and social strategies in second language acquisition.* Unpublished doctoral dissertation, Stanford University.

Fillmore, L. W. (1983). The language learner as an individual: Implications of research on individual differences for the ESL teacher. In J. Handscombe & M. Clarke (Eds.), *On TESOL '82: Pacific perspectives on language learning and teaching* (pp. 157–173). Washington, DC: Teachers of English to Speakers of Other Languages.

Furrow, D., & Nelson, K. (1984). Environmental correlates of individual differences in language acquisition. *Journal of Child Language, 11*(3), 523–534.

Gall, M. (1970). The use of questions in teaching. *Review of Educational Research, 40*(5), 707–721.

Gall, M. (1984). Synthesis of research on teachers' questioning. *Educational Leadership, 42*(3), 40–47.

Gallas, K. (1995). *Talking their way into science.* New York: Teachers College Press.

Garvey, C., & Baldwin, T. (1970). *Studies in convergent communication: Analysis of verbal interaction.* Baltimore: John Hopkins Center for the Study of Social Organization of Schools Report No. 88.

Garvey, C., Baldwin, T., & Dickstein, E. (1971). *A structural approach to the study of convergent communication.* Paper presented at annual meeting of the American Educational Research Association.

Gee, J. (1990). *Social linguistics and literacies: Ideology in discourses.* Bristol, PA: Falmer Press.

Genishi, C., & Di Paolo, M. (1982). Learning through argument in a preschool. In L. C. Wilkinson (Ed.)., *Communicating in the classroom* (pp. 49–68). New York: Academic Press.

Goffman, E. (1974). *Frame analysis: An essay on the organization of experience.* Cambridge: Harvard University Press.

Goffman, E. (1981). Replies and responses. In E. Goffman, *Forms of talk* (pp. 5–77). Philadelphia: University of Pennsylvania Press.

Goodlad, J. I. (1984). *A place called school: Promise for the future.* New York: McGraw-Hill.

Goodman, Y. M., Watson, D. J., & Burke, C. L. (1987). *Reading miscue inventory: Alternative procedures.* New York: Richard C. Owen.

Goodwin, C., & Duranti, A. (1992). Rethinking context: An introduction. In A. Duranti & C. Goodwin (Eds.), *Rethinking context: Language as an interactive phenomenon* (pp. 1–42). New York: Cambridge University Press.

Guszak, F. J. (1967). Teacher questioning and reading. *The Reading Teacher, 21*(3), 227–234.

Halliday, M. A. K. (1977). *Learning how to mean.* New York: Elsevier North-Holland.

Hardy, B. (1977). Narrative as a primary act of mind. In M. Meek, A. Warlow & G. Barton (Eds.), *The cool web* (pp. 12–24). London: Bodley Head.

Harwayne, S. (1992). *Lasting impressions: Weaving literature into the writing workshop.* Portsmouth, NH: Heinemann.

Heath, S. B. (1982a). Questioning at home and at school: A comparative study. In G. Spindler (Ed.), *Doing the ethnography of schooling: Educational anthropology in action* (pp. 104–131). New York: Holt, Rinehart, and Winston.

Heath, S. B. (1982b). What no bedtime story means: Narrative skills at home and school. *Language in Society, 11*(2), 49–76.

Heath, S. B. (1983). *Ways with words: Language, life, and work in communities and classrooms.* New York: Cambridge University Press.

Holquist, M. (1990). *Dialogism: Bakhtin and his world.* London: Routledge.

Holt, J. (1970). *What do I do Monday?* New York: E. P. Dutton.

Holzman, M. (1972). The use of interrogative forms in the verbal interactions of three mothers and their children. *Journal of Psycholinguistic Research, 1,* 311–336.

Hudelson, S. (1989). *Write on: Children's writing in ESL.* Englewood Cliffs, NJ: Prentice-Hall.

Hudelson, S. (1994). Literacy development of second language children. In F. Genesee (Ed.), *Educating second language children: The whole child, the whole curriculum, the whole community.* New York: Cambridge University Press.

Hunkins, F. P. (1995). *Teaching thinking through effective questioning* (2nd ed.). Norwood, MA: Christopher-Gordon.

John, V. P. (1972). Styles of learning—styles of teaching: Reflections on the education of Navajo children. In C. Cazden, V. P. John, & D. Hymes (Eds.), *Functions of language in the classroom* (pp. 331–343). New York: Teachers College Press.

Kearsley, G. P. (1976). Questions and question asking in verbal discourse: A cross-disciplinary review. *Journal of Psycholinguistic Research, 5*(4), 355–375.

Kehl, R. (1983). *Silver departures: Quotations to set the mind traveling.* San Marcos, CA: Green Tiger Press.

Kenzie, R. W. (1977). *Assessing and facilitating manipulative curiosity and experimental inquiry in young children.* Paper presented at the annual meeting of the American Educational Research Association.

Kirshenblatt-Gimblett, B. (1976). *Speech play.* Philadelphia: University of Pennsylvania Press.

Klima, E. S., & Bellugi, U. (1971). Syntactic regularities in the speech of children. In A. Bar-Adon & W. F. Leopold (Eds.), *Child language: A book of readings,* (pp. 412–424). Englewood Cliffs, NJ: Prentice-Hall.

Kozulin, A. (1990). *Vygotsky's psychology: A biography of ideas.* Cambridge, MA: Harvard University Press.

Labov, W., & Fanshel, D. (1977). *Therapeutic discourse.* New York: Academic Press.

Lakoff, G., & Johnson, M. (1980). *Metaphors we live by.* Chicago: University of Chicago Press.

Laughlin, P. R. (1968). Investigation of the manner in which young children process intellectual information. ERIC ED 036 313.

Lindfors, J. W. (1986). English for everyone. *Language Arts, 63(1).*

Lindfors, J. W. (1987). *Children's language and learning* (2nd ed.). Englewood Cliffs, NJ: Prentice-Hall.

Lindfors, J. W. (1990). Speaking creatures in the classroom. In S. Hynds & D. L. Rubin (Eds.), *Perspectives on talk and learning* (pp. 21–39). Urbana, IL: National Council of Teachers of English.

Mehan, H. (1979). *Learning lessons: Social organization in the classroom.* Cambridge, MA: Harvard University Press.

Michaels, S. (1981). "Sharing time": Children's narrative styles and differential access to literacy. *Language in Society, 10.*

Michaels, S., & Collins, J. (1984). Oral discourse styles: Classroom interaction and the acquisition of literacy. In D. Tannen (Ed.), *Coherence in spoken and written discourse* (pp. 219–244). Norwood, NJ: Ablex.

Miller, P. (1982). *Amy, Wendy, and Beth: Learning language in South Baltimore.* Austin: The University of Texas Press.

Miyake, N., & Norman, D. A. (1979). To ask a question, one must know enough to know what is not known. *Journal of Verbal Learning & Verbal Behavior, 18,* 351–364.

Morgan, N., & Saxton, J. (1991). *Teaching, questioning and learning.* London: Routledge.

Nath, I. M. (1994). Presentation, EDC 385G: Children's Questioning, The University of Texas.

Nelson, K. (1973). *Structure and strategy in learning to talk* (serial no. 149). Chicago: University of Chicago Press for the Society for Research in Child Development.

Nelson, K. (1981). Individual differences in language development: Implications for development and language. *Developmental Psychology, 17,* 170–187.

Nelson, K., & Gruendel, J. M. (1979). At morning it's lunchtime: A scriptal view of children's dialogues. *Discourse Processes, 2,* 73–94.

Nelson, K. E., & Earl, N. (1973). Information search by pre-school children: Induced use of categories and category hierarchies. *Child Development, 44,* 682–685.

Ninio, A., & Bruner, J. S. (1978). The achievement and antecedents of labelling. *Journal of Child Language, 5(1),* 1–16.

Noddings, N. (1993). *Educating for intelligent belief or unbelief.* New York: Teachers College Press.

O'Donnell, R. C., Griffin, W. J., & Norris, R. C. (1967). *Syntax of kindergarten and elementary school children: A transformational analysis.* Urbana, IL: National Council of Teachers of English.

Paley, V. G. (1981). *Wally's stories.* Cambridge, MA: Harvard University Press.

Palincsar, A. S., & Brown, A. L. (1984). Reciprocal teaching of comprehension-fostering and comprehension-monitoring activities. *Cognition and Instruction, 1*(2), 117–175.

Pappas, C. (1991). Fostering full access to literacy by including information books. *Language Arts, 68*(6), 449–462.

Pease, D. M., Gleason, J. B., & Pan, B. A. (1989). Gaining meaning: Semantic development. In J. B. Gleason (Ed.), *The development of language* (2nd ed.; pp. 101–134). Columbus, OH: Merrill.

Philips, S. U. (1972). Participant structures and communicative competence: Warm Springs children in community and classroom. In C. B. Cazden, V. P. John, & D. Hymes (Eds.), *Functions of language in the classroom* (pp. 370–394). New York: Teachers College Press.

Philips, S. U. (1983). *The invisible culture.* New York: Longman.

Piaget, J. (1955). *The language and thought of the child.* New York: Meridian Books.

Przetacznik-Gierowska, M. (1990). Cognitive and interpersonal functions of children's questions. In G. Conti-Ramsden & C. E. Snow (Eds.), *Children's language* (Vol. 7, pp. 69–101). Hillside, NJ: Erlbaum.

Ratner, N. K., & Bruner, J. S. (1978). Games, social exchange and the acquisition of language. *Journal of Child Language, 5,* 391–401.

Redfield, D. L., & Rousseau, E. W. (1981). A meta-analysis of experimental research on teacher questioning behavior. *Review of Educational Research, 51,* 237–245.

Rey, M., & Rey, H. A. (1966). *Curious George goes to the hospital.* Boston: Houghton Mifflin.

Rigg, P., & Allen, V. G. (Eds.). (1989). *When they don't all speak English: Integrating the ESL student into the regular classroom.* Urbana, IL: National Council of Teachers of English.

Rogoff, B. (1990). *Apprenticeship in thinking: Cognitive development in social context.* New York: Oxford University Press.

Rommetveit, R. (1992). Outlines of a dialogically based social-cognitive approach to human cognition and communication. In A. Wold (Ed.), *The dialogical alternative: Towards a theory of language and mind* (pp. 19–44). Oslo: Scandinavian University Press.

Rosenblatt, L. (1978). *The reader, the text, the poem.* Carbondale: Southern Illinois University Press.

Roser, N., & Martinez, M. (1985). Read it again: The value of repeated reading during storytime. *The Reading Teacher, 38,* 782–786.

Ross, H. S., & Balzer, R. H. (1975). Determinants and consequences of children's questions. *Child Development, 46,* 536–539.

Rowe, M. B. (1974). Wait-time and rewards as instructional variables: Their influence on language, logic, and fate control. Part I: Wait-time. *Journal of Research in Science Teaching, 11,* 81–94.

Sacks, H. (1974). An analysis of the course of a joke's telling in conversation. In

R. Bauman & J. Sherzer (Eds.), *Explorations in the ethnography of speaking* (pp. 337–353). New York: Cambridge University Press.

Savić, S. (1975). Aspects of adult-child communication: The problem of question acquisition. *Journal of Child Language, 2,* 251–260.

Saxe, R. M., & Stollak, G. E. (1971). Curiosity and the parent-child relationship. *Child Development, 42,* 373–384.

Schaffer, H. R., Collis, G. M., & Parsons, G. (1977). Vocal interchange and visual regard in verbal and pre-verbal children. In H. R. Schaffer (Ed.), *Studies in mother-infant interaction* (pp. 291–324). New York: Academic Press.

Schank, R. L., & Abelson, R. (1977). *Scripts, plans, goals and understanding: An inquiry into human knowledge structures.* New York: Wiley.

Schieffelin, B. B., & Ochs, E. (1986). *Language socialization across cultures.* New York: Cambridge University Press.

Searle, J. R. (1970). *Speech acts: An essay in the philosophy of language.* New York: Cambridge University Press.

Seifert, P. (forthcoming). Inquiry in the kindergarten. In J. W. Lindfors & J. S. Townsend (Eds.), *Teachers' voices: Language arts.* Urbana, IL: National Council of Teachers of English.

Shared Nomenclature, Ohio State University Film Lab Service, 4019 Prospect Avenue, Cleveland, OH 44103.

Sharp, C. (1991). Sense making during story time. Unpublished paper, The University of Texas.

Shatz, M. (1979). How to do things by asking: Form-function pairings in mothers' questions and their relation to children's responses. *Child Development, 50,* 1093–1099.

Shulman, L. S. (1965). Seeking styles and individual differences in patterns of inquiry. *The School Review,* 258–266.

Sinclair, J. McH., & Coulthard, R. M. (1975). *Towards an analysis of discourse: The English used by teachers and pupils.* New York: Oxford University Press.

Smith, F. (1975). *Comprehension and learning: A conceptual framework for teachers.* New York: Holt, Rinehart, and Winston.

Smith, F. (1983). Demonstrations, engagement, and sensitivity. In F. Smith, *Essays into literacy.* Portsmouth, NH: Heinemann.

Smith, F. (1988). *Joining the literacy club: Further essays into education.* Portsmouth, NH: Heinemann.

Smith, K. (1990a). Entertaining a text: A reciprocal process. In K. G. Short & K. M. Pierce (Eds.), *Talking about books: Creating literate communities* (pp. 17–31). Portsmouth, NH: Heinemann.

Smith, K. (1990b). *Literature study in Karen Smith's classroom.* A video. Tempe, AZ: Center for Establishing Dialogue in Teaching and Learning.

Smitherman, G. (1977). *Talkin and testifyin.* Boston: Houghton Mifflin.

Snow, C. E. (1977). The development of conversation between mothers and babies. *Journal of Child Language, 4*(1), 1–22.

Snow, C. E., & Ferguson, C. A. (Eds.). (1977). *Talking to children: Language input and acquisition.* New York: Cambridge University Press.

Stern, D. N., Beebe, B., Jaffe, J., & Bennett, S. L. (1977). The infant's stimulus world during social interaction: A study of caregiver behavior with particular reference to repetition and timing. In H. R. Schaffer (Ed.), *Studies in mother-infant interaction* (pp. 177–202). New York: Academic Press.

Strieb, L. Y. (forthcoming). Parents and language arts. In J. W. Lindfors & J. S. Townsend (Eds.), *Teachers' voices: Language arts*. Urbana, IL: National Council of Teachers of English.

Sulzby, E., & Teale, W. (1991). Emergent literacy. In R. Barr, M. L. Kamil, P. B. Mosenthal, & P. D. Pearson (Eds.), *Handbook of reading research* (Vol. 2, pp. 727–757). New York: Longman.

Tamir, L. (1980). Interrogatives in dialogue: Case study of mother and child 16–19 months. *Journal of Psycholinguistic Research, 9*(4), 407–424.

Tannen, D. (1984). *Conversational style: Analyzing talk among friends.* Norwood, NJ: Ablex.

Tannen, D. (1989). *Talking voices: Repetition, dialogue, and imagery in conversational discourse.* New York: Cambridge University Press.

Tannen, D. (Ed.) (1993). *Framing in discourse.* New York: Oxford University Press.

Teale, W. H. (1987). Emergent literacy: Reading and writing development in early childhood. In J. E. Readence & R. S. Baldwin (Eds.), *Research in literacy: Merging perspectives* (pp. 45–74). Rochester, NY: National Reading Conference.

Tizard, B., & Hughes, M. (1984). *Young children learning.* Cambridge, MA: Harvard University Press.

Todorov, T. (1984). *Mikhail Bakhtin: The dialogical principle.* Minneapolis: University of Minnesota Press.

Torrance, E. P. (1970). Group size and question-asking performance of pre-primary children. *Journal of Psychology, 74,* 71–75.

Torrance, E. P. (1972). Influence of alternate approaches to pre-primary educational stimulation and question-asking skills. *Journal of Educational Research, 65*(5), 204–206.

Townsend, J. S. (1991). A study of wondering discourse in three literature class discussions. Unpublished doctoral dissertation. Austin: The University of Texas at Austin.

Trevarthen, C. (1977). Descriptive analyses of infant communicative behaviour. In H. R. Schaffer (Ed.), *Studies in mother-infant interaction* (pp. 227–270). New York: Academic Press.

Trevarthen, C. (1992). An infant's motives for speaking and thinking in the culture. In A. H. Wold (Ed.), *The dialogical alternative: Towards a theory of language and mind* (pp. 99–137). Oslo: Scandinavian University Press.

Tyack, D., & Ingram, D. (1977). Children's production and comprehension of questions. *Journal of Child Language, 4,* 211–224.

Van der Meij, H. (1986). *Questioning: A study on the questioning behavior of elementary school children.* Den Haag: Svo's Gravenhage.

Voigt, C. (1982). *Dicey's song.* New York: Fawcett Juniper.

Vološinov, V. N. (1973). *Marxism and the philosophy of language.* Cambridge, MA: Harvard University Press.

Vygotsky, L. S. (1978). *Mind in society: The development of higher psychological pro-*

cesses (M. Cole, V. John-Steiner, S. Scribner, & E. Souberman, Eds.). Cambridge, MA: Harvard University Press.

Vygotsky, L. S. (1986). *Thought and language* (A. Kozulin, Ed.). Cambridge, MA: MIT Press.

Walther, K. E. P. (1978). Effects of naturalistic settings on spontaneous verbal information-seeking behavior of 6th grade girls. Unpublished doctoral dissertation. Austin: The University of Texas at Austin.

Wertsch, J. V. (1985). *Vygotsky and the social formation of mind.* Cambridge, MA: Harvard University Press.

Wertsch, J. V. (1991). *Voices of the mind: A sociocultural approach to mediated action.* Cambridge, MA: Harvard University Press.

Wertsch, J. V., & Stone, A. C. (1985). The concept of internalization in Vygotsky's account of the genesis of higher mental functions. In J. V. Wertsch (Ed.), *Culture, communication, and cognition: Vygotskian perspectives* (pp. 162–179). New York: Cambridge University Press.

Whitin, P., & Whitin, D. J. (1997). *Inquiry at the window: Pursuing the wonders of learners.* Portsmouth, NH: Heinemann.

Whitmore, K. F., & Crowell, C. G. (1994). *Inventing a classroom: Life in a bilingual, whole language learning community.* York, ME: Stenhouse.

Wilen, W. W. (1991). *Questioning skills, for teachers* (3rd ed.). Washington, DC: National Education Association.

Wolf, D., & Gardner, H. (1979). Style and sequence in early symbolic play. In N. R. Smith & M. B. Franklin (Eds.), *Symbolic functioning in childhood* (pp. 117–138). Hillsdale, NJ: Erlbaum.

Wood, H., & Wood, D. (1983). Questioning the preschool child. *Educational Review, 35,* 149–162.

Zahorik, J. A. (1971). Questioning in the classroom. *Education, 91,* 358–363.

Zimmerman, B. J., & Pike, E. O. (1972). Effects of modeling and reinforcement on the acquisition and generalization of question-asking behavior. *Child Development, 43,* 892–907.

Index

ABOUT THE AUTHOR

Judith Wells Lindfors is a professor of curriculum and instruction (language and literacy) at The University of Texas at Austin. She teaches courses in language acquisition and language arts, and is the author of *Children's Language and Learning,* winner of the Modern Language Association's first Mina Shaughnessy Medal.